threads of yoga

also by Matthew Remski

poetry
organon vocis organalis (1994)
syrinx and systole (2010)

fiction
dying for veronica: a sub-catholic dream with mind-music (1997)
silver (1998)

non-fiction
(with Scott Petrie) *yoga 2.0: shamanic echoes* (2010)

threads of yoga

a remix of patañjali-s sūtra-s

with commentary and reverie

matthew remski

ISBN: 978-1480100473

For more information or to order additional copies, please contact:

www.matthewremski.com
contact@matthewremski.com

cover and text design: ingrid paulson

"Yoga is like an ancient river with countless rapids, eddies, loops, tributaries, and backwaters, extending over a vast, colourful terrain of many different habitats. So, when we speak of Yoga, we speak of a multitude of paths and orientations with contrasting theoretical frameworks and occasionally incompatible goals."

Georg Feuerstein (1947–2012)

table of contents

Note: section 7.3 ("against isolation and the extraction urge") contains passages reworked from the opening chapter of *yoga 2.0: shamanic echoes* (Petrie and Remski, 2010).

acknowledgements

Special thanks to: John Bemrose, Anne Cloutier, Rita Dertkin, Lindsay Gamester, Sarahjane MacDonald, Simone Moir, Michael Stone and my parents, David and Jill, for encouragement and feedback; to the students of the original Advanced Yoga Philosophy programme at the old Renaissance Yoga and Āyurveda building in Cabbagetown for fostering an environment of philosophical and emotional adventurousness; to the staff of Yoga Festival Toronto for showing me contemporary yoga culture in its highest empathy-gear; to Joel Kramer and Diana Alstad, for blazing a path of critical inquiry in modern yoga discourse; to Jason Hirsch, for illuminating the homeodynamic/homeostatic distinction; to Luciano Iacobelli, for his thoughts on the "afterlife"; to For Life in Kensington Market, for bringing me food and *epoché*; to Miles Sherts, for the sauna, swimming hole, introduction to conscious communication, and the love of Skymeadow Retreat through the years; to Jody Kelly, for excellent discussion and proofing; to Cathleen Hoskins for polymath insight, grammatical acumen, additional proofing, the "failure of ambivalence", and for musing with me on the word "cleave"; to my partner, Alix Bemrose, for her enthusiastic, incisive, and expectant third-trimester editing.

I'd also like to thank my *ad hoc* editorial committee of online correspondents, who over the past three years have engaged many of these ideas with positive vigour. They have helped to nurture an open-source era of yoga philosophy: Frank Jude Boccio (who triggered a deeper look at "śūnya"), Shyam Dodge, Carol Horton, Priya Thomas, Julian Marc Walker, and many others. The frontispiece quotation from the late Dr. Feuerstein, which I believe describes the "multitude" within our discourse, is from the March/April 1990 issue of Yoga Journal.

This book is dedicated firstly to Scott Petrie, with whom I began to explore the heart of these subjects, and without whom this text would never have emerged. But also to my newborn son Jacob. I finish this book just as you emerge from the womb. I leave a part of myself behind in these pages, as I move forward with you.

1. quick-start guide

This book is many books at once. It is a "remix" of an ancient book. It is a meditation on how we translate things from different times and different cultures. It is a sharp critique of some old ideas that I believe no longer serve contemporary yoga. It is an invitation to yoga culture to begin to fully use the philosophical, psychotherapeutic, literary, and scientific tools of our age to enhance our self-inquiry and socio-political awareness. These threads are loosely woven together with the unfinished poetry of my life and how I have practiced so far. A brief road map might be helpful. I'll describe the original text first, and then how I've structured my presentation of it, and my reflections on it.

Patañjali's original text consists of 196 aphorisms that are notoriously difficult to translate, as is evident to anyone who reads multiple translations. The terse sayings are loosely organized into four chapters called pāda-s. Pāda means "foot", and as a chapter heading, it implies, according to some oral traditions, the amount of knowledge that can be transferred during a comfortable walking conversation with a friend. Given the complexity of the first pāda—*the book of integration,* in my language—we can say one thing absolutely for sure about the ancients: they walked a lot, and took their time. *Solvitur ambulando,* said Diogenes of

Sinope (an original mad yogi if ever there was one): "The question is resolved by walking."

The concerns of the book as a whole are woven through each of the four pāda-s, but they are also thematically distinct. The first pāda (which I unfold in Part 4) lays out the heart of the system's metaphysics. It announces the goal of practice—to unbind the patterned tensions of conscious and unconscious life through states of self-reflective meditation. It names the experiential patterns that it claims can be sweetened to the point of stable peace through diligent and relaxed practice, and lists the attitudes purported to help in this process. But then, with little instruction or preparation, the text leaps directly into a description of advanced meditative techniques, along with how they can alter the path of one's life and the very nature of one's consciousness. Many oral traditions tell students that because this first chapter lays out a superstructure of the yogic path in terms of an absolute beginning and end, it is meant for the most "advanced" readers who have already practiced (or somehow magically intuited) the various techniques that would guide them. Accordingly, I often advise the beginning student to bite first into the meat of pāda two, which focuses on the practical evolutionary methods that we most identify with yoga—ethics, attitudes, posture, breath, sensory refinement, and meditation—and how to feel and measure their results.

Pāda two (unfolded in Part 5), which I'm calling *the book of practices*, lays out the famed eight-limbed path in detail. For those of us who learn by doing, this is the place to start: brief but clear instructions on social ethics and internal attitudes, bodily poise, breathwork, sensory freedom, and the three general levels of contemplation. If you start here, the metaphysical speculations of pāda-s one, three, and four can be seen as supplemental and artistic reveries upon what may be possible when we sink into the complex peace of interdependence, and are able to focus ourselves with a minimum of internal conflict.

Pāda three (unfolded in Part 6), *the book of wonders*, makes sparkling correlations between areas of focused study and the natural insights that may flow from them. For example: *There is an intuitive relationship between internal light, atoms, hidden things, and things that are far away. Meditating on the sun gives insight into the earth.* In my presentation, this book presents meditation as an enhancement of our creative impulse.

The last pāda (unfolded in Part 7), *the book of overflowing*, presents meditation as an enhancement of our existential impulse. It plunges into questions of memory and change, then soars into the stratosphere of particle physics, to finally resolve into a relaxed vision of death as part of our continued learning:

> Under a clearing sky, the desire for knowledge wanes. Within you, gravity, urge, and resolution integrate. You can see the flow of time behind you, and you know how it happened. Immersed in integrated relationship, consciousness sees itself evolving.

How have I organized my presentation? How might you want to navigate it?

There are eight Parts to *threads of yoga*, counting this one. If you'd like to quickly engage with what a decade of practice and consideration has done to Patañjali-s old book through my hands, you can skip immediately to Part 3—"threads: the complete remix of the yoga sūtra-s of Patañjali". This section consists of my entire prose "translation" of the yoga sūtra-s. I've presented the work firstly in prose to normalize it for a contemporary audience, so that it can be read without prejudice as we would read any other text we happen upon.

After encountering the complete text, you may want to rewind to "Introductory Notes" (Part 2), for some background on the origins of this remix, along with general thoughts on "what yoga needs now", and the problems and opportunities of translation. Or, it might feel more useful for you to jump ahead into any of the core Parts of 4 through 7. Near the end of each of these Parts is a section called "my choices", which describes how each original sūtra evolved into my "thread" through a process of comparative and creative translation. Those who have prior familiarity with Patañjali might find these sections provide a good orientation for the issues I wade into in more contemplative sections. Those without prior familiarity might find them a tad technical.

Distinct from the prose presentation of the full remix in Part 3, each of the core Parts on the chapters (4 through 7) includes two textually and visually distinct presentations of the pāda in question. Each Part opens with a traditional setting in which the aphorisms are numbered, and ends with a setting of the pāda as a contemporary poem, with line breaks. Most students of Patañjali agree that the aphorisms themselves only "sink in" through numerous repetitions. For me, content that is repeated in different forms seems to integrate more quickly. I also believe aesthetic flexibility promotes philosophical flexibility. To me, an integrated presentation on yoga should yoke or unite the techniques of form (creativity breaks neurotic patterns) with the aims of content (yoga heals neurotic patterns). If we're going to write books about yoga, I think, we have to look carefully at the technology of writing and typesetting as an opportunity to reflect and perhaps release yoga's creative promise.

Between the visually distinct versions of the pādas and the "choices" commentary, I've inserted personal contemplations and reveries on the many themes broached by Patañjali, as well as on our historical and current interactions with his worldview. These sections are rather eccentric. Some offer broad praise to the old text, and many are highly critical of it. This ambivalence is consistent with my general feeling towards the original: it is a marvelous document with serious flaws. In my opinion, grappling equally with both its gifts and its weaknesses will help contemporary yoga practice grow and evolve as a living culture. Part 8, the "Coda", focuses in a more upbeat way on the feelings and questions that I hope will provoke further inquiry.

I'd like to say a few words about two key terms I use throughout this book. "Intersubjectivity" is the philosophical and psychological acknowledgement that experience and meaning are co-created through human relationship. It is an advancement from the "isolated mind" moods of earlier philosophies (Descartes), early psychologies (Freud), and most of Western science prior to quantum theory—all of which presume clear boundaries between the observer and the observed, the "I" and the "you". Intersubjectivity posits that although we often feel separated from each other in private bubbles of meaning, our fundamental condition is one of togetherness and unconscious empathy, in which we intuit that the interior lives of those we are with are similar to our own, that the "you" I encounter is another "I" looking back at a "you", who is myself. It is a crucial term to my presentation because Patañjali-s path is lonely to a fault, and rarely considers the impact of relationship upon psychic health. I read all of the possibilities and flaws of his system through this principle.

Another key term is "flesh". This is the common English translation of *la chair,* a concept introduced by the French phenomenologist Maurice Merleau-Ponty (1908–1961) to enhance dialogue around the problem of the word "body", which conveys a sense of separation from the world of which it is made and with which it is continuous. "Flesh" is anything but inert or unintelligent. "Flesh" feels, emotes, surges towards its goals, and even thinks. Replacing "body" for the most part with "flesh" also allows me to reduce reliance on the body's traditional foil: the "mind". Wherever possible, I have eliminated "mind" as an enclosed category discretely sequestered from "body", replacing it with "thought" or "thinking", which can both be felt activities of "flesh". If there is one thing that yoga has definitely shown contemporary practitioners, it is that it makes no sense to separate "mind" from "body". While multiple streams of inquiry are now breathlessly searching for the "mind-body connection", many yoga practitioners carry the feeling that this "connection" does not need to be found or forged—it was simply never missing. I propose that we might go further in our discourse, and altogether resist the binary language that provokes us to believe that this flesh we share can be carved up into categories and parts. Perhaps we can begin to mend our alienation by amending the language that seems to make it solid. Perhaps we don't need to search for the connection between things. We need to see that we are always-already living it.

2. introductory notes

2.1 restoring embodiment: a manifesto for a changing tradition

The legacy of yoga has been resurrected in our time through the innate pleasure of our flesh. The simplest techniques of breathing, spinal elongation, and joint fluidity have given countless flesh-alienated postmoderns a renewed sense of vitality, purpose, grounding, and connection. As media, technology, and hyper-urbanization abstract us from bodily experience, the reach of modern postural yoga has pulled our tissues into the daylight. And although there is considerable stretchy-pants spectacle involved, evoking complicated feelings about how the flesh should look or move, most practitioners know that yoga's real gift is that of internal sensitivity leading to internal resolution. In modern yoga we are given a physical culture that rewrites the meaning of flesh from the inside out. If the breath isn't relaxed, we know we're not quite there. If thought has not stilled and focused into the waves of present sensation, we know there's more (or less) work to do. Further: if the pleasure of musculo-skeletal alignment and warmed circulation does not somehow sweeten our interpersonal relationships, lend resilient courage to daily life, and inspire us towards social and ecological justice, we know we're missing something. Through modern postural yoga we have remembered that our flesh innately wants to rejoice, connect, and serve—and that it does not lie.

This yoga renaissance is quietly rewriting a central theme of its parent tradition. The flesh has rarely if ever been considered as its own hero in older yoga cultures. At best, the flesh has been seen as a vessel for an unseen higher essence, and therefore an instrument for its own transcendence, as per the many Tantric and Nātha yoga lineages. Less positively, the flesh has been seen as the definitive proof of separation from the embrace of "divinity", as in the bhakti yoga lineages. And perhaps the most negative view of all—the flesh as the repulsive devolution of consciousness and an obstacle to the recovery of self-knowledge (rather than the source of it)—has been the hallmark of ascetic views that in no way reflect our present values, yet echo stubbornly through our discourse and unspoken sentiments. The yoga sūtra-s of Patañjali fall squarely into this ascetic mood: compiled from the sayings of renunciates of many stripes who at the dawn of urbanization fled their families and social roles to tiny forest ashrams, where, with great austerity, they attempted to tame the unruly and desirous flesh towards their goal of transcendent epiphany.

Patañjali says little about the value of embodied sensation as he collates the wisdom of his harsh age. He says little about interpersonal love, and nothing of children or the environment. He presents an internalizing and subtractive path, in which ethics are a means towards social disentanglement, and the flesh has learning value to the extent we are disgusted by it (sūtra 2.40). In other words, Patañjali teaches exactly *against* the present zeitgeist of yoga culture. And yet the yoga sūtras is presented, largely uncritically, as a core text in most yoga education programmes throughout the world today.

The prominence of the old book may have more to do with its modern publishing history and the rise of global-yoga-guru-culture than to its fame within the broader tradition. Globetrotting Swami

Vivekananda published the sūtra-s (as part of his seminal work *Rāja Yoga*) to popular acclaim in 1896, and vigorously promoted its transcendental message with his other-worldly charisma. But now, over a century later, why is it still better known to global yoga culture than arguably more famous and utilitarian yoga texts? Consider the *Yoga Yājñavalkya*, 12 chapters delivered in the much more digestible (and perhaps equitable) form of a dialogue between a husband and wife philosopher-duo. This text declares *jīvātma paramātma saṃyogaḥ*: "yoga is the union of the individual to the whole." Or—the *Yoga Vaśiṣṭha*, a beloved text of 32,000 verses, consisting of a dialogue between the sage Vaśiṣṭha and Prince Rāma, who has returned disillusioned from his youthful world travels and is basically told by the old existentialist: "Good for you! Melancholia is the beginning of true growth."

Has interest in the broader literature of yoga simply paled in the shadow of Patañjali-s austere monolith? Do we associate impenetrable brevity with ultimate truth? Are the opacity of the aphorisms ideal for agenda-driven cross-cultural misprision, insofar as we can project upon them anything we like? Or, more problematically, does our adherence to a minimalist ascetic text conceal a hidden wish to console our complex interpersonal suffering through social withdrawal and meditative narcissism? I would suggest we're already accomplishing this consolation through consumerism, including the consumeristic aspects of contemporary yoga culture, and perhaps Patañjali-s original message of social disengagement subconsciously supports this.

But we are also powerfully enthralled by Patañjali-s unwavering attention to mental processes, not to mention the non-sectarian, do-it-yourself feel of the old text. There is something mystically attractive about an Axial Age description of thought and psychological patterning presented with such resonant authority. My experience is that many who encounter the aphorisms have the immediate sense that they arise out of a non-distractedness that our world and culture can rarely offer. They seem to suspend us in a mood of extended contemplation and confident stillness. One of the primary attractions of the text, regardless of its philosophical merits, is that it highlights the relative crudeness of our speed, our data-saturation, our ennui, our vulnerability to alienation and the banal. And in a world of limitless words, the economy of these aphorisms shines like the edge of a blade.

It is Patañjali-s close and precise attention that I wish to translate here, while leaving his metaphysics and asceticism behind. Philosophy will change through discourse: all tenets are temporary and unstable. What does not change is the quality of attention that makes our changing discourse evolutionary, as opposed to supplementary. I offer this text and commentary as an alternative speculation on what Patañjali-s attention and incision might offer us today, within a far different social-philosophical context than his own. A context in which renunciate withdrawal will not heal our interpersonal pain nor speak to our social diseases. A context in which we desperately need to be reminded of our embodiment, and grounded in ecological awareness. A context in which the magic of bodily pleasure that got us practicing in the first place becomes the basis for reaching out with love into the world that made us, has always held us, and which we never wish to leave.

2.2 on the method of "remixing"

threads of yoga is an experimental translation, insofar as *trans* means "to cross over or beyond", and *latus* means "to carry". To "translate" is to carry something over, and beyond.

The sounds of the word "translation" evoke their own meanings. *Trans* cues "trance". *Latere* means "the hidden", but comes into English as "lateral". Thus: "to translate" might also be to carry something hidden, over and beyond, yet beside us, while entranced.

Sūtra means "thread". Any translator of the yoga sūtra-s is carrying threads across time and culture, through revolutions of sentiment, thought, and technology, to be woven on new looms, into new cloth. Perhaps, in this metaphor, the warp-threads are the vertically constant frames of language, culture, audience, place, purpose, bias. And the weft-threads are our multiple responses, of varying colour and tension, shuttling across to bind the cloth. The warp is circumstance, the weft is creativity.

threads is not a direct translation from the Sanskrit. Even if I were a Sanskrit scholar, I'm sure I would be juggling too many sources of input and interference to ever hope for a 1:1 rendering into English. I'm enthralled by the old text itself and its aura, by dozens of previous translations and commentaries, fragments of oral tradition I have heard through the years, a thousand conversations with colleagues and strangers, vast cultural and historical divides, the new forests of contemporary psychology and neuroscience, and the strange, luminous fruit of my own practice. Thus, I've called it a "remix".

The purpose of a remix is equal parts homage, adventure, reclamation, and pleasure. It collects the raw beats of the past and brands them, transparently, with the pulse of the present. In a "yoga 2.0" idiom (Petrie and Remski, 2010), this pulse asserts that relationship is more important than meditative bliss, metaphysics distracts from presence, consciousness is evolving new questions, and yoga is always changing, because its practitioners are.

I have purposefully entangled the threads of Patañjali-s efforts with my own reverie, criticism, and commentary to tarnish the presumption of objectivity that haloes most presentations of canonical texts. My choice in this work is to be honest about the fact that any translation of anything is a subjective re-creation—a remix. I also intend for the weaving of root-text and reverie to reflect the dialectic of personal growth so important to the ethos of yoga. In my experience, learning does not spring whole from the past, but is rather created in experiential dialogue between other (what one hears), and self (what one wishes to echo, or add), and others (those who discourse with you). It builds like a story, which is why I've included parts of my own story here. The learning arc of a story pitches and rolls, at times unfocused and disorderly, yet bending towards coherence upon some unreachable horizon.

Through the entanglements and multiple views of a reader-centred text, I have also sought to undermine my authorial voice, and to place my own (sometimes very strong) opinions into a dialogical context. Yoga philosophy has opened me up because it invited me to experience and discern for myself what is evolutionarily helpful. Because the yoga tradition has no central authority, I feel its authors should presume none, and consciously share power with readers and listeners. If writing is to convey meaning about yoga, it should be writing that is co-created and shared. Dialogue eschews the comprehensive, and, continuing late into the night by flickering candles, elevates the elliptical.

The oral nature of the original yoga sūtra-s haunts my process, and me. Their compression, pulsing metre, and grammatical minimalism served as a kind of mnemonic shorthand for legions of (textually) illiterate practitioners who recited them trance-like throughout the generations, perhaps pausing between each section for impromptu commentary around the campfire. (I was brought up in a traditional Catholic environment: the pulse of plainchant may be the genetic root of my fascination.) Contemporary contact with the sūtra-s has mainly been broadcast through the flattened affect of typography, which by its static nature overdetermines its message, invites criticism but not dialogue, and stares vacantly at the lonely reader like an epitaph. The ossified text is like the Baudrillardian object: always already laughing at your incomprehension.

I've heard many oral tradition teachers say that the sūtra-s should never have been written down, because writing destroys both memory and the intimacy of oral instruction. And yet they are written: elsewhere, and now here. The question cannot be whether we should limit textual representations of important ideas, but whether we can leverage more indeterminate and therefore creative meaning into the representations we cast. For me, this invites adventurousness with the materiality of writing.

As I mentioned in the "quick-start guide", I have given the textuality of my remix a fluid mood, presenting it in prose form, in sentence form with contemporary poetic line-breaks, in its conventional mode of one aphorism per line, as well as aphorism-plus-commentary interlaced. I hope this visual flexibility helps to hint at the oral and performative quality of the aphorisms, and to loosen the feelings of calcification that often accrue to "important books". My thought was that if this book is visually variegated, as the oral tradition is variegated in accent, tone, projection, aural ambience, digression, and anecdote, perhaps it can actually begin to do the very yoga it describes: to disrupt and reprogram both conscious and unconscious patterning with moments of perceptual wonderment and unexpected integration.

Part of my method in this book is carried over from my earlier life in contemporary poetry, in which the elements of meaning—typographical marks and sounds—are played with like paint instead of being enslaved to symbolic systems that presume to offer precise definitions. My writing career began amongst "language" poets, who used sounds and typography as gestures, pointers, placeholders, objects of play and comedy, and pivots of irony. They taught me to juggle words and locate meaning within the air, rather than pinning it to where they fell. (You might feel this process resonate in the sections called "my choices" in which I cycle through the word-options offered by previous translators and my own reverie.) Language poetry taught me what I later went on to learn through chanting mantras: language is continually overflowing its consensus meanings. They reminded me of what I had learned thirty years before from my toddling brother as I watched sounds and words blossom from the space between his head and heart: language is much more than a descriptive tool. Language is a fountain (a font) of primal urge and emotion. It is the aural trace of the endless play of our internal voices. When we use it playfully, it co-creates with us. But when we domesticate it to a conceptual purpose, our most serious grammar and richest vocabularies become very fragile nets through which most of the world escapes. The philosopher who wishes to think newly must contend with the limitations of language, as Wittgenstein shows. Or they must defy the limitations with creativity, as we see in the neologisms of Heidegger. For there are more things both revealed and concealed in our language alone, to paraphrase the Bard, than are dreamt of in all our philosophies.

My central goal is to bring the yoga sūtra-s back into relationship with us as yogis, creative readers, and closet philosophers. This first requires a kind of de-familiarization, which chips away at the banal authority of the canonical. Whenever I encounter a book that seems to project authority or canonicity, I feel entranced but disconnected: I am both mystified and blasé. It's not unlike the feeling I have towards my iPhone: it is beautiful, seems complete, and yet I haven't a clue how it works, and I become resigned to my ignorance. Somehow it shoves me towards melancholic withdrawal from its closed perfection.

Demystifying Patañjali is like unlocking the phone and open-sourcing its code so that everyone can play with it, altering its values, and perhaps its very purpose. It changes from a product into an object of relationship. The tone is not declarative, and the feeling is one of "never-finished". We have moved from an "exegetical" mode, in which our goal is to render old ideas with faith and reverence, to a "hermeneutic" mode, in which we are reflecting as much upon the old ideas as we are upon how we respond to them, and how we use them in the present tense. Leaving exegesis behind, we move away from an implicit endorsement of the artifact (the original yoga sūtra-s, in this case) as a "perfect" or "complete" system, and recognize its innovative value as a collection of tools that we will use differently from our forebears, because we are building different things. Exegesis says, "Our goal is to faithfully reconstruct the eternally-relevant meaning of this old book, so that we can follow its holy intentions perfectly." Hermeneutics says, "Our goal is to understand what this text may have said to its audience at the time, and to investigate how it's been interpreted and used through the generations, and to explore our many responses to it now as we continue to grow in its light and shadow."

The hermeneutic flow from de-familiarization to open-source and demystification tends to have an embodying effect. We can feel it when our reading overwhelms linguistic habit or cognitive faculty, which is the goal of most contemporary poetry. When we read the unexpected, there is a bodily response. We gasp, sit a little straighter, or hug the page close to our hearts. I think that this is the primary learning response that we crave. It is fueled by newness.

I'm publishing this work in a venerable yogic tradition: solo—i.e., without the help of a formal publishing company and its marketing and distribution networks. I'd like to see if this remix has enough juice to naturally wick to wherever the discourse is dry. I'd like to see if this book can circulate the way I imagine yoga itself once did, before the age of academic validation or consumer branding: by word-of-mouth and from heart to heart. By using print-on-demand technology, I will also be able to amend this text according to the feedback and criticism I receive, and release new editions with relative ease.

Such points return me to my main theme. In my experience, the discourse on Patañjali has seemed vertically-controlled, set-in-stone, theological, overly reverential, and penitentially nostalgic for an inaccessible time and place. That the vertical influence continues is not a surprise: the aphorisms can easily project a paternal certitude that consoles the postmodern heart. Nor is it surprising in terms of content: as I will show, Patañjali presents a transcendent, hard-dualist escape route for the despairing. His onward-and-upward path encourages dissociation from place, things, and people: hardly what is needed in a culture of disembodied hyper-individualism wrecking havoc on the environment. What we really yearn for are new strategies for nurturing the intersubjective: the recognition that by honouring and mirroring each other's unique needs and stories and internal lives, we come to know who we are. We see these strategies developing in contemporary yoga culture around the world, wherever it manages to resist consumerism: ecological stewardship, community-building, non-violent communication, the yoga of relationship. We value horizontal networks of knowledge. It seems only natural that such a progressive culture would begin to revise and even rewrite its oldest books.

I have been asked: "Why use or even refer to the original at all? Clearly, you are simply creating a new philosophy." Perhaps.

Though more accurately: I am blending philosophy, psychotherapy, literary theory, anthropology, and aesthetics. (I am specifically indebted to the legacy of psychoanalysis for my notions around the childhood-developmental and psycho-evolutionary stages displayed in yoga's history.) In any case, I rely on the original because like a parent it has been a touchstone of my individuation process. It gazes at me, and through me. Its aphoristic form carries mesmerizing power. Patañjali-s relentless focus upon the structural problems of consciousness remains the root yogic concern, and this unwavering gaze will continue to inspire generations. This project has shown me more clearly what the old book contained, and how this scans against what I have come to value, through practicing both with and against it. As the excellent philosopher he was, I think Patañjali would approve: I have tried to wrestle his truths down to the ground of my own.

The diversity of my sources mirrors the mode in which most of us come into contact with Patañjali today. In fragments, for the most part. Favoured quotations flash through yoga teacher training manuals and across social media, and under the e-mail signature lines of professional practitioner-teachers. *Now, the teachings of yoga.... The postures of meditation should be stable and filled with ease.... Suffering that has not yet come can be avoided....* It is a fragmentary text yielding fragmentary memes. The aphorisms seem to proclaim personal revelation, but in an open sense, as though they should be obvious to everyone. The vague quoting gives me the same feeling I get when walking by an old vinyl record shop, watching hipsters pore over obscure discs that radiate an eccentric and seductive authenticity. The experience of encountering bits of Patañjali is like hearing the hooks of several compelling songs and wanting to splice them together on top of a private rhythm. As anyone who goes to DJ shows has felt, the friction-point of where the hooks join is the heart of the dance. What will he lay down next, into this mix?

As postmoderns we are natural *bricoleurs,* naturally improvisational. We don't assume anything to be complete in itself, but rather that hints of completeness will emerge, temporarily, through shuffling and recombination. The best teachers are aware of the responsibility of remixing, because they know they have picked and chosen according to chance exposure and personal preference. The aphorisms of one zeitgeist meld seamlessly into the aphorisms of another: Patañjali, zen, mindfulness language, the *Tao*.

The best teachers can also see that the aphorism is energetically confusable with the branding tag-line, and they work to allow experience rather than fashion to be the glue that coheres their vision. The best teachers avoid scratching the discs as they transition from one to the other.

I've been told by orthodox practitioners that I would never really understand Patañjali unless I spent a decade studying it line by line with a qualified master. They're right: I would never understand the text *that* way, i.e., through a single lens. But I'm afraid that what I've seen in my fellow practitioners who are also devotees to one guru or another is that the strict student-teacher approach is as much motivated by an attraction to the social control of the learning group as it is by the yearning to receive a "complete account". Feeling that you have the inside track on the sutra-s seems always to be accompanied by feeling that you are unconditionally loved by your chosen authority figure. But do postmoderns feel unconditional love? Do we even want it? Do postmoderns centralize authority? Or do we crowdsource it?

Ironically, the impulse to bricolage in this text may be inspired by Patañjali himself or, more broadly, by the general production modes of ancient texts as they crystallize out of their watery orality. As Edwin Bryant (2009) and Georg Feuerstein (1989) suggest, Patañjali is collating the loops and hooks of several generations into a non-denominational heartbeat, nodding with equal appreciation towards the Jains, the Sāṃkhyans, and the bhakti-s of his day. He's spinning the discs, splicing and cutting, and we dance.

It is thematically appropriate that this project was born intersubjectively. It emerged in dialogue with my friend Scott Petrie, in a barn on a mountain in Vermont, during a month when all of our eccentric learning through the years seemed pulled through benign gravity into our hearts. We read, debated, deconstructed, and reassembled each aphorism countless times. We found ourselves re-animating this gleaming artifact of our adopted tradition with our uncertain breath. It felt like we proved to ourselves the treasured thesis: nothing true and useful emerges alone, but through relationship. Our intention was guided by an old oral translation of sūtra: "tool (tra) for the enhancement of the good (sū)".

As it moved towards this present form, which I consider to be provisional, the text and its commentary has continued to develop in the same cooperative way. Excerpts of earlier drafts posted online received widespread and swift editorial help from a growing global yoga philosophy movement. I've been able to test many individual threads through social media and feed public responses to them back into the mix. And two years after I'd begun the project with Scott, the whole remix passed through another complete rewrite with my partner at our kitchen table. Alix is a dancer, writer, and āsana teacher. She was seven months pregnant with our first child as we worked together. She brought her many disciplines to the reading, and baby rolled and kicked, and our hours were imbued with silent expectation.

My textual sources for both the remix and the commentaries include the translations and commentaries of Hariharananda Aranya, I.K. Taimni, Vyas Houston, Barbara Miller, Swami Sacchidananda, Swami Prabhavananda, Swami Vivekananda, Georg Feuerstein, Shyam Ranganathan, Edwin Bryant and Chip Hartranft. Through these authors I have also indirectly sipped at the old commentaries of Vyāsa, Śaṃkara, and Vijñānabhikṣu. I most often favour the translations of Bryant, Hartranft, and Miller for readability, when it is appropriate to contrast the "original" with my remix of it. I would encourage you to read this text alongside any or all of these resources, as well as anything else that catches your eye, wherever you are in life. And may this remix encourage others.

2.3 loosening the tyranny of certainty

Patañjali-s old book stimulates a subtle tension from the very first page: the desire for a complete answer to life. The sūtra-s begin with an implicit promise: the core problem of human life will be resolved. Instantly, a feeling of other-worldly authority pervades the text. For many of us, reading further involves a seamless seduction into this other world. What happens there? How is it different from our own? How much older and more serene? How much wiser are these words than those we hear within?

Meanwhile, the quiet integrations of any and every moment can slip like grains of sand through our fingers. Every breath contains a pause. The heart beats without effort. You watch tall grasses reveal patterns of wind. Food melts in your mouth. An emotion rips through the flesh, erasing your name. A preverbal child gazes at you and you remember the open sky. Your lover looks downcast, and your chest splits. Before sleeping, you float for an instant, suspended between gravity and space.

The power of Patañjali-s aphoristic voice vibrates deeply. But it would be a mistake to confuse elliptical charisma for truth. Perhaps he has the answers to life, and perhaps he doesn't. Ultimacy is the enemy of evolution: the paint is never dry. Of the very origins of the universe, the earliest poem of yoga culture, the *Ṛg veda,* offers: "Who really knows? Who can presume to tell it? Whence was it born? Whence issued this creation? He who surveys it in the highest heaven, he surely knows—or maybe he does not!" (Pannikar, 58). This much older view puts all metaphysical speculation into perspective, and keeps mystery as palpable as the unfindable edge between your fingers and this page. Holding and enjoying uncertainty keep all threads of thought and sentiment active, changeable, responsive—in a word: dangling.

One way of embracing Patañjali-s tone of certainty might be to remember that it is not only inherent to the impersonal compression of the aphoristic form, but may also be derived from that kind of teetering confidence we detect in our most artistic and adventurous thinkers. The greatest themes are often very anxious creations. We risk everything as we conceive of the whole.

On the other hand, we might also remember that the author is actually no-one to us. So little is known of the historical Patañjali that current scholarship can't even establish whether he is a single writer, or a collective pseudonym for several generations of seekers, echoing their aphorisms back and forth through time. Most commentators use the name Patañjali as though they were referring to a single enlightened sage who is giving a single enlightened discourse. (I'm guilty of this as well, because using the name makes for better flow, and I appreciate the drama of the personification. But really I don't think of Patañjali as a person, but as a community and its system.) The power of a text that is assumed to have come from an actual realized person is considerable. It makes it seem as though *Someone* really knows the truth, and one had better listen to him. This of course adds tension to the process of translation, as we become pious with concern about what "he" intended by a particularly obscure aphorism. But can intention really be discerned in a crowdsourced collection of sayings? There's definitely something about our psyches that makes it easier for us to accept and endorse the words of an individual than the words of a collective. But acceptance and endorsement is not our task: inquiry and creativity are. Perhaps remembering that Patañjali carries the voices of many will encourage us to add our own voices to the broad margins of his sparse pages.

3. *threads*: the complete remix of the yoga sūtra-s of patañjali

3.1 the book of integration

We all inquire into yoga. Yoga happens in the resolution of consciousness. Through yoga, consciousness can become aware of its interdependence. Otherwise, consciousness can become increasingly alienated, and awareness becomes inaccessible.

There are five common conscious patterns that can clash or harmonize: assertions, confusions, fancy, dreamless sleep, and remembering. Assertions may come from witnessing, inference, or belief. Confusions are the misalignment of words and reality. Fancy is language that drifts away from relationship, towards metaphysics. Dreamless sleep is a feeling of nothingness. Remembering is the present experience of the past. These patterns can be loosened through consistent practice and presence.

Practice is any intentional re-patterning of feelings and thoughts towards interdependence. Re-patterning may occur over a period of consistent and focused effort. Presence is felt when you hold no expectation or assumption. Awareness of interdependence is the fullest presence.

Reasoning, reflection, wonderment, and the awe of being alive are the initial gateways to integration. Through integration, these gateways dissolve, leaving unseen traces. At death, these unseen traces are resolved into their surroundings and recycled. In yoga, this resolution can come through the efforts of confidence, energy, deep memory, focus, and intelligence.

The intensity of practice reveals yoga's nearness. Intensity has many different facets, including the focus of devotion. Devotion can feel timeless and resolved. In that feeling is the awareness of interdependence. We have always felt it. It can be heard in primal sound, which, when sung, can reveal hidden things. Then, obstacles to inner spaciousness become transparent. Those obstacles are disease, apathy, doubt, carelessness, joylessness, addiction, false perception, unsteady focus, and restlessness. Their symptoms are stress, pain, depression, trembling, and irregular breathing. Calming practice alleviates these symptoms.

Calmness arises from friendship, empathy, delight, and equality towards others, or spaciousness in breathing, or a feeling of stillness in sensuality, or when experience is light and joyful, or when you observe the senses without expectation or assumption, or by meditating upon dreams or sleep, or by holding in your heart something you love. In time, the heart can hold the smallest thing, and the uncontainable.

When stillness is held, experience absorbs and reflects the things that surround it like a jewel. Its facets can deconstruct the object, its components, its energy, the act of perceiving it, and the mystery of perception. This experience can hold language, or it can be empty of words. The experience of worded or wordless wonderment plunges down to the quantum level.

In deep meditation you can witness how experience is woven together. Such witnessing leaves traces. Your hidden aspects become integrated. A feeling of authenticity arises. It is deeper than what you can hear or study. It begins to unravel future patterning. Bearing no future patterns, you become unbound.

3.2 the book of practices

Yoga applies endurance, learning, and commitment. It reduces alienation and cultivates empathy.

Ignorance, individualism, addiction, dissociation, and the "afterlife": these alienate. Ignorance enables alienation in all forms, from seed to tree. Ignorance involves not learning about change in objects, ideas, sensations, or self. Individualism sees things instead of relationships. Addiction turns pleasure into a thing. Dissociation runs away from experience. The "afterlife" devalues life.

The causes of alienation are interwoven. Loosening one begins to unravel them all towards empathy. Concentration stills alienating thoughts.

Fruitlessly seeking consolation, alienating patterns of thought tend to repeat. This repetition can impede self-perception, relationship to time, and the capacity for enjoyment. Alienating patterns predispose you to continued alienation.

For one who takes responsibility for his or her existential condition, life will be felt fully as ever-changing, echoing with loss, limited, unknowable, and chaotic. But the future is unwritten.

Pain is caused by the blurring of authenticity with fabrication. We feel gravity, urge, and resolution surge through the elements, and these feelings can lead to ecstasy. Gravity, urge, and resolution appear in all stages of form, from the object we name and hold to the nameless quanta coursing through it.

Consciousness seems distinct from the flesh, and yet pours through it. Consciousness delights in giving meaning to the flesh, as though it were its source. As consciousness evolves, meanings change or are taken away, for different people at different times.

Consciousness projects meaning onto things but then, forgetting its projection, assumes those given meanings belong to those things. But the conjunction of consciousness and things invites both to feel their interdependence.

These assumed meanings are another kind of ignorance. When ignorance fades, the original source of projected meaning is seen as consciousness and not the thing. A burden lifts. This becomes clear through contemplation on the difference. As veils of assumption fade, the depth of perception expands, and begins to explore the unknown.

The practices of yoga diminish alienation, allowing for the radiance of clear sight. The eight practices are relationship to other, relationship to self, poise, freedom of breath, freedom of senses, focus, contemplation, and integration.

Good relationship to others requires protection, honesty, fair trade, sexual responsibility, and self-possession. These five means of good relationship work for everyone, all the time. Good relationship to oneself requires ecology, contentment, endurance, learning, and commitment.

Negative thought patterns can be altered by embodying what balances them. When thoughts of oppression in any degree are held, acted upon, delegated to another, or colluded with, whether through greed, anger, or delusion, one must realize this pattern leads to shared suffering and ignorance, and work hard to reverse it.

When one protects others from harm, this produces a feeling of connectedness and safety. In the aura of honesty, causes and their results make sense. When you practice fair trade, your feeling of wealth is enhanced. Sexual responsibility enables intimacy. Self-possession allows you to define yourself according to your own actions, while revealing your interdependence with all things.

Ecology allows you to honour your flesh, and the flesh of others. Ecology enables clarity, brightness, joy, insight, sensual harmony, and inquiry. Contentment makes one at home in the world. Endurance allows the flesh and senses to be more fully enjoyed. Learning connects you with your archetypes. Commitment to relationship invites integration.

Poise is steady and well-spaced. This occurs when restlessness fades and feeling is boundless. Then, even oscillations are peaceful.

Breath is free when its movement is first easy and then voluntary. You can feel yourself making the breath smooth and subtle by observing the number, length, and placement of inhalations, exhalations, and pauses. Breath observance can also suspend the division between what is inside and what is outside. This feels like an unveiling of light. And concentration blossoms.

As consciousness draws inward, it becomes the object of the senses. When the senses are free, they will not disturb contemplation.

3.3 the book of wonders

Focus can channel diffuse thoughts into one theme. Contemplation is focus that attunes to its object. Integration can dissolve the subject-object barrier through attunement, allowing both to share a single form. These three work together. They give flashes of brilliance and understanding. They unfold in stages. They are more internal than the first five limbs. Yet they can feel external to even deeper states.

Deeper states build momentum and depth through feedback, changing hidden patterns. Meditative feedback can create a continuous flow that overwrites alienation. As this happens, wandering thoughts find their home, and the feeling of integration deepens. As integration deepens, there is equanimity between things rising and dissipating. Such practices give insight into what we sense, how we sense, and the passage of time.

All forms share the same basic particles through time. The sharing and recycling of particles in various patterns causes different forms to continually emerge.

Understanding what we sense, how we sense, and the passage of time can yield narrative intuition. Deconstructing the blend of sounds, meanings, and intentions within language gives insight into the grammar we share with all beings. Uncovering your latent patterns gives insight into your past. Understanding your mind gives insight into another's mind, but not insight into the things that other sees. Meditating on flesh resolves the feeling of being objectified. Understanding the narrative of events gives insight into how things end. Contemplating the grace of others strengthens you. Meditating on the non-human world gives shamanic energy. There is an intuitive relationship between internal light, atoms, hidden things, and things that are far away. Meditating on the sun gives insight into the earth. Tracking the moon teaches you the stars. Meditating on the North Star reveals how we move. Meditating on the core shows the elegance of physiology. Meditating on orality gives insight into appetite. Focus on the thyroid can give bodily stillness. Meditating on the halo connects you to the heritage of genius. All such insights can be spontaneous. The heart shows you thought.

Seeing the difference between consciousness and the self-sufficiency of things sharpens self-awareness. From this can come heightened sensuality. But such peak experiences are not always the point.

When the flesh is free and relaxed, you are open to intimacy. Rising energy can make you buoyant amidst oppressors, thieves, and puritans. A shining core can be seen. The art of listening is the marriage of ear and space. Movement feels like flight when the flesh is wedded to space. Abstract consciousness seems to blaze with light. By living intimately with nature and learning the large and the small, the still and the dynamic, and how things work together, one feels blessed by the world. Experience can then shrink into a bead of pleasure, or countless other things.

The freed flesh pulses through the facets of beauty, grace, and glowing strength. When you see how the sense organs work, weave you together, and commit you to the world, they become gateways of pleasure. These gateways can also encourage the exploration of internal worlds at the speed of light. Seeing the difference between consciousness and the self-sufficiency of things makes all of these experiences possible.

Equanimity towards even these wonders, while burning the seeds of alienation, grants even deeper liberation. Otherwise, one can become seduced by spiritualism.

Meditating on both a single moment and the flow of time gives insight born of différance. This insight deconstructs experience down to its raw data. This raw data communicates to consciousness all possibility at once. Then consciousness can be aware of even itself as raw data, co-creative with materiality.

3.4 the book of overflowing

The wonders of integration can also come through the conditions of one's development, intimacy with plants, conscious communication, ardour, or meditation.

Evolution is an overflow of identity. The overflow is natural, and only needs gardening. Individuation creates selves. These selves share collective consciousness.

Of the means towards wonder, meditation is the most stable. For those experienced in integration, the judgment of moral actions becomes subtle.

Past action binds a memory; present circumstance unlocks it. Memory can outshine the details of identity. Memories, like desire, are without beginning. An undigested memory resolves when its cause, effect, context, and neurosis are integrated into present awareness.

A thing reveals its past and future as its particles dance. The particles dance to the music of gravity, urge, and resolution. The dance is so entrancing, a dancer appears. Each person will see a different dancer. But no single gaze can understand or define or possess her.

Things colour consciousness. Matter produces and is known by consciousness; consciousness produces and is known by awareness. Consciousness can be seen by awareness. But it is difficult for consciousness to be aware of itself seeing. The attempt can lead to a hall of mirrors and an alienation from time.

When consciousness is still, it can become aware of itself. Consciousness is fulfilled when it warmly intermingles with matter and awareness. It delights in being seen. Being aware of this process imbues individuation with connection. This awareness re-integrates the part and the whole, and feels inexorable.

At this point, alienating thoughts are fleeting memories. And you already have experience in releasing them. The exalted is common, and the common exalted, and living feels like a summer downpour. Standing in it washes away alienating thoughts and isolated footprints.

Under a clearing sky, the desire for knowledge wanes. Within you, gravity, urge, and resolution integrate. You can see the flow of time behind you, and you know how it happened. Immersed in integrated relationship, consciousness sees itself evolving.

4. pāda one: integration

4.1 the book of integration

1.1 We all inquire into yoga.

1.2 Yoga happens in the resolution of consciousness.

1.3 Through yoga, consciousness can become aware of its interdependence.

1.4 Otherwise, consciousness can become increasingly alienated, and awareness becomes inaccessible.

1.5 There are five common conscious patterns that can clash or harmonize:

1.6 assertions, confusions, fancy, dreamless sleep, and remembering.

1.7 Assertions may come from witnessing, inference, or belief.

1.8 Confusions are the misalignment of words and reality.

1.9 Fancy is language that drifts away from relationship, towards metaphysics.

1.10 Dreamless sleep is a feeling of nothingness.

1.11 Remembering is the present experience of the past.

1.12 These patterns can be loosened through consistent practice and presence.

1.13 Practice is any intentional re-patterning of feelings and thoughts towards interdependence.

1.14 Re-patterning may occur over a period of consistent and focused effort.

1.15 Presence is felt when you hold no expectation or assumption.

1.16 Awareness of interdependence is the fullest presence.

1.17 Reasoning, reflection, wonderment, and the awe of being alive are the initial gateways to integration.

1.18 Through integration, these gateways dissolve, leaving unseen traces.

1.19 At death, these unseen traces are resolved into their surroundings and recycled.

1.20 In yoga, this resolution can come through the efforts of confidence, energy, deep memory, focus, and intelligence.

1.21 The intensity of practice reveals yoga's nearness.

1.22 Intensity has many different facets,

1.23 including the focus of devotion.

1.24 Devotion can feel timeless and resolved.

1.25 In that feeling is the awareness of interdependence.

1.26 We have always felt it.

1.27 It can be heard in primal sound,

1.28 which, when sung, can reveal hidden things.

1.29 Then, obstacles to inner spaciousness become transparent.

1.30 Those obstacles are disease, apathy, doubt, carelessness, joylessness, addiction, false perception, unsteady focus, and restlessness.

1.31 Their symptoms are stress, pain, depression, trembling, and irregular breathing.

1.32 Calming practice alleviates these symptoms.

1.33 Calmness arises from friendship, empathy, delight, and equality towards others,

1.34 or spaciousness in breathing,

1.35 or a feeling of stillness in sensuality,

1.36 or when experience is light and joyful,

1.37 or when you observe the senses without expectation or assumption,

1.38 or by meditating upon dreams or sleep,
1.39 or by holding in your heart something you love.
1.40 In time, the heart can hold the smallest thing, and the uncontainable.
1.41 When stillness is held, experience absorbs and reflects the things that surround it like a jewel. Its facets can deconstruct the object, its components, its energy, the act of perceiving it, and the mystery of perception.
1.42 This experience can hold language,
1.43 or it can be empty of words.
1.44 The experience of worded or wordless wonderment plunges down to the quantum level.
1.45 In deep meditation you can witness how experience is woven together.
1.46 Such witnessing leaves traces.
1.47 Your hidden aspects become integrated.
1.48 A feeling of authenticity arises.
1.49 It is deeper than what you can hear or study.
1.50 It begins to unravel future patterning.
1.51 Bearing no future patterns, you become unbound.

4.2 openings: the evolutionary democracy of yoga

What an opening! What a rich and exciting invitation extended towards us—every bit as inspiring now as it was to the young wanderers who first heard and memorized it so many centuries ago. Unique to its time and fascinating to our own, Patañjali-s path presents a democracy of evolutionary seeking, a do-it-yourself spirit, and the radiance of brevity. For those of us whose root spiritual texts were mythic/heroic (Exodus and the Gospels), elegiac/romantic (the Psalms), legalistic/neurotic (Leviticus), confessional/didactic (the letters of Paul) or hallucinogenic (Relevations), Patañjali offers something very different, something that sounds every bit like a rational and customizable road map for a very personal journey.

While the text holds numerous problematic philosophical assumptions (which I'll go on to scrutinize), these are not burdened by cultural anachronisms or belief-requirements. The universality of its voice makes the text feel as though it has no country or history. Patañjali presents many options to those who would pursue his goal—especially in the "immanent" mindfulness techniques of 1.33 to 1.39. Throughout, he reveals nothing of his person or context: he steps out of the way of his collation-job to present the knowledge of his day with transparency and openness. His stripped-down verse sparks an abrupt kind of hope—that through centuries and across incomprehensible language and cultural divides, there might be truly accessible guidelines for self-inquiry. Many who stumble upon his first chapter feel the thrill of a text that doesn't care who you are or where you come from or when you live, but is solely and plainly interested in handing over the keys of contemplative resolution. Patañjali doesn't ask for devotion: attention and open-hearted effort are the only admission requirements to his school, built of breath.

The scope of Patañjali-s project is magnificent: What is our internal strife? He presents no fatalistic creation story, no overt narrative of a great fall from grace. His therapy begins without explicit blame, *in media res*, with a brave act of epistemological humility, giving an outline of what can be clearly known by everyone: the vṛtti-s ("fluctuations of consciousness", according to many translators). Assertions, confusions, fancy, dreamless sleep, and remembering (1.5). Then he begins to parse the veil of words—"Confusions are the misalignment of words and reality" (1.7), to be able to describe more fully the limits of external and internal language: "This experience [of integration] can hold language, or it can be empty of words. The experience of worded or wordless wonderment plunges down to the quantum level" (1.42–4). He gives us permission to relax the anxiety of learning: "Presence is felt when you hold no expectation or assumption" (1.15). He names the actions and qualities that grant access to our most tranquil and uplifted states: "Reasoning, reflection, wonderment, and the awe of being alive are the initial gateways to integration" (1.17). In sūtra 1.41, he introduces a deconstructive idea: that at a certain level of trance, the mechanisms of perception and consciousness become transparent. What greater theme could be pursued by self-reflective travellers than to ponder how we know *what* we know, and how we know *that* we know? With the entirety of pāda one, Patañjali truly hands us the black box of consciousness, and says, "Open this, and free yourselves."

In my opinion, and setting aside the accidents of its publishing fame, the yoga sūtra-s deserves our continued attention as a wildly exciting text for four interweaving reasons. Firstly, it breaks with most previous paths of spiritual growth in its attempt to help the seeker excavate the tensions of inner life in a self-directed manner, without reliance on gurus or corporate bodies of authority. It is openly ambivalent to religious attitudes, going so far as to equate breath-awareness (1.34) with religious devotion (1.23) as a technique of evolution. From the outset, it contains no self-validating list of lineages, no creation story or deference to divine power: the text is a non-denominational and impersonal list of quiet discoveries. Secondly, the sūtra-s generally (if we remix pāda three) move away from the magical thinking directed at cutting deals with unreachable gods and invisible spirits for a better life—an approach that continues to pervade our current spiritual milieu, from the remote prayer experiments of evangelical Christians to the "think methods" popular in this new age of *The Secret*.

Thirdly, Patañjali offers a substantive and startlingly modern map of psychomentality, dividing out conscious faculties for our observation, and alluding to how the unconscious shadows that seem to motivate our actions might be illuminated. I render saṃskāra and vāsanā as "trace" and "pattern", following Feuerstein, who describes saṃskāra as a "sublimilinal activator", and vāsanā as a "chain of similar karmic activators" (1998, 241). Bursting forth from the Vedic tradition, which sought to pacify the external forces of adṛṣṭa ("unseen" gods and energies), Patañjali relocates the unseen within us, invites us to introvert, to open our eyes to why we are who and how we are. This puts the notion of "trapped memory" front and centre, allowing a clear reckoning of karma: our traces, habits, and grooves. Patañjali suggests that we can slowly free ourselves of the unseen. This relentless excavation of hidden thought as the source of our pain, this dive towards whatever is unconscious, represents a clear displacement of his ancestors' obsession with the whims of external gods.

This leads to the fourth gesture: the opening chapter of the yoga sūtra-s elevates the capacity for internal observation to the level of a virtue previously occupied by notions of "godliness". The sincere human no longer needs to adhere to a perfect ideal, whether social or philosophical, to attain wisdom. She simply needs to watch her experience unfold, and to enrich her action with tender watching.

These four gestures amount to a broad gift: the text places implicit value on the power of internal authority. Our consistent attraction through the ages to sources of external and often authoritarian power makes this gift as radical to us as it was to the Axial Age. We are collectively burdened with a Daddy-complex several millennia old, and the yoga sūtra-s stand as a rare call to the power of self-authorization.

The faith-based mechanisms of authoritarian religions and regimes alike propose stark claims. First and foremost: human life is valuable to the extent that it is possessed and directed by an external god, ideal, national identity, or social convention. Further: the road to perdition is paved with the delusion that you can find meaning in your own way. Further: you have fallen into this fallen world inevitably through your own fallen nature, and you can't learn your way out. Further: you need a saviour, and a book. Monotheistic systems add an additional dire warning: you'd better choose wisely, because there's only one true path, one true book. In 2010, Reverend Albert Mohler, president of the Southern Baptist Theological Seminary in Louisville, Kentucky, took a harsh stand against his followers who practice yoga, presenting his authoritarian view quite succinctly: "Christians are not called to empty the mind or to see the human body as a means of connecting to and coming to know the divine. Believers are called to meditate upon the Word of God—an external Word that comes to us by divine revelation." Patañjali-s compilation of aphorisms proposes the opposite tack. It suggests that because human suffering comes from habitual patterns of anxious relationship—between flesh, breath, emotions, others, and environment—we actually come pre-equipped with the ability to resolve these patterns through daily practices that quietly reorganize these relationships. Our innate and internal healing wisdom can be tripped into action by *any* fragment of inspiration: a god (1.23), or "something you love" (1.39).

Staying with this one example of authoritarianism among the many that are globally current, the Bible-centered Christianity of Mohler asserts that knowledge and authenticity come from a specific allegiance to a specific religious-historical person and event. It asserts that deviating from this authorization opens a doorway to eternal peril. Mohler's follower cannot be self-defined nor self-possessed. She may be permitted to stretch her muscles with the thought of having been made in god's expansive image, but must stop before her flesh becomes her own source of pleasure or even revelation. Mohler can't let his followers practice mindfulness, lest their minds become their own source of wonder. His Christianity works through the powers of church and god owning and directing the internal reality of believers. If there is pleasure, it comes from god, and not from within. If there is mental peace, it comes from god, and not from within. Mohler's follower seems to be forbidden to enjoy that which yoga practice holds dearest: personal agency that drives personal evolution. The most powerful and revolutionary statement that Jesus makes about our condition—"The kingdom of God is within you" (Luke 17:21)—is a sentiment that Mohler's authoritarianism must either reject or twist beyond recognition, but which Patañjali would encourage us to embrace with open arms.

This is not semantic: I'm afraid that this clash of worldviews may begin to play itself out in very negative ways throughout (especially exurban) North America, as well as many Islamic regions that have issued qualified *fatwas* against yoga practice—as has recently happened in Indonesia. When my ex-wife and I opened our first studio together in a small town in Wisconsin in 2002, the local Lutheran evangelical preacher announced from his pulpit that his hundreds of parishioners were forbidden from crossing our threshold. Soon after his sermon, our studio was vandalized. Looking back on this, I wonder whether we should have complained to the (nominally secular) state that we were suffering from religious persecution. But of course, we weren't practicing a *religion*—and that was exactly the preacher's concern. We were practicing self-inquiry, and there's nothing more threatening to the authoritarian mindset. The preacher would rather lose devotees to another church, I'm sure, than to watch them discover that they need no church at all.

My yoga-studio-in-the-heartland story has, I believe, a wider resonance. Yoga tends to show up wherever the dominant paradigm is wearing thin and creating internal conflict, wherever the emperor is losing his clothes, wherever people begin to say: "What I have been taught is not working: I need to find my own answers, together with those who speak to my heart." As such, it is part of an ongoing, often unseen, revolution in human culture that seeks unity through diversity and speaks silent truths to the bombast of established power. It's a revolution that has been with us throughout human history, and consistently meets resistance from those who do not yet have the courage or tools to find their certainty and peace through looking within themselves, while connecting to each other in relationship.

But we as contemporary practitioners have far less to fear than our forebears, who lived in deplorably worse times than our own. As I'll partially explore in section 4.12, the life from which the yoga sūtra-s emerges is inconceivably "nasty, brutish, and short", in the phrase of political philosopher Thomas Hobbes. We would do well to pause in wonderment and gratitude to consider that a few young dropouts of the Axial Age managed to overcome the horrors of infanticidal parenting, as well as constant war and raiding, starvation, inexplicable disease, terrifying superstition, caste slavery, constant violence against women and children, and barbaric laws and judicial systems—to learn how to simply sit still under a tree for long enough to enjoy the freedom of breathing, and to wonder at the deeper potentials of life.

In summary: pāda one is a gift of possibilities that have not tarnished through the millennia. Yet—we have to look very closely at what the chapter offers, for beneath the promises of its opening lies a largely unexamined worldview that no longer serves us as it once did. Drawing it out of the text may help us draw it out of ourselves.

4.3 looking closer: to join or not to join?

Patañjali begins by pinpointing obstacles that consciousness throws in the way of embodied peace: patterns of mental activity that tend towards the repetitive, neurotic, self-referential, and compressed. He names these patterns "vṛtti-s", a word that has been translated as "modifications" (Aranya, Taimni, Sacchidananda), "turnings" (Miller), or "changing states" (Bryant) of the mind. The implication is that habitual mental movement is innately problematic and self-perpetuating. He then hints at the active unbinding of these patterns through both transcendental and mindfulness practices. I have preserved much of this argument throughout my remix. But in the process I have also rewritten a fundamental claim of the text. This rewriting is central to everything that follows.

Sūtra 1.3 is typically (and more accurately) translated as "Then [through the practices of yoga] The Seer Abides In Itself" (Aranya). Or: "When thought ceases, the spirit stands in its true identity as observer to the world" (Miller). Or: "Then pure awareness can abide in its very nature" (Hartranft). In other words: if the movement of consciousness ceases, a primal, underlying function emerges (seer, spirit, observer, pure awareness), which can self-sufficiently enjoy itself, distinct from the rest of experience, and even from the world itself, as Patañjali suggests by the very name of his fourth book (kaivalya pāda: "The Book of Isolation", as it is conventionally rendered). The original text paints a vision of contemplative attainment that literally separates us from what we know—sensation, emotion, thought—and points us towards a post-cognitive state of luminous stillness. Edwin Bryant calls out this separative drive in his commentary quite plainly: "[The term] Yoga [insofar as it popularly translates to 'joining'] is best avoided in the yoga sūtra-s since...the goal of *yoga* [in the system of Patañjali] is not to join, but the opposite: to unjoin, that is, to disconnect puruṣa [seer, spirit, observer, etc.] from prakṛti [the material consciousness we seek to erase]" (Bryant, 5).

But is Patañjali-s promise of disconnection something that we find useful, or even comforting?

From my own practice and therapeutic work, I find it to be neither. But it is perhaps more important to clearly state that the premise is simply impossible. Patañjali-s claim that disconnecting one's identity from the internal voices of thought exposes an *a priori* self-awareness that carries all of the properties of a soul is directly contradicted by every thread of evolutionary theory that we have accepted into our culture through peer-reviewed research. The faculty of pure observation (draṣṭuḥ: "seer") that Patañjali wants to isolate and return us to has many monikers in both mindfulness culture, psychotherapy, and neuropsychology: the watcher, witness-consciousness, the observing ego, mentalization, self-consciousness. In our era, each one of these ideas refers not to something that preexists our everyday experience, but to a faculty that we develop through a socialized neurology. We are not born conscious, let alone *self*-conscious. We attain consciousness, and then awareness, slowly, methodically, through relationship and language, through seeing ourselves in mirrors, through seeing ourselves as others see us. Macrocosmically, some argue—Julian Jaynes (1976) is one—that self-consciousness is also an anthropological evolute that comes into our species history only three or four thousand years ago, at about the time that the first-person construction—"I am that I am" (Exodus 3:14)—first enters our poetry. Patañjali claims that the seer or the witness is eternally present, while developmental and evolutionary psychology show that witness-consciousness is born at about eighteen months in a child's life, and, macro-culturally, at the dawn of agriculture, when the fortunate among us gained new chunks of time with which we could sit and watch things grow, in the fields, and in our hearts.

Why is this issue important? If we take Patañjali-s forgivably archaic view uncritically—if we refuse to remix it—we subconsciously evoke a *devolutionary* narrative, which can have profound implications for our self-perception on the path of yoga. The belief that the normal functioning of our consciousness is an aberration covering over a pristine and original nature may strengthen our latent Judaeo-Christian "fall from grace". It can give a penitential air to the entire project of self-inquiry and growth, which may lead to subconscious puritanism and perhaps an undue seeking of clerical or saintly authority. And sadly, it fails to acknowledge the natural miracle of our developmental and anthropological growth: from unconscious perception, to involved cognition, to the capacity to witness—with this latest faculty including the previous two.

A primary argument of *threads* is, therefore, that the chatter of consciousness is indeed problematic, but not because it simply exists, as Patañjali-s vision suggests. Rather, I propose that consciousness is vulnerable to a kind of arrested development, in which the perpetual motion of thinking, imagining, and remembering becomes a default reactive mode that dissociates from the perceptual richness of the present moment. This dissociation crystallizes an alienating sense of individuation (asmitā), which must then struggle to rise above its fleeting concerns to participate in its broader ecosystem. After cognition begins in early childhood, we are vulnerable to numerous internalized abstractions that give rise to our science and artistry, but also can lead us away from interconnection:

> Through yoga, consciousness can become aware of its interdependence. Otherwise, consciousness can become increasingly alienated, and awareness becomes inaccessible.

The evolutionary perspective is crucial, I believe, to any goal of integration we might hold as postmoderns. In aphorism 1.16,

Patañjali claims: "When the ultimate level of non-reaction [i.e., the stilling of conscious movement] has been reached, pure awareness can clearly see itself as independent from the fundamental qualities of nature" (Hartranft). This reification of ultimate disconnection (ayoga) runs contrary to everything we currently know about the foundations of psychological wellbeing, as well as every effort we are currently making in our social and material sciences at healing the mind-body hard dualism of Descartes. For most of us, I believe, peace and authenticity arrive with a sense of things coming together, rather than things being split apart or cast out. Our healing drives are more reunitive than rejective. In stark psychoanalytical terms, Patañjali-s vision might be described as a disturbance gathered into an infantile avoidant fantasy of perfect self-sufficiency, in which the person wants to ultimately extract himself from every dependency and float, disembodied from his ecology—we should remember that this is impossible—beyond all waves of human care and concern. Ironically, this drive likely stimulates an increase in the anxiety-ridden thinking, planning, and imagining from which Patañjali wishes to save us. It is as if he wishes to reduce the alienation of mind-body disjunction by amplifying it. My remix of this thread drives the other way: *Awareness of interdependence is the fullest presence.*

It is worth noting again, however, that Patañjali does not seem entirely settled into this transcendental one-way flight from nature. While aphorisms 1.23 through 1.29 do focus on the goal of self-extraction from the world through the metaphysical ideal of Īśvara (an encouragement I supplant with a contemplation on the value of the *feeling* of devotion), aphorisms 1.33 to 1.39 offer techniques that feel right at home amidst current mindfulness culture. It would seem that the text is quite comfortable in socio-phenomenological discourse as it suggests integrating conscious thought with compassion (1.33), breath (1.34), or sensation (1.35). In these ways, Patañjali actually does teach a yoga we can recognize: the reunification of consciousness with the ecology from which it so hurriedly flees. This is the arc I choose to highlight.

4.4 considering "consciousness", "awareness", "perception"

The way in which I play with ("understand" would be an overstatement) the terms "consciousness" and "awareness" deserves a close look.

The first thing to say is that I use the former term in agreement with how it is used in contemporary neuroscience: "consciousness" is "that which introspects" (Jaynes, 1976). According to this model, nervous functions that have evolved both in our species-history and in the individual's life to be able to think, to know one is thinking, and to have a self-sense, all express the attainment of "consciousness". I use the term "awareness", by contrast, in alignment with how contemporary mindfulness culture uses it (Siegel, 2007): to express a refined function of consciousness that feels open, flexible, observatory, and non-reactive. "Becoming aware of…" is now common parlance for the psychological insight, patience, equilibrium, and empathy that all come with the purposeful grooming of regular consciousness. Awareness is consciousness with a diploma in Chillax.

One problem with this division that you will notice in picking up other texts on Patañjala-yoga is that the ranking of these terms is often reversed. "Consciousness" is the word used to describe the "purest" part of ourselves (puruṣa/draṣṭuḥ, in Patañjali's terms), and "awareness" is used to describe everyday mentation (citta) (Gerald James Larson is a good example, in White 2012, 78). "Pure consciousness" is further elided in the broader Indian literature with bliss, which is sometimes characterized as innate to human experience, and sometimes attributed to the divine. A common translation for the famous line, *cidānandarūpaḥ śivo'ham śivo'ham* of Śaṃkara-s Ātma Śatakam, is "I am Śiva: the form of pure blissful consciousness." If you read enough about Patañjali and hang out for long enough in the various streams of his oral heritage, you'll get the sense that few within the field are really clear or consistent on the distinctions between these terms. This is why I've reached outside of the traditional literature for distinctions that can describe evolution in yogic experience in language that makes reference to new neuroscientific standards while also respecting the changing flow of common usage.

According to my use of these two terms, it is clear that Patañjali wishes to elevate human experience beyond the swirling ambiguities of consciousness (citta) and into the unitary peace of awareness (puruṣa). But Patañjali's path is not evolutionary because he does not present puruṣa as something we move towards as we evolve in complexity, but rather as something that we recover: an original soul. Patañjali's puruṣa carries a speculative theology: it is eternal, ineffable, and independent of its material containment. In other words, it is most unlike how we know ourselves, and yet strangely fetishized as our primary aspiration. Although the sūtra-s do not explicitly announce a post-diluvian narrative, a basic transcendental guilt informs the entire psyche of the text: humans have fallen out of puruṣa/awareness into the delusion of citta/consciousness, and are only redeemable to our original purity by a subtractive suicide of flesh, feeling, and thought (a cessation of the vṛtti-s). Only by stripping ourselves of everything we actually know will we return to our original and forgotten souls: so says the sage.

But if we accept even a single sentence of Darwin, we are forced to acknowledge that development moves forward, not back. Consciousness is a complex evolute of the feeling flesh. This means that the highest achievements of consciousness—the capacities for self-reflexivity, non-reactivity, and dis-identification with the ego structure, to name a few—are the yet-further evolutionary refinements that we might call "awareness". Awareness blossoms for the human species in the same way it occurs to the human being—bootstrapping itself in a developmental surge out of a mystically complex foundation of consciousness, which itself hums with autonomic (involuntarily responsive) materiality. If we have awareness or souls, we have *evolved* them. Our souls are the last guests to the party. Awareness is not "original", but supplementary. We needn't crucify or starve ourselves to behold the soul, but rather continue to evolve towards the increasing illumination awareness seems to offer. Further, growing towards the soul—if that's our fancy—necessitates nurturing and adoring its mother: this flesh, this earth.

In my practice, "consciousness" and "awareness" exist along the same spectrum of meta-material abstraction. "Consciousness" refers to that aspect of waking and thinking experience that is capable of introspection, but also tends to forget its material origins through the ungrounding climb of cognition. "Awareness" refers to the temporary resolution of that ascent, through which a feeling of embodied re-integration may be felt. Awareness implies the non-reactive capacity to "hold" or "observe" the movements of consciousness with receptivity and empathy. It also implies for me a space of reverberant stillness in which consciousness has become content with its experience and refrains from doing anything to change it. Poet Lyn Hejinian expresses the dawn of advanced consciousness or awareness for me as she begins her book *My Life* (1987) with "A pause, a rose, something on paper."

Throughout the threads and their commentary, I will sometimes contrast "consciousness", which, according to our present neuroscience, accounts for a very small percentage of lived experience, with "perception"—our immediate, sensual, seamless, pervasive, intimate, wordless and thought-free coherence with the livingworld. The neuroscientists are now describing this livingworld relationship in terms of mirror neurology, which unconsciously moulds our experience in relationship to the other and the earth, and "neuroception" (Stephen Porges, 2011)—the pre-cognition interface that assesses environmental risk and safety. It is starting to look like our very flesh is programmed for intersubjectivity. Neuroscience is breaking new ground, and yoga philosophy will have to sharpen its language to catch up. I propose that if the evolute we call "soul" or puruṣa has a purpose, it should be to become more and more aware of this intersubjectivity. Thus my rendering of 1.16: *Awareness of interdependence is the fullest presence.* With awareness, our conscious life seems to reintegrate with our perceptual ground: the livingworld.

Perhaps the easiest way of showing how for me perception, consciousness, and awareness interweave is to simply quote from my remix of pāda four (4.18–26):

> Matter produces and is known by consciousness; consciousness produces and is known by awareness. Consciousness can be seen by awareness. But it is difficult for consciousness to be aware of itself seeing. The attempt can lead to a hall of mirrors and an alienation from time.
>
> When consciousness is still, it can become aware of itself. Consciousness is fulfilled when it warmly intermingles with matter and awareness. It delights in being seen. Being aware of this process imbues individuation with connection. This awareness re-integrates the part and the whole, and feels inexorable.

"Livingworld" is an important term for me that helps to braid these threads together. It is a translation of *Lebenswelt*, with which Edmund Husserl (1859–1938) inaugurated the current era of phenomenological philosophy. Phenomenology, briefly defined, is the consideration of "what appears" to subjective experience, stripped of any speculation about who is experiencing it and towards what end. Running with Husserl's term ever deeper into embodiment-philosophy, David Abrams (1996) describes the livingworld as our always-already present perceptual condition: the pressure of gravity upon your spine before you think of it, the ambient light and air-movement of the room you are sitting in before you consciously "name it to know it". Livingworld expresses our ecological interdependence prior to the alienation and abstraction consciousness brings to it. (I'll sometimes interchange "ecology" with "livingworld" in this book, and I intend both words to carry these meanings of general environmental support. "Ecology" as a word has the advantage of also being able to signify a disposition—*Greek:* "words or thoughts about our home"—which is why I also enlist it as a direct translation of śauca, which is otherwise rather narrowly rendered as "cleanliness".)

I once asked a friend and teacher of mine whether he believed in reincarnation. We were standing naked at the edge of a frigid swimming hole in early spring. He said "I really don't know, and I never think about it. Whenever I have a question about anything I try to just plunge into experience to feel the answer." Then he jumped into the black livingworld water with a war-cry that echoed through the mountaintop meadow. I stood and shivered, not quite ready to answer consciousness with feeling. But then I dove in, and became irrevocably aware of the moment, and was, in a sense, reborn. *A pause, a rose, something on paper*: awareness is perceptual presence plus conscious openness, stillness, and contentment, made possible not through heroic austerities (although a little cold water can help) but through allowing ourselves to feel the implicit support of our environment, which has never abandoned us, no matter what we have dumped into it nor how we have tried to flee it.

It is important to note that, perhaps with the exception of deep sleep (nidrā), the vṛtti-s that Patañjali seeks to pacify (nirodhaḥ) through various yoga practices (1.2) do not include this raw perceptual union between person and environment: the *a priori* fact of sense and sensibility. In effect, Patañjali ignores the already-given intimacy of the pre-thinking state. His list of vṛtti-s resides mostly within the conscious stages of mentation. Pramāṇa and viparyaya, for example, are typically translated as "right" perception and "wrong" perception. Vikalpa (fancy) is obviously conscious, while smṛti (memory) seems to cross the conscious/unconscious threshold with ease. Nidrā alone seems thin on conscious presence. If one is in relationship during deep sleep, the relationship is liminal. (Although my experience of the practice of yoga nidrā—meditative sleep—suggests that deep states of rest give a kind of porosity to the self-sense that perhaps opens me up to an ever-broader sense of relationship.)

A revisionist reader of Patañjali might feel that puruṣa is resonant with the open and nameless nature of perception according to the phenomenologists, preexisting the jagged shards (vṛtti-s) of consciousness that are his target. However, the cosmology upon which Patañjali relies (the Sāṃkhya system of 24 experiential elements) clearly divorces puruṣa from sensual contact, placing it outside of experiential relationship altogether—so much so that the very goal of yoga practice is to be able to return puruṣa to a purely disengaged state (the kaivalya or "isolation" of pāda four), in which it contains nothing, reflects nothing, and responds to nothing, basking only in the radiance of its own internal mirroring. Puruṣa is posited as outside and beyond materiality and consciousness altogether, existing eternally, a creator-god with nothing to create. (In psychoanalytic terms, it might be called a "masturbatory" fantasy, an image of bliss-through-aloneness.) Before the sublime isolation (kaivalya) that yoga practice is said to provoke, puruṣa is inaccessible to us, paradoxically, because of our "lower" material and conscious constituents—those same constituents we must use to try to attain it.

In essence, the original yoga sūtra-s invite us to resolve our anxiety and despair by rejecting and dissolving what we know about ourselves—and perhaps all that we can know about ourselves, our physicality and consciousness (citta)—into a null state, so that some yet-unknown but purer part of ourselves (puruṣa), which allegedly pre-exists physicality and consciousness, can emerge, unsoiled by the illusion of experience. Patañjali-s entire presentation hinges upon our re-identification with the allegedly eternal, *a priori* existence of a part of us, soul-like, that does not arrive, leave, grow, change, or think. It is strange that commentators still argue about the theism of this system: puruṣa itself is a passive *deus ex machina*. It doesn't sweep down out of the wings to save the heroes and transport them to heaven. It hovers above the stage, waiting for us to ascend out of lives purported to be unreal.

From what human feeling might this separative notion of puruṣa be derived? I believe that the jewel of our awareness is simply that very still, receptive, buoyant, vibrant state that most of us have experienced, marked by feelings of openness, abstract possibility, and the "long view" in which our personal identities lose their edges and our personal narratives pause their grinding forward motion. An hour of freedom, gazing at the sea. A suspension of time, a release of need, a radiant blankness in which both the form and content of life are empty of all questions and pressure. It is related to the qualia of "resolution", which I'll describe further in section 4.11. Often there is a sense of "laying down": I lay down my book, my laptop, my internal monologue. Things are almost suspended, and luminous. Awareness is not revealed by the erasure of an obscuring or illusory physicality and consciousness, but rather by the temporary deceleration of their swirling movement. It is any instance of quietude and brightness. For many of us, it is no more mystical or uncommon than a swimming hole, cold and deep.

4.5 thread 1.16 vs. phenomenology

More faithful translations of 1.16 than my remix show how it describes the ultimate goal of separating awareness from its object by neutralizing desire. Miller translates: "Higher dispassion is a total absence of craving for anything material, which comes by discriminating between spirit and material nature." Discriminating between "spirit" and "material nature" to the point of their mutual isolation (kaivalya—pāda four) is precisely what contemporary phenomenology and now neuroscience says is impossible. Awareness ("spirit") is always built upon "material nature", which provides all of its content.

From the phenomenological perspective of Maurice Merleau-Ponty, awareness is always "awareness-of" the manifold objects that call out the subjectivity of what we sense, feel, think, wish, and dream. Awareness does not have action or power or meaning outside of its object and their relationship. (As there cannot be a parent without a child.) In fact, the object seems to both precede and provoke awareness of it.

Neurologically, even if the content of awareness seems to be its *own* nature and qualities, it is still riding upon a material autonomic foundation. It sounds almost too obvious to say, and perhaps this is why we miss it: *the flesh is an absolute prerequisite for the meditator.* Internally mirroring self-reflection does not entail self-isolatability. Thoughts can fantasize about material withdrawal, and can even convince the thinker that this is happening, but can only ever do so through an act of denial as they ride upon the very materiality they claim to escape. To say that awareness can self-isolate into a state in which it alone exists is the arrogance of cognition forgetting its root. It is also a suicidal fantasy, or, in a less dramatic sense, the wish to disengage from our pervasive encounter with presence and otherness. It seems to be a flight from the stresses of contact and change. Unfortunately: it is a flight as well from the key junctures of learning and expansion and human development itself.

The inseparability of puruṣa and prakṛti is at our very fingertips. A meditation inspired by Merleau-Ponty may help. The technique is one of *chiasm*: the interdependent dialogue between one's flesh and the flesh of the world within the act of perception. David Abrams (1988) describes this interweaving as an "ongoing communion between divergent aspects of a single flesh."

Lay your hand down on a wooden floor. With as little conscious thinking as possible, allow adjectives to rise that describe what you feel. Perhaps: *hard, smooth, grained, supportive, resistant.* (These last two adjectives are almost transitive in nature, previewing the coming point. "Supportive" suggests *supportive-of* something, while "resistant" suggests *resistant-to.*)

Now ask yourself: are any of the words you used to describe the floor not also descriptions of your hand, but in shadow-form? "Hard"—as compared to what? *Your hand.* "Smooth"— in relation to what? *Your hand.* You took on the task of describing your world through your hand contact. You feel as though you became "aware" of the "floor". But, considered closely, your names for the floor actually described both you and the floor equally, and in relationship. The floor gave you an awareness of yourself. This subject-object intrinsicality is happening constantly on a stealth-perceptual level, and once in a while you can become aware of your sublime entanglement: the fact that the world gives you to yourself. Sensual engagement is *a priori* to every lived experience. You are feeling before you are conscious of feeling. You are conscious before you are aware of consciousness. Awareness is awareness-of.

4.6 on "yoga creationism" and the eternality of consciousness

The *a priori* and separative puruṣa of Patañjali inspires an undercurrent of eternalism that permeates yoga discourse to this day. We refer to "ancient teachings" while we defer to "sages of old". A thousand books speak of yoga's emergence from the "timeless Himalaya". Patañjali is an historical figure to the extent that we want to assert that he existed. But if we pin him down with dates (the scholarship argues between 200BCE and 300CE), many are quick to assert that he is not the "founder" of yoga: no—the mythical figure of Hiraṇyagarbha is. Hiraṇyagarbha (the "golden womb") is associated with the creator-god Brahmā in classical Purāṇa literature. Unconsciously, we begin to elide the origin of yoga with the creation of the universe, to the point that we often speak as if our art came from god. This feeling is sadly reinforced whenever yoga teaching takes on a sanctimonious or paternalistic air. Unfortunately, there is never a shortage of demagogues.

The notion of an eternal yoga might be consoling to those who crave certainty over learning, but all available evidence suggests that yoga evolved in tandem with our own developing needs for mood-regulation, other-awareness, and personal/social integration. "Yoga creationism", which tacitly denies this evolutionary perspective (and with it all too often the miracle of our own intelligence and adaptability), mutes the deeper conversations to be had about what we're doing, why we're doing it, how it is changing us, and how we are changing. It fancies a psychic return to Eden, rather than a sober grappling with what is here and now. Given the bizarre and reactionary rise of Biblical creationism in mainstream discourse, I believe we are compelled to do better than to offer a slightly hipper take on "what god says". It is much more valuable to contribute to the project of discovering who we are.

Embedded in yoga creationism is a self-similar flaw: devotional belief in yoga's eternality is mirrored by yoga's positing of eternalistic concepts. We easily intermingle the supposed eternality of yoga teachings with yoga's own eternalistic views of consciousness, mind, spirit, soul, etc. (which we can group together under the banner of "internality"). The eternal and external god/saint/sage who gives birth to the path of yoga at the beginning of time is mirrored by eternal and internal notions of the pure soul. But the obvious fact is that neither human consciousness nor the techniques that arise to manage and regulate it are eternal. Human yoga has evolved in response to the evolution of human consciousness—particularly to our faculty of internality, which has made us vulnerable to novel forms of alienation.

In the next section I'll turn to one possible story that we can tell about the emergence of the human consciousness that is both Patañjali-s target, and his medium. This story was first told by psychoneurologist Julian Jaynes in *The Origin of Consciousness in the Breakdown of the Bicameral Mind* (1976), and opens a door onto the perspective that yoga is a response to a new evolutionary complexity, rather than a rear-guard attempt to return to the Eden of puruṣa. Jaynes' evolutionary-psychology theory describes the birth of interiority and introspection in the era just prior to and continuous with the Axial Age. Aspects of his theory have been controversial for close to forty years now, and I use it with some circumspection. But regardless of the granular detail, general evolutionary thinking demands that we account in some way for how we began to rise up out of the purely phenomenal relationships of the animal world, and somehow began to abstract ourselves into the very private and interior isolation that Patañjali wishes to heal. Jaynes may or may not be right, but the fact remains that introspective consciousness had a beginning, that it continues its rising abstraction from the livingworld into the present day, and that we're still dealing with what this means and how to manage it.

Our consideration of the evolution of yoga will be mature when we consistently begin to feel good about what we are doing now according to our best knowledge and efforts, as opposed to the melancholic task of trying to reconstruct the purity of an invisible past, or to reanimate the corpses of saints and gods.

4.7 hard dualism as an outcome of the novelty of introspection

Julian Jaynes (1976) postulates a paradigmatic shift in human experience occurring at the dawn of agriculture and subsequent urbanization. He shows with startling poetry and interdisciplinary virtuosity that, within the space of a single millennium, we moved from claustrophobic perceptual coherence with the natural world to a state of internalized self-consciousness prone to alienation, which becomes both the object of and modus operandi of our earliest philosophies. The "self" that Vedānta tries to locate and reify (ātman), and which Buddhism strives to deconstruct (anātman), is in this view one and the same internality and isolatable individuality that did not exist in prior cultures. Thus, Patañjali is not remembering what the ancients taught, as many of the orthodox will preach. In fact, he is collating the improvised answers of his fellow yogis to a relatively new dilemma: the emergence of modern personhood.

According to Jaynes, our tribal ancestors inhabited a phenomenologically seamless world. The ecosystem left little space for feelings of private agency in the millennia prior to agriculture, and the further withdrawal from the sensual world brought by the dawn of literacy. We felt ourselves in direct communication with our surroundings: a blend of weather patterns, animal migrations, and daemons. So possessed were we by ecological forces (totems of wind, rain, animal, forest sprite) that we had little sense of decision-making or self-assertion. In the *Iliad,* Achilles does not *decide* to kill his foe: the wind in his lungs moves his arm to lift his spear. Abraham does not *decide* to kill Isaac: a voice from wind and fire commands him so. Nor does self-reflection stay Abraham's knife: it takes another exogenous force—an angel—to save the boy. We moved from campsite to campsite *in conjunction with* prey-movements, not because the *signs* of prey gave us the *idea* that it might be good to move camp. We did not use to *read* nature. We *were* nature. Puruṣa was unknown to us—and unneeded.

Our visceral, dreamlike, and often claustrophobic oneness between world and flesh was slowly pried apart by tool development, animal husbandry, and stuttering rises in health, longevity, and resulting population density, which forced neighbouring tribes into closer contact and commerce. Trade necessitated the accommodation of differing points of view, if constant conflict was to be avoided. Higher mental faculties emerged out of these first experiences of a wider-ranging social intersubjectivity. As inter-tribal trade spread, we began to translate languages and concepts, to use symbols, currencies, and other abstractions of value. Our survival became dependent less on being hardwired to the environment than upon the manipulation of multiple perspectives, protocols, diplomacies, languages, and goals. We began to use different voices in different social situations. By necessity, we began to create multiple inner selves. Human consciousness leapt from its nest into its network. This change was then compounded by the contemplative leisure time afforded to the wealthy by larger-scale agriculture and technologies of grain storage, codified with the rise of textuality, and corporatized by the emergence of legal and religious institutions.

In just a few thousand years, humanity progressed from the sensual coherence of an immediate and animalistic relationship with livingworld to the complexity of inner selves negotiating a representational society. Suddenly, going to market meant leaving your gods and forests behind; livingworld is no longer your governing principle. Your local gods cannot be shared with the other, who has his own. You must now be many things to many people and situations: a coherent broader community demands consensus. What was previously "true" is now displaced by the "efficacious" in the realm of social exchange and spectacle. In the midst of this new need for consensus, the burning questions arise. Out of these many roles, amongst many tribes, we ask: *Who am I? What is true*? No pre-modern human being asks these questions, because there is literally no separate internal agency to ask them, Jaynes suggests. But the social mask will give birth to an inner person, and when, like a three year-old, that inner person begins to ask the unanswerable, yoga must be born: a quest to commune, to rejoin, to feel grounded in a simpler mood. And where are the answers? They can no longer be outside us, for everything outside us changes and is subject to interpretation. For those who find uncertainty intolerable, constancy has to be relocated within, and then projected outwards into the unseen. From the soul, to heaven: so begins metaphysics.

In the Indian context, the crisis that attends our evolution into self-conscious life can be read within the very structure of the *Bhagavad Gītā*, in which the doubtful and introspective hero Arjuna seeks to individuate from the entanglements of his tribal responsibility on the threshold of its greatest expression—war. But his internal voice cannot yet have the final say. As if the tribal god is in his very skull, he receives direct instruction from Kṛṣṇa on staying the course of engaged action, on binding (yoking) himself to the natural/tribal purpose, and taming this new abomination of individualizing self-inquiry that threatens to extract him from active/phenomenal relationship. Arjuna is a modernizing human, plagued by the dawn of self-consciousness and its impact upon social complexity. Kṛṣṇa speaks for and from an older order, calling the hero back into harmony with a kind of devotional precognitive action we might associate with childhood, or with falling in love.

To summarize: the ascetic impulse (which Kṛṣṇa urges Arjuna to reject), with its hard-dualistic abstractions and anti-social, world-denying behaviours, was perhaps a traumatized response to exploding population density, compressive self-awareness, and the turning-inward of a new kind of private self. The Jains, Patañjali, other late-Vedic self-realizers, the Buddhists, and even the Platonists were all dealing with the same new and unknown quantity: the mysterious and seemingly infinite space of the hidden internal. Their impulse was to escape the growing chaos of social complexity by colonizing this new internal space and building within it protective scaffolds of language and symbol. The ascetics stood at the edge of a new human dilemma: it was now possible for us to feel separate from our environments, conceptually and, soon enough, technologically. It was now possible, through the reveries of abstract consciousness, to begin to imagine qualities unlike those we see in any other part of life: the eternal, the unchanging, the "perfect". It was now possible to chill out for extended periods of time in a new inner light, which seemed so much simpler, so much safer.

Patañjali-s stream of yoga seeks an inner home, inner identity, and inner truth. To find these, this stream retreats from our original livingworld: prakṛti. Now, our most pressing dilemma is whether or not we can re-enchant ourselves with the home we never really left. Do we now trust our livingworld—and each other—enough to resist this separative thrust, or have we come to believe (as most metaphysical traditions would teach) that this world is not our home, that we share it with other deluded souls, and that our bodies are entrapping and dragging these souls through the mud? Is an Axial Age solution to the search for safe internal space alienating us from the livingworld—the actual source and support for that search?

4.8 hard dualism as a failure of ambivalence

Earlier, I offered a psychoanalytical assessment of Patañjali-s dualism: "Patañjali-s vision might be described as an infantile avoidant fantasy of perfect self-sufficiency, in which the person wants to ultimately extract himself from every dependency, and float, disembodied from his ecology—we should remember that this is impossible—beyond the waves of human care and concern."

This is a little harsh. For an avoidant fantasy to emerge, consciousness must be terrified of *something*, and want to escape it. For all of us, this is a tender and painful story, and it follows a shared theme. As we come to know ourselves as separate from our mothers, we come to know the mother as other: unknown, uncontrollable. Where once her flesh literally was our own—the ocean from which we were born—we begin to see it as both source of nurturance, and, by virtue of her separateness, the very source of unreliability. She who once fulfilled all of our needs now may only meet some, and according to her own inscrutable will. The mother becomes two mothers to the child: a "good mother" and a "bad mother". Pierre Janet, Sigmund Freud, and Melanie Klein (Klein, 1987) all explored the ramifications of such splitting, and how, over time, the splitting of the mother becomes introjected, internalizing into a "good self" and a "bad self".

Klein in particular went further to describe how the infant begins to dissect the mother's flesh into the "good breast" (source of comfort, food, attention), and the "bad breast" (the possible denier of each). She called this stage the "paranoid-schizoid" period, in which the baby's world is divided into "all-good" things, and "all-bad" things: a condition that might shed light on the psychic roots of all hard-dualist positions. Klein called the psychological achievement of understanding that both mothers exist within the same flesh "the depressive position": a painful, slowly-won, but utterly fulfilling understanding that there is ambivalence within all life experience.

The hard dualism of Patañjali that imagines enlightenment as withdrawing from the "bad mother" of prakṛti expresses what the Kleinian line of thought might call a "failure of ambivalence". For Patañjali, prakṛti will always mortally disappoint: there's no choice but to escape or transcend it. It will never attain the rich and complex status to which psychoanalyst and pediatrician Donald Winnicott refers when he describes the maturity involved in loving the "good-enough mother"—the mother we accept as embodying both what we need and what we can never fully have (Winnicott, 1967). We might say that any hard-dualist stance within yogic thought expresses a psychological development arrested at the paranoid-schizoid phase of late infancy, in which the child has been unable to accept the good and the bad together. Without repairing this split, which Klein cautioned might lead to psychosis, how can yoga heal our primary maternal relationship with the earth?

Pressing further: the black-and-white thinking that divides experience into the corrupt and incorrupt cannot come from observing our livingworld. The natural world does not etch boundaries, and our ancestors felt this. Shapes, colours, movements, living, and dying elide and intermingle. Every edge is porous. Approaching the glow of a village fire will provoke the rising feeling of coming home, but light alone will not create thresholds of home and not-home. Human art and literature emerge from liminal dream-time, paintings of flowers emerge on rockfaces, and our stories are filled with mystical birds who conjoin the worlds. There is no cartography in our early history, no *Chicago Manual of Style*, no rules of evidence, no sterile environments, no closed canons.

Perhaps our tendency to divide things into opposing categories is not in-born, but a cognitive/linguistic overlay that develops when the psychic stress of ambivalence is not digested. When we felt our mothers becoming two, we either split the world along with them, or we transferred their strange changeability onto and into everything we felt, including our developing sense of self. The vast majority of humanity did the first, and has since used the same splitting skill to carve up land, time, flesh from mind, the worthy from the unworthy. Even agriculture demands that we separate wheat from chaff in a way that foraging never did. Mother, other, and world became wheat and chaff. Yoga has so far not escaped this pattern of cleaving, but now it might.

4.9 healing the presumptuousness of consciousness, healing the inner family tree

My argument so far is that human consciousness is our youngest faculty, laying itself over the phenomenal world, seeking to interpret it, and yearning to become co-creative with it. It is capable of many wonders—naming, theorizing, manipulating, exalting—but also of losing itself in abstraction, ambiguity, and forgetfulness towards its sustaining relationships. Human consciousness is a new and powerful agency that doesn't quite know how to use itself or how to make itself feel at home in its material seat. It is the child of matter, suffering from separation anxiety, neurotic with self-preservation and self-consolation, ebullient with creativity, surging with pride. It fantasizes about killing its material parent, and expresses this fantasy through the transcendent urge. Consciousness is matricidal. Metaphysics is its gleaming dagger.

Patañjali (and most yoga philosophy, to be fair) gets the genealogy backwards, suggesting that flesh is the child of consciousness and must be tamed by its parent to the point of invisibility. The ascetic wish is to perfectly manage his alienation by erasing all traces of material connection, by cutting down his family tree. He wants to heal his separation-trauma by convincing himself he was never really dependent upon anything or anyone. He forgets perhaps the oldest translation of prakṛti: "she-who-creates" (Feuerstein 2007, 242). If he isolates himself perfectly from the mother of materiality, he believes, his conviction might stick. The development of modern consciousness brings alienation along with introspection; the ancient yogi often chose to make this a virtue.

Most new yoga, however, as it plays out throughout the world today, suggests that the separation of consciousness from phenomena (child from parent) must simply be recognized, so that we can progress towards re-integration. Most of us who practice yoga feel our relationships improve over time, perhaps because by consciously sinking into every sensation we are implicitly healing the root "family" trauma of our evolution of consciousness. Perhaps familial tension itself is in some ways a projection of the tension of inner psychic genealogy. As we re-integrate conscious and perceptual life, we heal the crisis of individuation on multiple levels. Sinking back into the mother—"she-who-creates"—reconnects us with our full lineage.

4.10 evolution through hacking

There is an old riddle: the blade of a knife, no matter how sharp, cannot cut itself. The problem with looking at consciousness is that *we* are consciously looking. The *I* that looks for itself looks through the lens of the I's eye. Consciousness is the black box of experience. Consciousness is like proprietary software both produced by and sold to the end-user: our sense-of-isolated-self.

The yogi is a hacker dedicated to breaking the protected and protective code of our self-enclosed conscious life with awareness. She reverse-engineers how we went from being immersed in our livingworld to believing in our separation and its permanence. Key hacking codes include evolutionary biology, developmental psychology, neuroscience, and language theory. Evolutionary biology provides us with a working model of how everything makes itself, changes, and improves according to innate desire, rather than divine *fiat*. Developmental psychology allows us to empirically unfold layers of mental function so that we can clearly see what we are treating through meditative practices. Neuroscience smashes mind-body dualism. Language theory shows our self-referential circularity, illuminating the problem of black-box consciousness. And then there is meditation itself, in which all cognitive ventures come into a still focus. Meditation is like a key generator. Each moment of integration (and there are so many we haven't been invited to recognize!) spits out a key-code to unlock the product of our self-possession. Consciousness wants to make money (identity) out of its privacy. But the yogi is a self-hacking Robin Hood.

By strict cultural code, hackers share everything they learn. The discoveries of any individual must enrich the hive. And as they do, the individual expands, and her boundaries become more porous, and she craves yet more intersubjectivity. Yoga should in the end be completely open-source, where open-source is the medium of empathy, so that everyone can read the code, reflect each other's creations, and alter it towards their novel applications.

The proprietary attitude of various schools over "yogic truth" can provide for a while the engaged heat of dialectic. But like passionate and aggressive lovers melting into each other, the proprietary schools could resolve their quarrels with a fire that illuminates, as the notion of ownership burns.

Nobody *has* the truth. Truth is the product of sharing what seems to be true. *We* all *inquire into yoga.*

4.11 meditation on the qualia (guṇa-s) of existence

In the moments before sleep, there is buoyancy. The day rises up to disappear as the night sinks down to settle in. Both day and night, light and dark, pass through the flesh, which is both pressed up and hangs in the balanced resolution of accomplishment. The "I" that worked through the day dissolves at the edges, becomes plural. The story of time pauses. Thought rests in the margin. There is luminous satisfaction. The qualia of resolution (sattva) abides, for a while.

(If you are sitting by a window, now might be a good time to let your eyes lift from these words to gaze unfocused into the middle-distance. *A pause, a rose, something on paper.*)

Beneath the timeless feeling, time passes, and gravity overcomes the buoyant. Sleep becomes heavy. The flesh sinks into the bed more than it rises, and then does not rise at all, and feels like it never will again. The expansive "I" shrinks back into its margins, and becomes a stone, the centre of a story that has been forgotten. Circulation slows, nerves dull, and tissues become heavy. Consciousness slides from a positive to a negative charge. Internality inverts from presence to absence. The qualia of gravity (tamas) abides, for a while.

Everything that falls must rise, it seems, as if the pull of what is above limits every downward range. At a certain level of density, deep beneath the earth, or at the bottom of the well of sleep, heat begins to gather and glow. Compression is felt as pressure, and resistance awakens to press back. The flesh twitches with a nameless need, breath deepens and quickens, the eyes move beneath the lids and the root of the tongue quivers deep in the throat. Things rise out of the dark towards something: a want or hunger, a need. The impulse to go somewhere, to reach and grab something. The qualia of urge (rajas) moves forward, accelerating, for a while.

Urge, as desire, fixes upon an object, and moves to be near it, to grasp it, or consume it. It is fire reaching out for fuel, predator moving towards prey, lover reaching for beloved. At the point of contact and consumption, the fire burns brightest, and then, sated, resolves to radiant resolution: a satisfaction that abides for awhile, until rest becomes heavy, and turns into a swoon.

The qualia of gravity, urge, and resolution play out visibly through the sleeping-waking-sleep-cycle. But also macrocosmically through the seasons, with the urge of spring resolving to the radiance of late summer's accomplishments, before the fields and gardens are put to bed for the winter of gravity. And microcosmically: through the cycle of each task, beginning with a burst of inspiration, driving towards accomplishment, which elides into the stasis of mild boredom, before the next inspiration strikes. And existentially: in drive, crisis, death, compost, regeneration. In the *Saṃkhyakarika* of Īśvarakṛṣṇa, it says "The guṇa-s successively dominate, support, activate, and interact with one another" (12–13).

Perhaps the clearest play of the qualia is felt in the erotic. Desire for communion builds to fever. So many jagged edges rise to be resolved: the crisis of individuation, the need to atone (to make "at-one"), the need to re-member the flesh through the pleasure at its root. Movement quickens, heated fluids release, gazes meet through shared flame. Orgasm is a bright fire, enraged or exuberant, or both. And then the sharpness of its heat softens and floats as the gazes cool, sweat glistens and begins to dry, and gravity pulls the lovers to the undifferentiated earth.

But if this connective flow of energies, moods, and feelings sounds beautiful to you, Patañjali thinks you are naïve. In 2.15 he places this exact cycle of energies at the root of human suffering. Aranya translates:

> The Discriminating Persons Apprehend (By Analysis And Anticipation) All Worldly Objects As Sorrowful Because They Cause Suffering In Consequence, In Their Afflictive Experiences And In Their Latencies And Also Because Of The Contrary Nature Of The Guṇas (Which Produces Changes All The Time).

In other words, Patañjali proposes a nirguṇa ("without qualia") vision of salvation. ("Nirguṇa" is a word more commonly used to describe a certain Advaita Vedāntin approach to describing "the Absolute", i.e., with as few words as possible. I'm using it more simply here, because Patañjali is literally *against* the qualia.) According to the text, life reaches its perfection when all of its irritating changes are sent packing. The sad absurdity of this notion becomes clear if you read Aranya's rendition above with a whining Droopy-Dog impression.

The original describes the guṇa-s as "virodhāt": in "conflict", or "opposition" (Hartranft), "turning against themselves" (Miller), or "ever-warring" (Prabhavananda). The message is one of agented and willful conflict, as though the livingworld were in a continual state of psychic tension, rather than anabolic/metabolic/catabolic oscillation. Like the metaphysical hard dualism that emerges from a failure of ambivalence, I believe this is another instance in which yoga philosophy projects a tension internal to human consciousness onto the livingworld. The forces of nature are "vy[ing] for ascendancy" (Hartranft), because our own internal and often contradictory voices are doing the same. The anthropomorphization of livingworld in this way is an attempt to make it more understandable, surely, but it also appropriates it into our humanly narrow framework, which lacks the implicit support and nourishment of what is always-already here.

The flow of what is always-already here is insufficient to Patañjali because of what it is: always-already changing. But what exactly is without qualia? What exactly is without oscillation and change? Not even the fantasy of the changeless thing or state is without change, as is clear from the history and language of metaphysics: the "soul" or the "Absolute" has gone through countless theoretical edits and amendments.

The etymology of "guṇa" suggests "bond", as in a force that binds a group of experiences together, but also a force that binds the jīvātman, or individual soul, to the uncertainties of nature. Throughout much of Indian philosophy, the guṇa-s are presented as agented, semi-divine forces that will seize and enslave human life to their qualities without warning. This sense, in which the guṇa is felt to overtake or possess consciousness, enhances a deep layer of the puruṣa/prakṛti hard dualism that I have worked to resist throughout this text. I used to translate guṇa as "mood", but have come to feel that this doesn't carry enough weight, and also that it restricts the range of the word to the human realm, when, like bhūta (element) or doṣa (psychosomatic humour), the word actually describes actions and experiences ranging across the entire flesh of the world.

To translate guṇa, I have turned to "qualia", a Latin word meaning "what kind" that is often used to denote the general notion of what things are like, or how things feel in their "rawness". I use it to continue to point to the level of experience before and beneath language and the conscious: the realm of the perceptual. "Qualia" picks up a rich thread of discourse in the philosophy of science and mind that endeavours to explore the ineffable textures of subjective experience and whether they can ever be fully known through physicalist explanations. Some thinkers say that qualia are self-existent: that experiencing the "redness" of red, and the "pain" of injury (both common examples of qualia) can never be fully explained by the causal language of science and therefore always reside at least partially outside the cognitive realm. Others say that qualia are merely metaphors that obscure the concrete mechanisms of experience: that "redness" is simply light with a certain wavelength, or "pain" is an inflammatory response. "Qualia" serves quite well for guṇa insofar as it holds this argument, but not as an argument that seeks resolution. "Gravity" to me is *both* an irreducible raw feeling that can only be expressed through metaphors of sleep and post-coital swoon *and* the atomic weight of a heavy metal. To me, the finest words, like "love", carry a charged play between vast and granular meanings. I also appreciate that the argument over the substantiality of qualia/guṇa-s is self-similar: like the oscillation of the guṇa-s themselves, it will never end.

4.12 from infanticide to deconstruction: exploring the origins and legacy of the nivṛtti and nirguṇa impulses

Spiritual paths tend towards the subtractive or the immersive. Subtractive paths focus on what must be taken away in order for a presumed purity of identity and experience to re-emerge, while immersive paths seek to integrate a fragmented world and psyche. Patañjali offers a subtractive path that advocates stripping experience of vṛtti-s (mental movement) and guṇa-s (qualia of existence).

I have argued in 4.7 that his asceticism may emerge from a traumatic phase within the evolution of modern consciousness (Jaynes, 1976). But I also believe that his and other subtractive paths may also emerge at least in part from a darker psycho-historical trauma that provokes the defenses of rejection, denial, and escapism. In our time, we have sublimated this trauma into a penetrating skepticism that serves us very well, while concealing the pain of an old wound. Understanding where it comes from might allow us to move forward with a little more transparency. This is a difficult idea that demands much further development. I offer it here in speculative form.

Subtractive paths are austere in nature, and often sparse in aesthetic. The robes of the Zen monk and Benedictine friar express the same renunciation: the first tries to strip himself of separative ignorance, that *satori* may flash through him; the second has abdicated his personal agency, that his soul may not distort the reflection of Christ. The sky-clad Jain is the most extreme exemplar of this drive. The purpose of the subtractive path is to empty out personhood, to scrub individuality, shed distinguishing clothes and ornaments, to vacate society and its prescribed roles, to fast, to shave one's head, to unsex oneself, to resign from economy, to become pure to the point of invisibility, to leave no footprint, to sublimate, to become homeless, to seek only the horizon, to be without lover, country, or children. To seek, as the old man in the Hemingway story: "a clean, well-lighted place." Or perhaps to disappear altogether: nirvāna translates literally as "extinguished".

The overall feeling of the subtractive is penitential. There is a debt to be paid, a rage to be soothed. One's head stays bowed. One is haunted by a vague school-boy sense of always being in trouble. The subtractive seeker feels he has somehow overstepped his bounds, abused his welcome on earth, and must pay something or someone back. But why? Why should anyone feel inherently unwelcome in this life? What is our original sin? Perhaps it is the psychic burden of having survived the holocaust of human history.

Interpreted through the psychogenic stages of human parenting as theorized by Lloyd deMause, the morbidity of these systems might be said to have arisen out of the "infanticidal mode", prevalent in many human cultures from prehistory until the 4th century CE. Let us be clear: the root of every conventional spirituality that we know and practice today, from the Abrahamic faiths to all Indic religions prior to medieval Tantrism, lies in the gore of this incomprehensibly savage era. A full survey is neither possible nor appropriate here, but suffice to say that throughout the ancient world, childhood was a nightmare from which many did not awaken. Ritual child-sacrifice to appease dark and chaotic fears was common, hardening through millennia into formidable cycles of fear and abuse. Parents offered children to their gods in exchange for the mercy of having survived their own infancies. This is what makes the Calvary narrative so poignant in our imagination: Jesus is the archetypal sacrifice of son to father (in the guise of a father's sacrifice of his son to us). The promise of his story is that his was the ultimate and salvific child-sacrifice—no others need follow. And yet they do. In later phases of the infanticidal period, exposure of infants to death (often twice as many baby girls than baby boys) accounted for staggering neonatal mortality rates (estimates range up to 50%) and gender disparities. The exposure of infants continued to be so globally common that moral sentiment against the practice only began to be enshrined into legal codes beginning in the 19th century.

In *Foundations of Psychohistory*, deMause states the obvious with regard to this horrifying history: "When parents routinely resolved their anxieties about taking care of children by killing them, it affected the surviving children profoundly" (deMause, 61). Let us be clear: Abraham, the Saptarṣis of Vedic lore, Moses, the Hebrew prophets, Zoroaster, Mahāvīra, Gautama, Patañjali, Jesus, Śaṃkara, Dattātreya, and Nāgārjuna are all survivors of cultures of widespread infanticide. The paths they go on to establish are imbued with two powerful sentiments: that of being "chosen" by God or *karma* to fulfill a supernatural purpose (but perhaps "chosen" is more properly understood as "spared" from amongst their siblings), and profound distrust for what should be more natural systems of support: parents, family, ecology. These two feelings are wrapped in a powerful group-fantasy that perpetuates the pursuit of sacrificial disciplines to grant psychic release: we have fallen into the chaos of sin or ignorance and we must atone. Abstractive concepts of transcendent realms devoid of human relationship and the values of growth and change become the spiritual ideal. Traumatized by the horrific psychic pressures of the infanticidal context, the forefathers of world religions dream of escape: inwards to an imagined soul or upwards to an imagined heaven. Either direction requires self-subtraction, especially from family life, even though the real source of pain is usually too terrifying to name. Infanticidal violence is internalized: the child is the parents' unconscious scapegoat, and is compelled to purify himself for reasons he will never consciously know. Still, the geniuses seem to intuit the enemy: Mahāvīra and Gautama run away from their tyrannical fathers. Jesus says to his mother: "What have I to do with you?" (John 2.4). St. Francis of Assisi strips naked before his imperious father in the piazza, burns the garments of his pedigree, and then wanders the hills above the town as an outcast. And Dattātreya sings of the wishful conclusion to familial withdrawal in Avadhūta Gītā, 1.63: "[In truth] you have no mother, no father, no wife, no son, no relative, no friend. Why is this anguish in your mind?"

I can only imagine that the grown children of a culture of infanticide would be deeply unsettled by survivor's guilt, in which the senselessness of one's luck indentures one to an unseen magic. Or it becomes so intolerable to realize that one is alive because others have died that only self-negation will ease the pressure. In this sense, a powerful way of rebalancing the guilt of surviving would be to limit the scope of being alive—through self-mortification, or by becoming stoically "dead" to the world. ("I die daily," says St. Paul.) This would especially apply to the denial of pleasure. In today's language, in which survivor's guilt has now become a symptom-category within post-traumatic stress disorder, such pressures are thought to lead to severe anxiety and clinical depression. In our day, more soldiers commit suicide after returning home than die on the battlefield. Is survivor guilt one of the mental health contexts from which the metaphysics of transcendence arises?

Self-erasure makes strategic sense for the guilt-tortured psyche. The ascetic withdraws and hides from violent parents and a volatile society, disappearing physically into the forest and mentally into mantra and abstract contemplation. Perhaps he seeks a perfectly disembodied parent in his god, or to identify with god by stripping away his own non-divinity, or for a source of consolation that lies beyond relationship altogether. He rejects childhood relationship by fleeing his parents. He rejects the childhood of citizenship by fleeing the state. He becomes no-one and nothing in his pursuit of dissociative bliss. Śaṃkara echoes Dattātreya in his Ātma Śatakam: "I have no father or mother, I have no birth. I have no relatives, nor friend, nor guru, nor discipline. I am Śiva: the form of pure blissful consciousness." Śaṃkara is central to understanding what we have inherited of Patañjali-s legacy: his commentary on the sūtra-s has governed the discourse since the 9th century CE.

For the guilt-ridden survivors of infanticidal culture, I imagine that the self-subtractive behavioural arc might also be the root of the philosophical technique of *via negativa*: the manner of describing reality, transcendent states, profound truths, or god/gods in terms of what they *cannot* be, because we fear our language fails the task of sublime description. Or, more poignantly, we fear to speak at all. For example: god is met in the "Cloud of Unknowing", according to the nameless English mystic of the late Middle Ages. Similarly, "ultimate reality", which several Buddhist systems of meditation aspire to experience, is framed as śūnya—devoid of characteristics. We dare not name god, for to name god would be to presume to share power with god. We are in hiding from god's murderous wrath: better not to call god anything for now, nor to make images of god, according to the *negativa* way. Silence is our safety.

Perhaps the technique of philosophical negation extends the process of external self-subtraction down to the cognitive level. Just as one's flesh, social role, libido, family, appetite, and homeland must be stripped away to appease the murderous father or god, so too must our deluded conceptual language be stripped of its positive and presumptuous descriptive power. Our common lives cannot honour the largesse of divinity, and our common language dares not serve it but through silence. Śaṃkara's hymn is a litany of negations driving towards a pristine dissociation. Singing as though he has become one with Śiva, he not only denies being a body, or having sense organs, elements, and prāṇa through a process of external subtraction, he also denies having intellect, ego, subjectivity, and even emotions in verses of internal subtraction. He is running away from something. The language of *via negativa* suits the traumatized subtractor well. He needs to hide. He will speak when given permission. And when he speaks it will be reductive. Jesus says: "Simply let your 'Yes' be 'Yes,' and your 'No,' 'No'; anything beyond this comes from the evil one" (Matthew 5:37).

I now risk wondering aloud if *via negativa* philosophy, so haunting in tone, is a sublimation of the cry from the nursery/abattoir of antiquity. Screams of "no" emerging from the horror of our infanticidal root elide into the anti-social "no" of ascetic withdrawal, to finally resolve into the internal "no" of neti-neti ("not this, not this"), which is used to push feelings and thoughts away from contact with all phenomenal and even abstract objects, into a realm of self-referential isolation, where, theoretically, abandonment and pain is impossible. "Always *not this, not this* to both the formless and the formed" sings Dattātreya in 1.62 of *Avadhūta Gītā*.

When I contemplate this progression of *no*'s, I feel it in the flesh as an old gestural pattern. I think first of the thrashing of my head from side to side while screaming during my circumcision (a memory of vestigial infanticide I have recovered through trance-work). Later, I remember the firm head-shake of rebelling against authority and renouncing the social structures and expectations I knew to be oppressive. Later still, I can feel the half-head-shake-half-head-bobble motion of philosophical discernment or bafflement—a movement I was surely mimicking from my Indian and Indophile teachers, but which also felt natural to the ineffable themes we spent our days contemplating.

Deeper than this, I have noticed in my yoga experience a repeated refrain of negation that is inherent to my desire for meditative peace. I have so often entered my room, closed the door, and sat down into the psychological posture of "not-this, not-this". My ex-wife used to say I was entering my Śiva-pod. (It sounded funny, but she wasn't really laughing.) I wanted the complexity of everything to simply fade into white. An outer shell of complexity consisted of unresolved childhood stresses, my career uncertainty, my relationship issues, Republicans, creationists, global warming. Banishing these from my conscious mind soon elided seamlessly into rejecting conceptual frameworks, spiritual platitudes, and even language itself. Every single day I elided a renunciation of things and conditions into a renunciation of ideas about things and conditions. External withdrawal was the model for internal withdrawal. I wanted to escape both the violent world and the seeming violence of my mind. I just said no, or rather, *not-this*: first to pain, and then to thinking about pain, and then to thinking altogether.

One day my therapist seized on a pause in my own holy litany of similar rejections, looked me straight in the eye and said, "I know all about what you're running away from. What I want to know is what you're running towards. Who and what are you living *for*?"

How is this relevant to our consideration of Patañjali? Broadly speaking, subtractive paths are described as nivṛtti in Indian philosophy: "having turned away", i.e., from the turnings of the world. This not only resonates with Patañjali-s 1.2, but with the yoga sūtra-s repeated reference to the desired end of guṇ-ic activity. Coherent with his erasure-plan for the vṛtti-s, Patañjali also dreams of an end to the cycles of gravity, urge, and resolution. Bryant translates the end of the path in 4.32: "As a result, there is a cessation of the ongoing permutations of the guṇa-s, their purpose now fulfilled." We can also come back to the key thread, 1.16. Bryant has: "Higher than renunciation is indifference to the guṇa-s." To things that conflict, cycle, change, resolve, and begin again, Patañjali says: *not-this*. He predicts the later philosophical dream of a nirguṇa (without-qualities) ecstasy. To desires, attachments, and the flesh, he says *not-this*. To assertions, confusions, fancy, dreamless sleep, and remembering, he says *not-this*. To the social responsibilities of Vedic culture, he says *not-this*. To words that would presume to define happiness, he says *not-this*. At the top of his hierarchy of meditative attainment is asaṃprajñāta samādhi: "integration without thinking".

Current levels of abusiveness in parenting are rarely murderous. Except for the moments of intense pain and autonomic fear that attended my circumcision, I have never felt mortally endangered by my protectors, and I doubt many of those I know ever have. I was strapped and beaten in my incredibly anachronistic Catholic boy's school, but the fear wasn't mortal. (Citizens of more oppressive regimes are not as fortunate.) As a global community, most of us have not walked through 19th-century London and Paris and seen rats gnawing on the corpses of abandoned babies in the gutters. We have not witnessed wet-nurses smothering the unwanted (deMause, 32). The fear of being killed as a child, along with the guilt of surviving infanticide, is slowly beginning to evaporate from the human psyche. If we're not still barely surviving, do we have as much need to transcend something? Is transcendence becoming obsolete? Even if it is, it seems that the primal *no* that initiates the transcendent reflex remains with us in a sublimated form.

The nivṛtti-cum-nirguṇa views of Patañjali and others may be rooted in escape-drives and death wishes, but they have themselves become the roots of cognitive deconstruction, tinged with an old trauma. This might be a hidden attraction to us as postmoderns: the neti-neti head-shake of the Advaita Vedāntist ("Non-Dualist-Perfected-Philosophers") inheritors of Patañjali-s austerity is deeply resonant with our own critical impulses. The sensitive among us are constantly shaking our heads "no" in rejection and disbelief. Our zeitgeist overflows with, as Jean-François Lyotard describes, an "incredulity towards metanarratives". Institutional religion? *Not-this*. The Great Man Theory of history? *Not-this*. Romantic idealism? *Not-this*. Capitalism? *Not-this*. Revolution of the proletariat? *Not-this*. Social Darwinism? *Not-this*. The green revolution? *Not-this*.

The allopathic model? *Not-this*. Consumerism? *Not-this*. Ecological salvation through scientific manipulation? *Not-this*. Modern gurus? *Not-this*. From the nirguṇa gesture we have developed a very powerful tool for discernment that we now freely apply to all signifiers of distorted power dynamics or tepid banality.

I've felt that in this vast collective refrain of *not-this*, our hearts open to possibilities we are often not bold enough to describe or commit to. There is a melancholy to our deconstruction. I believe that if we can find the unconscious source of this sorrow—perhaps in the bloody cradle of our prehistory—and really listen to how much species-hurt we carry with us, we will perhaps fall in love with how far we have come. We might let go of our need to purify, self-subtract, and be-against as we look at each other and ask, "What, dear friends, are we living for, now?"

My partner was seven months pregnant when I wrote this. At that moment, I had my what-am-I-living-for answer. I gazed at her swollen belly and shuddered with love and longing, with the thought of how different a home and family and world baby will be born into, compared to that of our traumatized forebears. I can't even imagine the philosophy this baby may write or dance or sing.

4.13 further reverie on śūnya and zero

A friend wrote to me with a reflection on an earlier draft of the previous section:

Your mention of your baby soon-to-come makes me want to remind you that the root of the word "śūnya" implies "being swollen" and indeed used to refer to the belly of a pregnant woman. To my mind, this is the deep meaning of "emptiness"—not an "ultimate reality devoid of characteristics", but the fact that at this very moment, all "objects" are already-empty of any transcendent, un-changing essential nature or svā-bhāva (self-essence). So they can be what they are: swollen with possibility.

Patañjali uses śūnya four times, the most prominent being in thread 1.43, describing levels of openness as awareness builds: *it can be empty of words*. As my partner prepares for birth, she often goes inside herself to "speak to baby". "But we don't use words," she says.

The pregnant belly embodies the roundness of zero, the number which gives all other numbers creative meaning. "Śūnya" in Sanskrit elided into the Arabic "ṣifr", which also meant "empty", and was used in its earliest form as a "cypher"—a placeholder between numbers. Slowly, "ṣifr" melded with the Italian "zefiro", which also meant "the west wind": the wind arising from sunset and the end of things, to blow one's sails eastward toward the dawn. The Venetians refined *zefiro* to *zero* as they built their castles on water. The symbol of water element in Indian systems is a circle. It is the shape of the lips saying *om*. And the earth itself is a sphere.

It seems that in the shadow of the negations of Patañjali and his Advaita Vedāntin interpreters—all of these not-this's and nothings and nevers—embedded within a language of pain, something generative swells and waits.

4.14 my revisions of key patañjalian views

What *should* a root yoga text say, given what we now understand from evolution, phenomenology, and psychoanalysis? From neuroscience, humanism, feminism, and deconstruction? To ask such a question would be to be honest about what we need, and to take full and excited responsibility for how our lineage evolves.

Here are some of my revisions, broadly. It's an unfinished list:

1. Awareness is not an eternal, abstract or extractable ideal: it evolves through time, and in intrinsic relationship with every bit of biology that supports it.
2. Our suffering is not the result of our connection with the world, as the ascetic mood suggests. Nor is it an illusion, as the

Vedāntic interpreters of Patañjali insist (Śaṃkara and those who follow). Our experiences of *disconnection* and *dissociation* are suffering.

3. Human flesh and feeling is continuous with the feeling flesh of the world: we cannot find a division between them.
4. The movements of gravity, urge, and resolution are endlessly interwoven and pervade all experience. Escaping from their influence would be both impossible and boring.
5. Samādhi —the integrated moment—is commonplace, available to everyone, and cued by everyday intimacies.

4.15 my choices: the book of integration

1.1 We all inquire into yoga.

"Now, the teachings of yoga" is the standard translation (Bryant, Hartranft, and others). I have fertilized this simple opening with some of the central themes of *threads*. Starting with "we": if we take yoga to be conjunctive—psychologically, socially, politically, ecologically—its study and practice will be intersubjective. This would mean that it is not passed from a self-as-subject to an other-as object, but understood by those sharing it that it comes alive because we recognize each other as subjects-in-relationship.

With the first person plural, the aphorism becomes self-reflective: yoga is, among many other things, communion through dialogue. The first person plural also implies the "now" of the original opening word atha: dialogue can only take place in the present. "All" invokes inclusivity: if we share anything as a human family it is the drive towards re-integration. "All" also suggests the trans-historical invocation of Patañjali: his atha indicates his process of collating the extant teachings of his day. *threads* is a similar project. While Patañjali brings together the observations and experiences of the ascetic tribes he knows, I try to integrate the threads of any and all disciplines that shed light on intersubjectivity and eco-harmony. As my view of "what yoga is" has expanded over the past decade, I have come to see every integrative pursuit as sharing the root of yoga. The "all" of "we all" includes for me scientists in labs, sociologists in the field, dancers on the stage, and writers in their garrets.

The sound of "all" also retains the phonetic impact of the first syllable of atha, the guttural opening of the throat that begins the Sanskrit alphabet, said to be the first sound of both creation and human speech.

1.2 Yoga happens in the resolution of consciousness.

The common rendering of this sūtra invokes the goal of constricting experience. "Yoga is the *cessation* of the turnings of thought," writes Miller (emphasis mine). I remix to "yoga happens", implying that a state is to be revealed when an habitual tension is relaxed. In translating nirodaḥ as "resolution", I stay away from "suppression" (Aranya), "inhibition" (Taimni), "restraint" (Sacchidananda), and "control" (Prabhavananda)—none of which would be helpful in the realm of self-evolution practices such as psychotherapeutic care and somatic healing, which always seek to open and add space. "Resolution" implies a sensation of integration, which occurs both naturally and occasionally through willful action. "Turnings of thought" (vṛtti-s) is generalized here to "consciousness".

1.3 Through yoga, consciousness can become aware of its interdependence.

This thread is a first gauntlet thrown down against the isolationist arc of Patañjali-s thought. In line with the Sāṃkhya philosophy he builds upon, he divides experience into a "seer" (draṣṭuḥ) and a "seen" (prakṛti—implied by omission in the original sūtra). The "seer" is presented throughout much of the text, commentary, and oral culture as a kind of blissful and eternal homunculus, embedded within flesh, peering out through and into the world of "nature" (another common translation of prakṛti), like someone trapped within a projection booth at a cinema. I de-homunculize the "seer" by simply naming the faculty involved in self-awareness: "consciousness [that] can become aware of". Patañjali teaches that the blending of seer and seen constitutes our fundamental suffering. The seer has forgotten that it is in a projection booth, and therefore cannot abide "in its own true nature" (Bryant), leading to, as Miller offers for 1.4: "...the observer identifies with the turnings of thought." In other words, the non-yogi thinks he is in the movie, rather than the watcher of a movie. (The movie metaphor resonates with how prakṛti is consistently presented as "less real" than puruṣa throughout the literature.) Our salvation, according to Patañjali, lies in cognizing the split between viewer and movie, and then shutting the projector off through various extractive meditation techniques. My threads begin with a different claim: that our pain comes from the feeling of being trapped and isolated from the livingworld—not within the unreal, or an illusion. The seer (the observatory function of consciousness) must therefore re-member its interdependence with perception and the other to avoid the result of thread 1.4. Yes, it can feel at times as though "we" are "within" and "looking out". This is the problem of the undigested interiority that Jaynes describes. The answer, I believe, cannot lie in shutting off the movie (the guṇa-s, the world, relationship) but by recognizing that we are the guṇa-s, world, and relationship. We are within the thing that is within us.

1.4 Otherwise, consciousness can become increasingly alienated, and awareness becomes inaccessible.

"Increasingly": consciousness can be a continually self-abstracting evolute of the human experience. Our disembodiment and dissociation seem to hurtle blindly forward and upward, as evidenced by our eco-crises.

1.5 There are five common conscious patterns that can clash or harmonize:

For Patañjali, patterns of consciousness (vṛtti-s) are kliṣṭa (clashing) or akliṣṭa (non-clashing). It's crucial to remember that *neither* category is acceptable to the ascetic view, which dreams of complete and permanent un-patterning.

1.6 assertions, confusions, fancy, dreamless sleep, and remembering.

1.7 Assertions may come from witnessing, inference, or belief.

For agamah, I use "belief", replacing "testimony" (Miller and others) and "competent evidence" (Vivekananda), to emphasize the co-dependence of authority and faith. Direct perception and inference are not so mediated.

1.8 Confusions are the misalignment of words and reality.

Words can obfuscate presence. The word is not the thing, and a rose by any other name, or by no name at all, would smell as sweet. I conceal as much as I reveal as I choose words to represent myself and my thoughts. But in the "confused" pattern of consciousness (viparyaya), the gap between signifier and signified begins at an immediate perceptual level and creates an unintentional fiction. The classic example from Indian philosophy is that of mistaking a coiled rope for a snake at twilight. Here, the general obfuscation of words becomes explicit inaccuracy that will immediately confuse another and distort consensus reality. Confusion is a supplementary veil of language-driven consciousness laid over the livingworld. In Vedic linguistics, confusion occurs only at the level of vaikharī (any spoken word as the audible distortion of the inner impulse to speak), which arises from madhyamā (the speech of dreams, emanating from the heart), which arises from paśyantī (the speech of deep sleep, emanating from the navel, with which we can communicate with animals), which arises from parā (the speech of a perceptually integrated state, emanating from the perineum).

1.9 Fancy is language that drifts away from relationship, towards metaphysics.

Miller has: "Conceptualization comes from words devoid of substance." Here, I place "fancy" (Miller's "conceptualization", *vikalpa*) on a scale of language-abstraction, which drifts from the relational to the disembodied. This thread accounts for Patañjali-s focus on our capacity for semiotic ungroundedness, but goes farther to associate this capacity with the language-habit that informs the entire discourse of the sutra-s. To the extent that Patañjali speaks of such metaphysical quantities as puruṣa and Īśvara, he is in the language-realm of the abstract-disembodied, which cannot engender relationship in the same way as does language that describes what we can all see and work with. I was inspired to choose "fancy" when a novelist friend reminded me of how Samuel Taylor Coleridge divided up the acts of consciousness (especially as they manifested in language) into "Primary Imagination" (our universal and connective conscious tissue), "Secondary Imagination" (its echo in the individual), and "Fancy"—the capacity to abstract through "a mode of memory emancipated from the order of time and space; and blended with, and modified, by that empirical phaenomenon of the will which we express by the word *choice* (Coleridge, 167)."

1.10 Dreamless sleep is a feeling of nothingness.

1.11 Remembering is the present experience of the past.

1.12 These patterns can be loosened through consistent practice and presence.

Vairāgya is usually translated as "dispassion". To choose "presence" turns away from a critique of sensual engagement to promote a relaxed sensuality that rests in the here-and-now. The word-choice retains a focus on the reduction of expectations, without stripping the practitioner of the passions involved in becoming still or, indeed, the passions of stillness. "Loosened" evokes the etymology of "analysis", which means "untying", and carries the mood of psychotherapeutic work.

1.13 Practice is any intentional re-patterning of feelings and thoughts towards interdependence.

"Intentional" is my choice for yatnah, instead of "vigilance" (Houston), "permanent control" (Prabhavananda), or "continuous struggle" (Vivekananda). I favour the language of cognitive behavioural therapy to the language of discipline and punishment, which alludes to a transcendental fall. Secondly, to me, "re-patterning" suggests actual change, providing a balance for "practice" (the rendering of abhyāsa by almost every translator), which implies continual preparation. In a phenomenological yoga, there is nothing to prepare for, no one moment more important than others, no future performance of an idealized state. There is simply the experience at hand.

1.14 Re-patterning may occur over a period of consistent and focused effort.

1.15 Presence is felt when you hold no expectation or assumption.

1.16 Awareness of interdependence is the fullest presence.

The original aphorism promises disconnection from the most fundamental building blocks of nature, the guṇa-s (gravity, urge, resolution—tamas, rajas, sattva). Bryant, again: "Higher than renunciation is indifference to the guṇa-s. This comes from the perception of puruṣa, soul." My thread suggests the opposite: that being immersed in the guṇa-s (the tangible media of interdependence) is "presence". Here, "presence" might be construed as "dispassion" for what is *truly* alienating: the abstraction of consciousness from the phenomenological.

1.17 Reasoning, reflection, wonderment, and the awe of being alive are the initial gateways to integration.

Yogic skill is akin to hacking the mainframe of consciousness from cognitive towards extra-cognitive states. The task is to become aware of the hidden mechanisms of consciousness so that they can be accentuated or altered with transparency. The sūtra suggests that this hacking flows in a forward motion, with analysis leading to insight, which leads to bliss, which leads to understanding how our individuality is generated. The commentator Vijñānabhikṣu stages this hacking by describing the order of deconstruction as a deepening of metacognition: first we become aware of the object *qua* object, and then of the act of sensing it, and then of the function of the sense organ, and then of the agency that owns the senses.

1.18 Through integration, these gateways dissolve, leaving unseen traces.

In 1.17–18, the difference between samprajñāta samādhi (the integration invoked by the "initial gateways" of knowledge) and asaṃprajñāta samādhi (the integration that dissolves the gateways of knowledge in a flash of non-thought) would be the difference between integrative experience that is self-conscious ("I'm here, doing this), and integrative experience in which self-consciousness vanishes: *pleasure soft pleasure, no thoughts at all, soft pleasure soft.* Patañjali suggests that at this point of clarity, only "unseen traces" (saṃskāra) remain in what is left of consciousness.

1.19 At death, these unseen traces are resolved into their surroundings and recycled.

The original sūtra distinguishes here between levels of humans according to meditative attainment: the greater ones (post-humans) disappear into sublime ether while retaining some self-sense, while the lesser ones (merely-humans) are confined to rebirth. I ignore the speculative metaphysics of reincarnation to focus on how the constituents that propelled the yogi towards integration—the saṃskāra-s embedded in flesh and thoughts—are commonly and simply recycled into the web of life. The original implies that meditative perfection culminates in the disappearance of the yogi from prakṛti, which reinforces the escape-narrative of asceticism. When we subtract the subtraction of the metaphysical narrative, there is, happily, no escape from the world that makes us and receives us.

1.20 In yoga, this resolution can come through the efforts of confidence, energy, deep memory, focus, and intelligence.

For śraddhā, I replace "faith" (as virtually all translators render it) with "confidence", which implies the attitude motivated by faith. This avoids the question of the *object* of faith in favour of the *energetic disposition* of faithfulness.

1.21 The intensity of practice reveals yoga's nearness.

Aranya has: "Yogins With Intense Ardor Achieve Concentration And The Result Thereof Quickly." My construction here democratizes the revelation of an already-present yoga. Attainment is married to action, and not the virtue or identity of the person. Inclusive language is a core value of this text.

1.22 Intensity has many different facets,

Sacchidananda has: "The time necessary for success further depends on whether the practice is mild, medium, or intense." My choice is to de-emphasize levels of intensity and the pressure of success-seeking to focus on inclusive genres of authentic practice. Of 1.22, Bryant says: "Śaṃkara says the purpose of this sūtra is to fortify the enthusiasm of the practitioner." I want to do exactly this here by eschewing the attainment-oriented anxiety of the original and invoking a student-centred model.

1.23 including the focus of devotion.

From this thread through 1.29, Patañjali proposes forms of meditation upon metaphysical ideals. Miller has: "Cessation of thought may also come from dedication to the Lord of Yoga." I eliminate the transcendental signifier while continuing the syntax from 1.22.

1.24 Devotion can feel timeless and resolved.

Here Patañjali describes the deity Īśvara as the perfect object of devotion. Miller translates: "The Lord of Yoga (Īśvara) is a distinct form of spirit unaffected by the forces of corruption, by action, by fruits of action, or by subliminal intentions." To establish the most inclusive stance possible, my choice is to reify the *feeling* of devotion rather than its object. Devotion is a powerful psychological method that, while believed to provoke communication or beneficence from a deity, may rather simply stimulate the process of healing the alienation of consciousness which finds itself alone and withdrawn in modern selfhood. For me, the description of a metaphysical quantity is far less useful than a description of an energetic attitude. Forests have been felled to print books on the attributes of beings we cannot verify. I feel it is more useful to simply acknowledge the pleasure and evolutionary efficacy of falling and feeling deeply into love.

1.25 In that feeling is the awareness of interdependence.

Here the original describes the omniscience of Īśvara. Bryant has: "In him, the seed of omniscience is unsurpassed." To me there is only one relevant meaning of "omniscience". To understand interdependence, even imperfectly and in microcosm, is to sense how *everything* works. Instead of claiming that this is a property of or blessing from God, I suggest that the feeling of devotion within the process, or even to the process itself, can encourage this epiphany.

1.26 We have always felt it.

The original focuses on the lineage of Īśvara-worship. Miller: "Being unconditioned by time, [Īśvara] is the teacher of even the ancient teachers."

"We have always felt it" democratizes everyday human samādhi-s, distributing the power of the sages to all, past and present. I am changing the focus from the exclusive lineage-ownership of an eternal abstraction of God to the ongoing availability of inspiration for everyone.

1.27 It can be heard in primal sound,

The original says: "*Īśvara* is represented by a sound, om" (Hartranft). "Om" begins most of our days: the first waking spinal and pelvic movements, the first humming and opening. I expand "om" to include any primal (and perhaps preverbal) sound. I have found such sounds to be especially revelatory of deep memory and connection. I am nostalgic for the intimacy of an oral culture in which sounds were felt as creative, perhaps as much as I am nostalgic for the pleasure I experienced in learning to speak.

1.28 which, when sung, can reveal hidden things.

Hartranft has: "Through repetition its meaning becomes clear." I both personalize and generalize in this thread: while I have recited this simplest of mantras for years, I cannot come close to saying "its meaning becomes clear". But I can say that it has acted as an aural key to unlock early childhood memory and some of the mystery of language acquisition. It has also triggered and supported a feeling of blended expansion and resolution. For me it is the shorthand sound of being okay with being here and being myself, and expressing gratitude for these facts.

1.29 Then, obstacles to inner spaciousness become transparent.

1.30 Those obstacles are disease, apathy, doubt, carelessness, joylessness, addiction, false perception, unsteady focus, and restlessness.

For avirati, I use "addiction", instead of "sexual preoccupation" (Houston), "indolence" (Miller), "sensuality" (Sacchidananda), or "craving for sense-pleasure" (Prabhavananda). I believe that no pleasurable sensual experience, sexual or otherwise, is in essence unhelpful. However, the neurological feedback loop of numbed pleasure-responses leading to the amplification of desires is a common pattern leading to despair.

1.31 Their symptoms are stress, pain, depression, trembling, and irregular breathing.

1.32 Calming practice alleviates these symptoms.

Miller has: "The practice of focusing on the single truth is the means to prevent these distractions." Here I remove the reference to "single truth" (eka tattva) being the object of practice, to avoid the anxiety of deciding what such an exclusive truth could possibly be.

1.33 Calmness arises from friendship, empathy, delight, and equality towards others,

Where Patañjali advises "indifference", "neutrality", "impartiality", "disregard" (the renderings of upekṣaṇam by Aranya, et al) towards others as a path towards calmness, I offer "equality", which does not imply withdrawal from discernment or protective action. Withdrawing from the other is no longer a viable option for our species.

From this thread through to 1.39, he proposes perceptual or mindfulness-based meditation practices.

1.34 or spaciousness in breathing,

1.35 or a feeling of stillness in sensuality,

1.36 or when experience is light and joyful,

1.37 or when you observe the senses without expectation or assumption,

1.38 or by meditating upon dreams or sleep,

1.39 or by holding in your heart something you love.

I fully democratize samādhi here by giving it to anyone who has fallen in love. I utilize threads 40 through 44 to allude to the delights of being in love.

1.40 In time, the heart can hold the smallest thing, and the uncontainable.

1.41 When stillness is held, experience absorbs and reflects the things that surround it like a jewel. Its facets can deconstruct the object, its components, its energy, the act of perceiving it, and the mystery of perception.

The motionless jewel of integrated consciousness (in samādhi) blossoms with a series of meta-cognitions. Not only is the origin and construction of its object apparent, but so are the components and process of perceiving it. Holding the construction of both object and subject in mind brings a pleasurable flood of interdependence.

1.42 This experience can hold language,

1.43 or it can be empty of words.

In 1.42–3, the original describes how meditative wonderment progresses from worded to wordless. As the flow of cognition halts, timelessness rises.

1.44 The experience of worded or wordless wonderment plunges down to the quantum level.

Here I invoke a contemporary expression of sūkṣma-viśaya: "subtle objects", which will be picked up again in pāda three, "The Book of Wonders". Patañjali is invoking the tanmātrās of the Saṃkhya cosmology he and most Indian philosophers of his day are drawing upon: the sensory potentials of sound, touch, form, taste, and smell, which are said to precede their elemental media of space, air, fire, water, and earth.

1.45 In deep meditation you can witness how experience is woven together.

Here I imagine the end result of meditation as a contemplative union with livingworld.

1.46 Such witnessing leaves traces.

The original describes how the meditation of integration rewrites the latent impressions (saṃskāra-s) that normally lead to rebirth (i.e., continued relationship) into latent impressions that encourage the continued experience of integration. The vision is one of a feedback loop that spirals the yogi up and out of prakṛti. Here I strip out the self-subtractive teleology to hint at something less determined. What "traces" might the repeated experience of integration create?

1.47 Your hidden aspects become integrated.

Bryant has: "Upon attaining the clarity of nirvicāra-samādhi, there is lucidity of the inner self." I take a Jungian tack here, suggesting that meditative clarity by nature involves the illumination of shadows. The "inner self" in my experience is revealed in layers of often fearful surprise, in a process that invites me to greater internal harmony.

1.48 A feeling of authenticity arises.

Miller has: "Here, wisdom is the vehicle of truth." Avoiding the overdetermination of "truth", I invoke a central value of existential psychology. Answering the call of authenticity is the primary goal of Jean-Paul Sartre, Viktor Frankl, Carl Rogers, and Rollo May.

1.49 It is deeper than what you can hear or study.

1.50 It begins to unravel future patterning.

1.51 Bearing no future patterns, you become unbound.

Paraphrasing from 1.46 to the end: contemplative integration reconciles our shadows, feels authentic, goes beyond cognition, unravels patterns, and gives a feeling of freedom. My aim is a powerful demystification of integration that avoids the complex semantics of the levels of samādhi (1.42–4, 1.46–8) and "truth" (1.48) as transcendental signification. Stripping Patañjali-s vision of its complex categorization and obscure abstractions is an implicit invitation to practitioners to value the eccentricity of their own wonderment-trances, rather than to interrupt them with constant comparison to hoary ideals. Let's remember that the sage is describing indescribable experiences in difficult-to-parse aphorisms in a language that almost no one can now read. No sūtra can define, quantify, or prescribe the quiet openings of the heart.

4.16 the song of integration

We all inquire into yoga.
Yoga happens through the resolution
of consciousness.
Through yoga, consciousness can become
aware of its interdependence.
Otherwise, consciousness can become increasingly
alienated,
and awareness becomes inaccessible.
There are five common conscious patterns
that can clash or harmonize:
assertions, confusions, fancy,
dreamless sleep, and remembering.
Assertions may come from witnessing,
inference, or belief.
Confusions are the misalignment of words
and reality.
Fancy is language that drifts away from relationship, towards metaphysics.
Dreamless sleep is a thought pattern about
nothingness.
Remembering is the present experience of the past.
These patterns can be loosened
through consistent practice and presence.

Practice is any intentional re-patterning
of feelings and thoughts towards interdependence.
Re-patterning may occur over a period
of consistent and focused effort.
Presence is felt when you hold no
expectation or assumption.
Awareness of interdependence is
the fullest presence.

Reasoning, reflection, wonderment,
and the awe of being alive are
the initial gateways to integration.
Through integration, these gateways dissolve,
leaving unseen traces.
At death, these unseen traces are resolved
into their surroundings
and recycled.
In yoga, this resolution can come
through the efforts of confidence, energy,
deep memory, focus, and intelligence.

The intensity of practice reveals yoga's nearness.
Intensity has many different facets,
including the focus of devotion.

Devotion can feel timeless
and
resolved.

In that feeling is
the awareness of interdependence.
We have always felt it.
It can be heard in primal sound,
which, when sung, can reveal hidden things.

Then, obstacles to inner spaciousness become transparent.
Those obstacles are disease, apathy, doubt,
carelessness, joylessness, addiction,
false perception, unsteady focus, and restlessness.
Their symptoms are stress, pain, depression,
trembling, and irregular breathing.
Calming practice alleviates these symptoms.

Calmness arises from friendship, empathy, delight,
and equality towards others,
or spaciousness in breathing,
or a feeling of stillness in sensuality,
or when experience is light and joyful,
or when you observe the senses without expectation or assumption,
or by meditating upon dreams or sleep,
or by holding in your heart something you love.

In time, the heart can hold the smallest thing, and
the uncontainable.

When stillness is held, experience absorbs
and reflects the things that surround it
like a jewel.
Its facets can deconstruct the object,
its components,
its energy,
the act of perceiving it,
and the mystery of perception.
This experience can hold language,
or it can be empty of words.
The experience of worded or wordless wonderment
plunges down to the quantum level.

In deep meditation you can witness
how experience is woven together.
Such witnessing leaves traces.
Your hidden aspects become integrated.
A feeling of authenticity arises.
It is deeper than what you can hear or study.
It begins to unravel future patterning.
Bearing no future patterns, you become unbound.

5. pāda two: practices

5.1 the book of practices

2.1 Yoga applies endurance, learning, and commitment.
2.2 It reduces alienation and cultivates empathy.
2.3 Ignorance, individualism, addiction, dissociation, and the "afterlife": these alienate.
2.4 Ignorance enables alienation in all forms, from seed to tree.
2.5 Ignorance involves not learning about change in objects, ideas, sensations, or self.
2.6 Individualism sees things instead of relationships.
2.7 Addiction turns pleasure into a thing.
2.8 Dissociation runs away from experience.
2.9 The "afterlife" devalues life.
2.10 The causes of alienation are interwoven. Loosening one begins to unravel them all towards empathy.
2.11 Concentration stills alienating thoughts.
2.12 Fruitlessly seeking consolation, alienating patterns of thought tend to repeat.
2.13 This repetition can impede self-perception, relationship to time, and the capacity for enjoyment.

2.14 Alienating patterns predispose you to continued alienation.

2.15 For one who takes responsibility for his or her existential condition, life will be felt fully as ever-changing, echoing with loss, limited, unknowable, and chaotic.

2.16 But the future is unwritten.

2.17 Pain is caused by the blurring of authenticity with fabrication.

2.18 We feel gravity, urge, and resolution surge through the elements, and these feelings can lead to ecstasy.

2.19 Gravity, urge, and resolution appear in all stages of form, from the object we name and hold to the nameless quanta coursing through it.

2.20 Consciousness seems distinct from the flesh, and yet pours through it.

2.21 Consciousness delights in giving meaning to the flesh, as though it were its source.

2.22 As consciousness evolves, meanings change or are taken away, for different people at different times.

2.23 Consciousness projects meaning onto things but then, forgetting its projection, assumes those given meanings belong to those things. But the conjunction of consciousness and things invites both to feel their interdependence.

2.24 These assumed meanings are another kind of ignorance.

2.25 When ignorance fades, the original source of projected meaning is seen as consciousness and not the thing. A burden lifts.

2.26 This becomes clear through contemplation on the difference.

2.27 As veils of assumption fade, the depth of perception expands, and begins to explore the unknown.

2.28 The practices of yoga diminish alienation, allowing for the radiance of clear sight.

2.29 The eight practices are relationship to other, relationship to self, poise, freedom of breath, freedom of senses, focus, contemplation, and integration.

2.30 Good relationship to others requires protection, honesty, fair trade, sexual responsibility, and self-possession.

2.31 These five means of good relationship work for everyone, all the time.

2.32 Good relationship to oneself requires ecology, contentment, endurance, learning, and commitment.

2.33 Negative thought patterns can be altered by embodying what balances them.

2.34 When thoughts of oppression in any degree are held, acted upon, delegated to another, or colluded with, whether through greed, anger, or delusion, one must realize this pattern leads to shared suffering and ignorance, and work hard to reverse it.

2.35 When one protects others from harm, this produces a feeling of connectedness and safety.

2.36 In the aura of honesty, causes and their results make sense.

2.37 When you practice fair trade, your feeling of wealth is enhanced.

2.38 Sexual responsibility enables intimacy.

2.39 Self-possession allows you to define yourself according to your own actions, while revealing your interdependence with all things.

2.40 Ecology allows you to honour your flesh, and the flesh of others.

2.41 Ecology enables clarity, brightness, joy, insight, sensual harmony, and inquiry.

2.42 Contentment makes one at home in the world.

2.43 Endurance allows the flesh and senses to be more fully enjoyed.

2.44 Learning connects you with your archetypes.

2.45 Commitment to relationship invites integration.

2.46 Poise is steady and well-spaced.

2.47 This occurs when restlessness fades and feeling is boundless.

2.48 Then, even oscillations are peaceful.

2.49 Breath is free when its movement is first easy and then voluntary.

2.50 You can feel yourself making the breath smooth and subtle by observing the number, length, and placement of inhalations, exhalations, and pauses.

2.51 Breath observance can also suspend the division between what is inside and what is outside.

2.52 This feels like an unveiling of light.

2.53 And concentration blossoms.

2.54 As consciousness draws inward, it becomes the object of the senses.

2.55 When the senses are free, they will not disturb contemplation.

5.2 practice begins with other

The second book lays out the heart of Patañjali-s practical advice in eight themes (2.29 onwards). Often these themes are assigned an ascending teleology, such that ethics and attitudes (yama and niyama) are seen to be lower prerequisites for stabilizing the physiology (āsana), and the more internalizing and abstract feats of energetic direction (prāṇāyama), sensory control (pratyāhāra), and contemplation (saṃyama). This staging of themes reinforces the transcendental mood that permeates this text. When ethics are presented as elementary to meditative bliss, the practice implicitly moves away from the interpersonal and towards the ultimate value of the private. In this hierarchical model, ethical relationships with others are not valued as their own gifts (nor as obviously essential to our survival), but rather are to be used for personal gain. The ascending interpretation seems only interested in others in an avoidant mode—to the extent that the practitioner is able to pacify her reactivity to others towards a radiant self-sufficiency.

For our purposes, there may be pedagogical value in emphasizing the "mastery" of the yamas and niyamas as foundational, insofar as this may root modern postural yoga culture within an ethical foundation. Still, I've seen this same teleology prove to be a stumbling block for āsana practitioners who are convinced that they are not ready for meditation until their postures are perfected, which of course will never happen.

The etymology of aṣṭa-aṅga seems to push back against the teleological view. Aṅga means "limb": as from a tree. (Aṣṭa simply means "eight".) One also might think of the spokes of a wheel. Or the multiple arms of Indian deities, with each hand holding a different implement of guidance, inspiration, or discipline. Or the eight planet-like factors surrounding the earth in the art of Vedic astrology. The aṅga-s radiate out from the centre of an evolutionary intention: the desire to become more whole. Or, more to the point, how to re-member more and more wholeness.

Viewed in this circular mode, the limbs of yoga practice oscillate between external and internal contingencies in much the same way that our very psycho-somatic development occurs. We come into existence through relationship, and it is through the surfaces of our relationships that our internality evolves. We begin our lives as tissues that are virtually indistinguishable from the tissues of the mother's flesh, and our process of individuation arcs through infinite degrees that arguably never quite achieve the status of the separate. If we are not intrinsic to the mother's flesh, we are intrinsic to the flesh of the world. External sensations of the proto-epithelium in the zygote are the stimulus for the invaginating growth of the central nervous system: we gain the capacity to feel and to think quite literally by being surrounded and touched. Such material intrinsicality with the (m)other forms the basis for our internal selves. Even now, our mirror neurology quivers as we watch sparrows alight upon the power line, and we shiver when we see that our baby is cold. Our neurology is a reflective web of bio-social interconnections. We are constantly weaving our relationship experience into our internal tapestry of mood and thought. Ethics and psychic health are indistinguishable.

The circle of the limbs suggests that our interiority can be groomed to pour its contemplation back out into the interpersonal. Our capacity for integrated sensation and wordless pausing can flow outward into the economy of our relationships. Contact with the other (yama) establishes your personhood (niyama), which is enhanced by groundedness (āsana). Silent reverie upon the internal space of selfhood (prāṇāyama through saṃyama) prepares you for a richer experience of otherness. Ethics is both the inspiration for and the handiwork of meditation. Meditation gives us first-hand experience of an enriched interiority that we naturally project onto the other. One of the jewels of refined awareness is the capacity to hold a theory of other minds. Going inside allows us to expand our intuitions of the other's interiority.

We began as other, and through relationship to other we feel internal space. We navigate internal space and re-emerge, hungry for more contact.

5.3 mother, other, world

Our lives begin with body-molding cohesion, an intrinsicality with the womb. The womb: an endless night, the sleep before time, extends in all directions, as do we. The flesh is not a container of selfhood but a site of limitless contact. Had we ears and language *in utero*, the womb would tell us we are whole and interdependent. But we have no need for self-description: we're not quite here yet, nor quite there. Soon, however, something will etch our silhouette in relation to the womb, and then the world.

According to the embryology of Āyurveda, fetal experience begins with sound, which surrounds us from somewhere and penetrates into something. Sound reveals the first possible threshold between self and not-self. But the experience is porous, non-local, and unfindable: the perfect introduction to the other, who creates you, pervades you, meets you, invades you, departs from you when you sleep, and returns as you wake. And what sounds does this other make? Do we hear her breath, her heartbeat, her digestion? Do we hear her voice cooing in love or snapping in conflict? Does she go walking in the surf? Does she rest the belly of a cello against her own belly, and draw her impassioned bow across the strings, and our own hairlike nerves? *You gave me ears to hear you*, says the Psalmist.

Add *m* to *other* for *mother*. Recall the mother through *om, there*. Perhaps we are drawn to mantra because sound stands at the threshold of supported stillness and individual action. Sound grounds perception (and is said to create the world) because it establishes pervasive presence.

Touch follows. The precursor of skin, ensheathing the delicate nerves, forms softly against the mucosa of the uterus. There is movement and rubbing, a trying and testing of boundaries, an exploration of containment. Sensing smoothness, rubbing it harder to feel the firmness beneath. As the fetus rubs, epithelial cohesion is chemically cued. Now we are inside something, *with* something. The other not only pervades, but now surrounds and contains. Being something slowly elides into being *in* something. Being in something slowly elides into being some*where*. Being somewhere slowly elides into wanting to explore *somewhere else*. Gestation is long for the human, and patience is required, and so an internal journey begins through dreams. The form, pressure, and silhouetting of sensation elide into visual distinctions: an inner flame throws shadows against inner walls.

These imperceptible oscillations between with-ness and apartness within the womb are accelerated and amplified by birthing, and then decelerate again after birth, resuming their gestational pace. The ideal is constancy and evenness. We need the mother's flesh to reveal itself as continuously present, even as parts of it (the distance between breast and face) teach us the tactile separations of space. We need the mother's flesh to reveal itself as unitive and distinctly segmented in gentle alternation. The mother's flesh, continuous in its nurturance even as we recognize our separateness from her, is so delightful and round and full that it imprints its presence within us. Some psychoanalysts (Kaplan, 1978) have suggested that we begin to carry an internal mother, whose constancy can bridge the gaps of the fleshly mother's occasional absences or distractions. We want this to happen slowly and gently. We hope that the new human discovers his internal mothering faculty, his integrity, self-enclosure, capacity to be separate—along with the painful needs derived from these discoveries—as slowly as possible, so that the memory of cohesion and wholeness is not destroyed on the path to separateness, but rather enriched by textured layers of newness. The first mother is the other. The second mother is the other, internalized. Wherever you turn, the other is there. Mother, other, world. It is possible that the life of separation can begin in trust. If it doesn't, yoga can help.

Often, as the experience of with-ness or oneness slides into differentiation, oneness is ruptured, and its memory invokes both loss and betrayal, something you long for and know you can't have. This might be the root of the split religious sentiment that both longs for and resents a singular god. But imagine that the experience of differentiation renders the old experience of oneness kaleidoscopic, or polyphonic. Imagine that the other could slowly shift in manifestation from the unified womb of pervasion to a quiet unfurling of diversity. As though you were awake, curled in the mossy hollow of a forest tree, on a moonless night. And then twilight softly stole up upon you, showing the edges of things beginning to silhouette within the cradling dark, so that before you realize anything has changed, you are sitting, still motionless, amidst a web of forms, a tangle of life, a tapestry that flows around and into your very flesh, tendrils connected to your flesh sensually and yet expressing their own life, beyond your will and understanding.

Otherness governs your individuation. It begins as the field in which you take root. Then it is the sheathe of your growth. You grow your flesh from otherness, and from the flesh and its sensual contact, a feeling of interiority emerges. Soon this other is the channel of your birth. Then it is the flesh of constant support, the flesh that transfers its power across a thickening boundary of skin, such that contact replaces immersion. Differentiation maneuvers to provide everything that coherence once did, but now within the increasingly complex context of many others—father, siblings, grandparents, nannies, friends—as opposed to one. The extent to which your differentiation at all stages unfolds with nurtured constancy will inform how you may be able in the future to accept and love the other, knowing otherness to be your origin and life. In the absence of a smooth differentiation process, a distorted relationship to the other may emerge. Having failed the relationship of constancy, the other may be avoided as a betrayer, or escaped-from, or hated as the withholder of pleasure, or someone/something whose power must be overcome, or your oppressor through her incomprehensibility. Or conversely: the other is clung to, merged with, and out of insatiable dependency, never surrendered. Mother, other, world: toward these you will throw the echoes of your differentiation-cries, and songs.

5.4 eight limbs therapeutic redux

Because our primary suffering is alienation, the yogic path of therapy begins with reestablishing relationship with other. Ethics (yama) comes first, because other people mirror your condition very plainly. Empathetic relationship with others open the door to a brightening of self-perception (niyama). Reconnecting with the flesh and breath (āsana, prāṇāyama) folds back into its phenomenal matrix. Feeling energy flow evenly back and forth between and phenomena is aided by understanding the sensory points of contact (pratyāhāra).

From here, contemplation of your condition has solid footing, because the most obvious *content* of alienation—lack of empathy, self-doubt or even self-hatred, and sensory overload—has been witnessed and engaged. One might then turn to witness the very *structure* of alienation (through saṃyama, the three degrees of meditation): how consciousness blends sense perception, meaning, concept, and memory into a fluid narrative, and then forgets it is doing so. Because it forgets it is a storyteller who takes dictation by chapter and verse from the phenomenal world, it suffers the anxiety of groundless creativity. Consciousness fears that it must create meaning alone. But this was never true. Consciousness attunes to meaning because it is embedded in larger meanings.

Saṃyama consists of focus (dhāraṇā), contemplation (dhyāna), and integration (samādhi). Focus allows concentration to narrow from the typically scattered state we have inherited from a more fearful era of constant sympathetic (defensive) nervous engagement (and now perpetuated in disembodied form through much of our news media). Contemplation imbues this focus with empathy, so that attunement between subject and object begins to hum. The peak of attunement is integration, in which the subject/object boundary is softened, and feelings of wholeness and connection saturate the flesh and mental flow. Sensing this pervasion of empathy, the yogi delights even more richly in the ethics of relationship (yama): the circle is complete.

5.5 some notes on the yamas: the language of learning the other

When considering how to meaningfully interpret the ethical principles (yama-s) of protection, honesty, fair trade, sexual responsibility, and self-possession, numerous contemporary nuances emerge.

The common translation of "non-violence" for ahiṃsā is problematic. It proposes a transcendental ideal that can punish us for normal defensive actions, allow us to overlook the intersubjective, and perpetuate wishful thinking with regard to our lived reality. There is no livingworld—from geology to the food chain to the immune system—that is devoid of violence. Nor is there any human posture within livingworld that does not involve at least some violent activity. Beings are constantly subjecting each other to unwanted and forceful intrusions. We trade life and flesh and calories back and forth, without mutual consent. The relationships between species oscillate between symbiosis and parasitism. We exist in a web of predator-prey relationships (Jensen, 2006), and although this fact is masked by contemporary agriculture and food distribution systems, it is disingenuous not to admit our painful, joyful and bloody participation.

Of course, we are all-too-capable of *calculated* violence that goes beyond survival to oppress the rights or lives of others for self-gain, or the profit of some favoured group. An active and intersubjective translation of ahiṃsā as "protection" invokes the need to resist this pattern, while acknowledging that violence might well form part of that resistance. The question becomes not "Am I non-violent?"—for no one can be. It becomes "Do I offer protection to the lives of others, and thereby reduce cruelty?" "Protection" implies a choice of who and what to protect in the given circumstance, giving flexibility between self-protection, other-protection, culture-protection, and world-protection.

"Protection" as a translation does have a few drawbacks, however. It might have a masculine ring and might carry a whiff of mobsterism. Certainly it raises many sticky issues of interventionism and meddling, as "protection" can easily slide into paternalism and other flavours of disempowerment, however well-meaning. Privileged, western, and very white yoga culture needs to be especially vigilant of this as it plays on the margins of "sēva tourism", in which practitioners go on retreat for two weeks to majority-world countries to practice āsana in three-star accommodations in the morning and visit malaria hospitals in the afternoon, before returning home to a studio culture that is almost invisible on the spectrum of political activism.

Also, as an active and muscular principle, becoming "protective" is perhaps unattainable by those who themselves need protection. But other options, such as "care" (resonant with Heidegger's *Sorge*) and "responsibility" are simply too broad, and cannot sufficiently prod the general political apathy that characterizes modern western posture-based yoga culture. The active quality of "protection" reverses the passive and double-negative tone of "non-violence" (a tone repeated with the yama of aparigraha, and the niyama of asteya). The double-negative structure shares a mood with the nirguṇa and nivṛtti techniques I am working to reverse in order to inject active and participatory energy into the socio-political culture of our studio networks.

"Honesty" works for satya, commonly translated as "truthfulness". It relieves the burden of certainty ("I have the truth"), which can lend a false power dynamic to relationship. "Honesty" pluralizes truth. Honesty might also be the *method* by which truths evolve collectively. One current standard for honesty in our discourse is held by the scientific method, which democratizes truth over multiple perspectives adhering to the same rules of evidence and peer-review. This "public" truth stands in bright contrast to the privacy of "spiritual" truth, which all too often is only validated by authoritarian power.

"Fair trade" is a timely broadening of asteya (commonly "non-stealing"), to account for the complexities of global economy, in which laying claim to property itself might be considered a form of stealing, and in which wage and resource disparities constitute gross violations of human rights. The letter of current law is insufficient when it comes to the ethics of economy. We must go farther, and ask: What are my relationships to food, shelter, labour, and information worth to my life? Does money accurately reflect and compensate effort and relationship? What am I really giving of myself to live in the developed world? Is my time and lifeblood worth as much as the time and lifeblood of the man who picked my vegetables? Further still: should knowledge be proprietary?

Taimni translates 1.38 as "On being firmly established in sexual continence, vigour is gained." "Sexual responsibility" derails the old celibate ideal of brahmacarya, while retaining some of the thematics of its etymology. Ācārya: "one who follows". Brahmā: "the path of expanding creativity". Our contemporary expressions and meanings of sexuality are polymorphously perverse and intertwined with our intersubjective evolution. We are slowly peeling away layer upon layer of puritanism. Dogmatic restriction from sexual contact—unless it is necessary for the process of recovering from addiction or abuse—cannot offer a balanced experience of intimacy or this central drive of flesh.

"Non-grasping" is the typical translation of aparigraha. By translating aparigraha as "self-possession", I affirm the grasping nature of desire as an intrinsic catalyst of growth and learning, but gently limit its scope to the field of self-responsibility. The kind of grasping we would most discourage would be that which arises from compensatory psychological need. Grasping at socio-economic justice, however, may be highly ethical. Of course, my translation does not even address the grasping that constitutes that basis of our consumer culture. My assumption in not directly engaging this most basic level of non-grasping is that a critical or ironic attitude towards consumerism would be the natural prerequisite to yoga training.

One of my colleagues suggested "humility" as a good translation for aparigraha. As an ex-Catholic, I feel constitutionally averse to this word. But perhaps it works for others.

5.6 love

If only Patañjali encapsulated his discussion of ethics with single reference to empathy or love! The text would resonate with our present concerns much more. I've often wondered how yoga culture can continue to canonize a text that makes no explicit reference to the experience with which we are perennially obsessed. The majority of our social sciences are fuelled by the impulse of empathy: we wish to discover the other, or how we behave in groups, or how our behavioural patterns arise and how they can be altered for the better. The vast majority of our art and literature worships at the altar of love: how our primal attractions seek dynamic bonding, how we surge towards the other into the terrified joy of intimacy and loss.

But the ascetic specifically avoids these concerns. His ethics are focused less upon the golden rule than upon the lonely golden path. He has left behind family life, and has pre-emptively broken every attachment that would bind his care to the everyday. The writers of the old ascetic texts are all men, and they tend to distrust love, sex, and women in equal measure. I wonder whether, through the glorification of this text, we secretly wish for a similar dissociation and continued gender conflict. Do we meditate with Patañjali because empathy is difficult and love is painful?

If we're going to continue to use this text in contemporary yoga culture, we must acknowledge the vacuum of love—in whatever way we use the term today—at its centre, and recognize that we have voices where Patañjali is silent. Perhaps we can start by reversing the purpose of his ethical discussion, so that our intention behind treating others kindly is not about internal equanimity, but about the exploration of empathy as a path to self-and-other growth.

5.7 niyamas: the language of learning the self

Śauca is usually translated as "cleanliness" or "purity". This might give problematic support to a culture overscrubbed by chemical cleaners and antibiotics. Within yoga culture specifically, it all too often amplifies the desire for "purification"—which can lead to everything from neurotically repetitive vinyāsa sequences to forms of spiritually-influenced disordered eating. In this sense, we carry a vestigial memory of the old ascetic disgust towards the polluted flesh. The ascetic attitude really offers no way out of impurity, since the very flesh itself is taken as the absolute sign of impurity. An obsession with purification often hinges upon an intractable paradox: one is trying to clean something that is either essentially dirty, or always on the verge of corruption. Purification is often a self-defeating proposition, if the self doing the cleaning has a self-image problem. You can't clean dirt itself.

As a new translation for śauca, "ecology" transforms a concern for personal purification into a pursuit of self-other and self-world balance. It also socializes the concept of cleanliness to resonate more closely with the homeodynamic model of contemporary wellness practice, with its focus upon public hygiene and environmental harmony. It feels as if neo-ascetic notions of bodily isolation and hyper-purification might lie at the root of the post-Renaissance medical model and its gaze, producing the homeostatic body: a paragon of health-unto-itself, hermetically sealed against impurity, existing outside of and beyond human interaction. I reject this separative and transcendent impulse in medicine and yoga equally. If yoga is to make us healthy, it will be because it ultimately coheres us more closely to our environment.

"Contentment" (saṃtoṣa) is a delicate issue for all of us. On one hand, general living standards have never been higher for the many of us who are privileged enough to read and write books about things. On the other hand, our living standards have primarily risen through incessant appeals to our dissatisfaction. To complicate matters further, our global community is torn apart by vast inequalities: contentment as a universal ethical prescription is something only the privileged can afford. Can we establish a median standard of living as a baseline for human contentment, or are our needs too diverse? Do countries with strong social infrastructures of child care, medical care, and advanced education establish more stable levels of contentment? Do they manage this by maintaining wealth domination over majority-world countries through international trade and finance? The seriousness with which we consider such questions will define the integrity of our yoga.

Beyond socio-political considerations, private contentments are always available to be enjoyed. Allowing the pleasure of the commonplace to shimmer is a lovely skill. Many of us have grown too far away from our precognitive skill for trance in childhood. We used to spend hours on the grass, gazing at the sky. We knew contentment, and somehow we unlearned it. We became busy.

Endurance allows the flesh and senses to be more fully enjoyed. Tapas is usually translated as "heat" or "burning effort". It is etymologically related to a range of Sanskrit words that suggest cooking and also sacrifice through fire. In Vedic mythology, heroes and yogis are constantly performing radical acts of tapas in order to gain boons and siddhis from the gods. The heat they generate is self-immolating: they are said to burn their impurities, and sometimes quite literally their flesh, in order to prove their worthiness for transcendence. In a way they embody the yajña of Vedic ritual, in which the fruits of the earth are offered to the sacramental fire to glorify the processes of transformation and to revel in the bright spectacle of self-loss.

To the extent that our own efforts in yoga can feel compensatory for our faults or punitive of our bodily dysmorphia or penitential in the face of gods in which we no longer consciously believe, shifting the focus from the self-immolatory to an ideal of stamina might provide a more accurate image of how we currently idealize our focus. Modern postural yoga is one of the very few physical cultures in which the sacrificial "no-pain-no-gain" attitude is actively resisted in favour of sensory attunement and the rediscovery of pleasure in movement. It is a physical culture with no real aesthetic or competitive goal, and thus constitutes one of the only kinetic opportunities in which sensory feedback need not be measured for value against a perceived appearance or attainment, or the clock. The posture is accomplished if it moves towards warming circulation, releasing breath, relaxing sympathetic nervous responses, toning the vagus nerves, and granting a sense of buoyancy. "Endurance" is a useful term to the extent that it suggests moving slowly and with perseverance towards these sensations.

Svādhyāya implies "self-inquiry", but it has usually been taken to mean a particular kind of scriptural study. To fully understand what Patañjali is advocating here we must know something about his pedagogical milieu. He is working in a time in which the textual literacy of many practitioners is low, but oral retention is astoundingly high. Adherents of the various Axial Age disciplines were expected to hear, repeat, and memorize spiritual poems and philosophical discourses *verbatim*. The skill for oral/aural memory reached its apex with the Vedācāryas, who held within family lineages the capacity to recite from memory up to all four of the massive Vedic root-texts, usually without a clear understanding of their archaic mantras. This feat was echoed by the memorization skills of the early Buddhists, who are said to have memorized Gautama's discourses as he spoke them, keeping them alive in aurality for some four hundred years before the Pali canon appeared on pressed tree bark. When Patañjali encourages svādhyāya, this is the heritage he speaks from: obsessive memorization of a narrow range of mystically-inspired poems that become essential to the social fabric of the discipline.

Our own educational context could not be more different. We have endless documents, high literacy, and multiple forms of textual storage. There are far too many texts for us to choose those we would commit to memory, and no impetus to preserve texts through memorization. With the exception of scriptural literalists, we don't commit to anything as if it were the final word: there are too many other words in our peripheral vision. We read comparatively, across periods, cultures, and even disciplines. Textual indexing, the folio format, and now the word search make data accessible by topic, allowing readers to pick and choose according to fancy. By contrast, the reciter delivers his poem whole and uninterrupted from the scroll of memory.

It used to be that through decades of apprenticeship, a student of yoga could become a "lineage holder", meaning that he (very rarely she) "held" a requisite number of the tradition's texts and practices in memory. Coming to hold the oral artifacts necessitated years of attention at the feet of various gurus, which often involved heroically dangerous travel. Lineage holders had to be collectors. Their bodies became precious vessels. But in our time data is ubiquitous and freely available. Our intelligentsia are not valued for their body-vessels—for knowledge held internally and exclusively apart from others—but rather for their capacity to create overviews, to be able to effectively refer to verified research, and to comment on the patterns that emerge in public data. We are not "holders" so much as conduits and processors. The value of data is dubious; the value of data organization is our real currency. In this way, learning has moved from possession to connection. Intelligence is expressed through the capacity to find patterns and weave threads together. Our information and knowledge revolutions enact an implicit interest in connectivity. We don't hold Truth: we co-create the process of truth.

"Learning" as a translation for svādhyāya expresses this simple democratization of knowledge and knowledge-making. But what do we choose to learn? What expands and refines us? What glints at us out the sea of data? It often seems to me that our ineffable choices of interest express the uniqueness of our very genome. Perhaps the subject matter is immaterial: the insatiable passion of learning is its own virtue.

Īśvara praṇidhāna invokes a humble and devotional disposition towards the mystery of being alive. Christian-influenced translators have rendered the phrase as "surrender to God", loading the object of devotion with a cultural heritage that is too vague to be meaningful in an Indian context. Bryant gives evidence for Patañjali-s Vaisnavism, and postulates that Īśvara points to the sustaining-deity-principle of Vishnu. Hartranft de-reifies the term as "pure awareness" in accordance with his non-theistic Buddhist interpretation.

Older resonances for Īśvara mirror the multiplicity of modern translations. In Vedic culture, one's astrological natal chart and physiological constitution formed the basis for the assignment of iṣṭa devatā: a titular deity said to specifically inspire one's unique skills and ameliorate one's circumstances. The devatā-s come from an enormous pantheon of local and often eccentric gods, each with their own mythology, skills, symbols, mantras, and implements. When Prabhavananda renders 2.44 as "As the result of study, one obtains the vision of that aspect of God which one has chosen to worship", he is recalling the liberality of this very individualized approach to devotion, which ideally spoke directly to the subconscious wounds and desires of each devotee. Which begs the question: who are our gods? Who are the deities of Toronto, the sprites of the San Andreas Fault, the Pyrenees, the Hudson River, the Rockies, or Regent's Park? Some contemporary yogis look for the forgotten aboriginal spirits of the lands they've guiltily inherited. But perhaps our gods are also embedded in our networks of technology, social media, and the dream-imagery of advertising.

The question is: what pulls us out of the banality of self-isolation, into the wonderment of continued learning? What makes us humble? What name, language, or symbol hurtles us into the depth of something, inspiring a sense of *commitment*? We are refreshed by our "incredulity towards metanarratives"—the "grand stories" told by metaphysics. And yet in our incredulity we are still drawn perpetually to the horizon, exhilarated and uncertain, even as we can no longer name what we love and reach for.

5.8 the beginning of āsana

When you stretch out a limb you spotlight the primary condition of your existence, your spatiality. Or: you call your already-present extension to conscious attention.

The limb seems to stretch out into empty space, but it plunges ever deeper into *contact*, now noticed. You stretch your arm upward, and the internal sensations—muscles relaxing, ligaments lengthening, and circulation finding underused pathways—are all responses to contact. Every movement of the flesh is a dive into space. Reaching up is really plunging your hand into a well of dark sweet water.

When you stretch out a limb you actively spotlight the given condition of always-having-been-touched. As a zygote, you floated in plasma, and an outer surface, a membrane, emerged through contact with that which nourished you. The membrane is porous from the beginning. Āsana seeks out its pores, to experience consciously the endless transfer of nutrition between what became a self, and what became a world.

The zygote is not closed, and its aloneness is a dream. It begins dividing from its first moment. It is never one thing, but begins with two and becomes a different two. It divides to extend into the amniotic space that nourishes it. Āsana is the conscious echo of this process. The amorphous breath channels into an invisible limb, probing the breath of the world. The amorphous flesh divides into spine and limb to extend into this unfolding womb, this welcoming earth.

You are not closed. Even if you were, you would be closed *against* something, closed *within* something, closed *in relation to* something. Whatever you are closed against is holding you, and waiting for dialogue.

5.9 aligning breath in space

Contemporary āsana practice offers two distinct gifts to our ever-more-sophisticated physical culture.

Focus on postural symmetry promotes a skeletal alignment that relieves the musculature of chronic gripping patterns. If key joints are stacked vertically along a plumb-line, musculature becomes responsible for movement and balance only—not for the resistance of gravity or the need to bind unstable joints together. With a gravity-coherent structure, the visceral flesh is not constricted by balance-compensating muscular movement. The organs can expand and contract freely with circulatory relaxation. This gives a sense of relaxed internal spaciousness. Hopefully, internal spaciousness can in turn inspire a sense of intersubjective spaciousness.

Secondly, lubricating movement with the smoothness of breath, as is the common instruction in contemporary vinyāsa, eases the typical nervous system reaction to strong physical effort. Our innate response to hard work is pneumatic contraction, which cues sympathetic (defensive) response. Held breath is often used to harden the abdomen, lending a kind of temporary and illusory solidity to the centre of gravity. While this can be effective for short and violent bursts of kinetic energy, it does not provide stamina, nor does it train us away from sympathetic nervous responses. Ideally, nervous system intelligence (a root of healthful ecology) can be trained away from over-reactivity, increasing our adaptive intelligence in the face of many forms of stress. Training in fluid āsana with fluid breath spreads out into emotional, social, and perhaps even political receptivity, by softening our instincts for self-preservation. To hold the breath while moving obstructs the movement from really getting in. Breath allows movement to motivate spaces of psycho-somatic stagnancy. The inhale penetrates what is uninspired. The exhale relaxes what is contracted.

But it would be disingenuous to ignore the many weaknesses from which contemporary āsana suffers. A brief list will indicate areas for continued development:

Vinyāsa moves primarily in a forward plane. There are relatively few of the hip-circling movements common to most forms of dance around the world, used for millenia to attract mates and, for women, to prepare for childbirth. By omitting the lateral sway, the forward concentration of most vinyāsa casts a predominantly masculine and transcendent energy to sequences, which may not be appropriate, given that the vast majority of contemporary practitioners are women. It is not surprising that contemporary dance vocabulary is beginning to influence vinyāsa. Hopefully, this will continue.

Āsana provides little bodily contact, except when teachers adjust students. It is a physical culture of solitary experience, and may not help the alienated with their interpersonal skills. In fact, I have seen many dedicated practitioners of posture who seem to have become more socially awkward, rather than less. Team or contact sports might provide good balance. It might be helpful to remember that some of the earliest usages of yogic posture were to prepare for the battlefield. Until the mid-19th century, many Tantric and Nātha yoga sects used āsana as training for anti-colonial guerilla warfare.

Different times breed different purposes. While modern vinyāsa yoga emerged primarily out of the cross-culturally created exercise regimes that attended anti-colonial revolutionary movements in India (Singleton, 2010), contemporary vinyāsa frames strength in much different terms. For women, strength-building sequences are often offered in the language of building personal power and creative autonomy, whereas the same sequences for men (a small minority of contemporary āsana practictioners) seem to encourage a genteel vision of strength. But for neither men nor women does the modern āsana vocabulary emphasize muscular power firstly. Length and flexibility is consistently emphasized over strength. "Opening" is the ubiquitous cue. Many practitioners become lax in the ligaments through overextension or overflexion of the joints, and their musculature often loses resilience through a fixation on over-stretching. There are relatively few postures or vinyāsas that build upper-body strength safely (the vinyāsa of downward-dog through caturaṅga through bhūjangāsana is notable exception, but often dangerous to those without good symmetry and shoulder-alignment training). Āsana in isolation can become catabolic to the musculature. In Ayurvedic terms, this can depress courage. Perhaps those who know this intuitively are those who consciously employ āsana to balance more forceful muscular activities like rockclimbing or martial arts.

We might ask whether the bias towards opening that softens the yoga-body also softens the yoga body-politic. A culture of muscular softness and relaxed ligaments might become overly pliant in the hands of power. This may not be what the acclaimed founder of modern postural yoga, T.S. Krishnamacharya, had in mind when he was training young men to be home-rule warriors in the Mysore Palace. The physical culture of yoga has taken a strange historical turn that reflects the fact that perhaps the social and political revolutions of today and tomorrow are internal in nature, or that at least we think they are.

5.10 prāṇāyama relaxes the self-other divide

Breath observance can also suspend the division between what is inside and what is outside.

The breath is a bridge between self and not-self. Crossing it with awareness will soften the boundary. It is impossible to say when air becomes you, but it does: feeding the metabolism behind all movement, tissue formation, and tissue repair. Simultaneously, air is "externally" ubiquitous. We wade through it as through water. We are pervaded by the source of our life: this breath-to-be. We think that the space between us is a mark of our separation, when in fact it contains what allows us to live. We are conjoined by the invisible source of life. It is not surprising that we express this in metaphysical terms, but the ungrounded language is unnecessary. Perhaps we invent metaphysics because it is difficult to trust the obvious beneficence of what we cannot see. Or perhaps we must rationalize being surrounded by life. Perhaps we don't feel we deserve this embarrassment of riches, this air, and so we must make up stories about how it is both bestowed and taken away by unseen authority. We convert an unseen source of life into an unseen authority. But invisible air is more wondrous than an invisible god or soul: it does something that can be felt. It is built upon what we are immersed within, what enters us beyond our will, what we suckle even in the deepest sleep, the breast we are unaware of.

You can consciously play with these sensations. You can willfully slow down your breath, and equalize inhale and exhale. You can decide to observe your respiratory movement and wonder when it becomes you, when it leaves you, when it enters the oak leaves above you, when it returns. Inhale is world-becoming-you; exhale is you-becoming-world. When attention to the breath is both focused and gentle, the diaphragm expands and flows: a circular muscle with neither origin nor attachment points. (The muscle that governs breath has neither beginning nor end.) The diaphragm first drew breath before the intercostals began to contract with a more conscious sense of will. When the diaphragm is both engaged and relaxed, we can slip easily into either supported song, or supported sleep.

Down through the ages, yogis have often attempted to stop the breath entirely (rechaka), to test and blunt the edge of the autonomic urge to inhale. Or, conversely, they hyperventilate, lowering the carbon dioxide content of the blood and initiating vascular restriction to the brain, slowing nervous response and disorganizing cognition. Various forms of breath-play provoke a range of swoons, giving rising or sinking sensations that open doorways to altered perceptual states. Breath-players are like pre-oxygen-tank pearl fishers—holding their breath as they swim along the coral seeking oysters. The longer they can hold, the better chance they have of retrieving a luminous prize. Breath-play is a neuroceptual way of making-strange, something yogis-as-artists do to see newly, to see more. Colours, floaters, and the deconstruction of space. Sounds, rhythms, the amplification of the breath-starved heart-beat. Pins and needles emerge from the soft surrounding air as inner air pauses. Breath is the source of life, and willful control over it (how prāṇāyama is usually translated and taught) is a free hallucinogen.

It's possible that breath-play, like drugs, may open a new perceptual world for the practitioner whose particular problem is psychological banality. But like drug-use, we can never be sure about what may be lost in the process. Will breath-play stress the nervous system over time? Or if practiced in a relaxed fashion, can it tone vagal response to better manage autonomic fear (Porges, 2011)? Does it encourage an addictive dissociation?

I neither practice nor teach any form of breath control or breath-play that does not encourage the regularization of breath, the lengthening of the respiratory cycle, the full use of the diaphragm, and the resultant relaxation of sympathetic nervous responses. I have simply seen no benefit otherwise. As a practitioner of Āyurveda, the only direct manipulation of breathing I sometimes mentor is to ask students and clients to see what it feels like to direct breath through one nostril or the other for several minutes at a time. To breathe at an even pace through the right nostril (sūrya bhedana) is said to stoke the solar energies of biochemistry. I'm not sure what the nervous-system explanation for this might be, but I would guess that if right-nostril breathing enlivens the left-brain activities that are biased towards cognition, this would have a systemically heating effect that can aid all metabolic actions. Many clients have reported clear digestive improvements after practicing right-nostril breathing before meals for several weeks.

Conversely, left-nostril breathing (chandra bhedana) seems to activate lunar energies, to cool metabolism, to hydrate, to soften mentation into right-brain intuitional presence, and encourage sleep. My clients have reported reductions in insomnia and anxiety through lunar breathing. In these two practices, the breath is not altered in terms of volume, pace, or intensity, but merely in terms of pathway. This makes a kind of eco-poetic sense to me: wind that has passed over mountains feels one way; over the desert plain, another; over the oceans, another. The differences between the nostrils are not geological, of course. But to excite the hemispheres individually could well cue different internal continents to unfold.

But honestly, even this might be overly complex. Is there any substitute for the sigh? Or for the simple, deep, diaphragmatic breathing that remembers the peace of childhood sleep?

5.11 pratyāhāra in the sensual world

Breath relaxation can be instantly deepened through peristaltic release. This is easiest to accomplish through conscious release of the tongue and jaw. Softening the tongue relaxes peristalsis all the way down the GI tract, so that breathing is no longer cramped by digestive gripping. (The small intestine is "grahaṇī" in Sanskrit: "the seizer", not only of nutrition but of desires and goals.) The tongue is also continually quivering with unconscious subvocalization: to release its muscular tension can slow down or even stop thought.

As the breath stills and the tongue relaxes its internal monologue, the upper pallet may also release upwards, such that a sphere of space is felt at the back of the mouth. In both yoga physiology and Āyurveda, this upper pallet tension-release begins to reverse the energetic flow of perception. For the majority of our conscious lives, we seem to reach out of our bodies to contact the objects of sense. This is especially palpable with the visual sense.

The extraocular muscles that move the eyes can release their almost perpetual tension, and will release automatically as the upper pallet rises. There is a feeling that one has been reaching out for forms, to see the edges of things, to discern. A willful holiday from this reach is possible, and seems to automatically cue an even deeper level of relaxation on the level of thought. As the stilled tongue stills the inner voice, quiet eyes seem to dissuade the very impetus to think.

This sensory relaxation is at the heart of pratyāhāra , which literally translates as "rejection (prati) of food (āhāra)"—implying an impossible renunciation of all inputs—but which I remix as "freedom of the senses". This division of the eightfold path is not as distinct in practice as those listed before, or as the meditative techniques that follow. It seems to naturally bridge what have been traditionally described as the "outer" methods of ethics through to breathwork and the "inner" methods of contemplative states. Although there are distinct techniques that are taught for sensory withdrawal, mostly involving physical blocking of the eyes and ears with various wrappings, pratyāhāra does seem to arise naturally out of āsana and prāṇāyama . In fact it is hard to practice any of the three in isolation from the others.

To me it's inaccurate to describe relationship to other, relationship to self, poise and freedom of breath, as "outer" methods, insofar as all of these practices work to reconfigure our neurology. The exercise of protection, honesty, and ecology, etc., literally rewires our very plastic social brains, as contemporary neuroscience is beginning to show. The common claim that the "outer" methods are preliminary to the "inner" methods in terms of complexity and effect is no longer tenable, nor is it useful to a global culture that needs relational answers to alienated suffering.

Perhaps we can say that pratyāhāra marks a threshold between external and internal inquiry. Feeling how we cross it, going in both directions, will tell us a lot about how we connect our personal and social ecologies. Heading into meditation, we hold the continuity of the other-phenomenal-world in relaxed trust by softening our sensory tension, and resolving our attention to the self-phenomenal-world. Heading out of meditation, newly self-regulated, we rejoin the other, reaching for her gently, with senses eager and receptive.

5.12 embodied meditation

Patañjali peels layers of meditation away from each other like the petals of a rose. I'll spend some time with these layers in Part 6. But in the meantime: what is meditation generally?

Start with any kind of pause. To stop moving forward, to relax the clenched circle of possession that has hardened the edges of how you meet what you want. To feel needs hover like mist, and then lift. The bones sink into the chair. Eyes relax back into the skull. Sounds become spatial again, and breath breathes you.

During any activity will do. Maybe it is easier when alone, in the midst of self-care. When the hand holding the washcloth feels it is washing itself. When the hands preparing food relax into the pleasure of hands being food. To fall asleep with one hand behind the head, and the other over the sternum. To melt your holding away, held by hands having no complex intention.

It might be easier when alone: this is what the ascetics claimed. Perhaps the mirror neurons relax their engagement with the being of others, and reflect the peace of flesh. The peace of things reveals you as a piece of all things. This all happens before and beyond language. The sentence of feelings can suddenly need no completion. Thought does not need to carry out its sentence. The page of the world is sufficient.

With others, this pause is intensified by the mutual gaze. To mutually gaze is to fall into the other's flesh, to pause the isolation of "you".

5.13 good-enough mother, good-enough practice

Patañjali raises a high bar: the erasure of consciousness. Deconstructing Patañjali-*s* subtractive drives doesn't necessarily lower this bar—it takes a lot of contemplation to rewire the pain of hard dualism. It takes a lot of effort to merely come towards yoga. But as I round up these reflections on the practices, a gentler perspective on goals might be in order. At the heart of losing heart in life and/or yoga we might find some deeply embedded, unreasonable expectations.

I've referenced Klein already with regard to the ascetic's failure of ambivalence. I've also referred to Winnicott, invoking his notion of the "good-enough mother" to describe how we might come into a mature relationship with the livingworld, and not reject it wholesale in our fetish for transcendence. We can apply the same concepts of maturation to our practice itself. Practice is like a parent: it gives, but it can take away. It supports you, but it can also abandon you to your own unformed devices. There are good days, and bad days. The maturity of ambivalence takes the long view.

Failing to develop ambivalence creates crushing expectations for practice. Without ambivalence, practice can never be good-enough. Some might say that Patañjali addresses this very problem with the invocation of vairāgya (a dispassionate attitude towards attainment) but I don't think we're getting the message. There's a lot of anxiety in the self-fixing energy of yoga culture. Many are driven by the not-good-enough. Paradoxically, many feel that they are not-good-enough at vairāgya! But honestly, how much better do we need to become? If you're reading this book, are you not already doing a substantial amount of self-work? How much more flexible do we want to become, or purified, or serene? I see many clients who feel stalled in their lives because yoga has presented them with a spiral of unattainable ideals by which they punish themselves to avoid moving forward. Students are governed by "I'm not good-enough", and fail to thrive in the world and relationship because they are obsessed with self-improvement. There's a fine line between being dedicated to evolution and the neurotic coping mechanisms of "not good-enough".

The drive towards a "perfect" practice is inspired, I believe, by Patañjali-s own failure of ambivalence, which posits peacefulness as a singular goal. So many of my yogi-clients—especially women—want to attain peace when in fact they are enraged, more often than not for very good familial, social, and cultural reasons. Often I try to help them realize that their years of āsana and meditation practice so far have given them good-enough skills: they are less reactive, more observant of their emotions, more aware of the long view, and generally able to tell when they are avoiding the challenge of being present. For them, wanting more peace is akin to wanting to disappear. With a little reflection on this point, the subtractive drive generally evaporates, and released rage turns the wheel of change. Martial arts can help a lot.

So far for me, yoga has given just the right amount of peace. My level of yoga-peace is good-enough. I'm suspicious of too much peace, in fact—it's a sure sign that I am splitting in some way and burying some shard of rage. These days I need my peace dressed with just the right amount of piss and vinegar to get things done. For those really interested in the yamas, peace is the hard-won, occasional byproduct of the passion for justice.

5.14 my choices: the book of practices

2.1 Yoga applies endurance, learning, and commitment.

For tapas, I favour "endurance" over "austerity" (Aranya, Taimni, Prabhavananda), or "accepting pain" (Sivananda), or "mortification" (Vivekananda). While "austerity" and "accepting pain" gesture towards yoga's interface with existential honesty, they both carry penitential overtones that I would rather avoid. "Learning" is the engine of evolution. Every adaptation sheds a layer of ignorance. "Commitment" is a resistance to dissociation.

2.2 It reduces alienation and cultivates empathy.

Miller has: "Its [yoga's] purpose is to cultivate pure contemplation and attenuate the forces of corruption." Here I directly elide samādhi with "empathy", as I build towards an emphasis upon Patañjali-s sole intersubjective topic: ethics. While meditative integration is typically framed as an internal event, I propose that the more important integration is available first through relationship.

2.3 Ignorance, individualism, addiction, dissociation, and the "afterlife": these alienate.

I quite radically remix abhiniveśa ("fear of death", "will to live", "clinging to life", etc.) as ""afterlife"". To posit our shared zest for life as some kind of mental distortion seems absurd and anti-human. Taimni's rendering is particularly deranged, stating that the "strong desire for life" is among "the great afflictions or causes of all miseries in life". This idea is dissonant and depressive to a suicidal degree. I feel compelled to introduce an entirely new position: that the notion of some experience *beyond* this life we are coming to know, which would presumably render this life meaningless to cling to, is itself a deep mental affliction. Patañjali argues that our reflex for self-preservation is delusional. I counter that the devaluation of this life in favour of an imagined non-living ideal is the real delusion. The quotation marks indicate irony.

"Afterlife" has a more immediate resonance for me as a kind of constant dissociation from presence. A friend said: "We're always living in the afterlife—reflecting upon what's happened. We're more in tune with the mental digestion of the previous moment than with the moment of eating. Except when we're eating or orgasming. The basic *mood* of cognition is past-tense." It made me think of the evolution of perceptual-to-conscious-to-aware life not only as an individual and species narrative, but also as the story of each passing moment. Our bias towards cognitive self-identification seems to put us a few steps behind the moment of life. As we ruminate upon the last moment, the new moment announces itself to our neurology. Language is slower than feeling: we are continually a step behind. We are literally after-life. Perhaps this is why we crave a literal afterlife: as a glorifying expansion of our natural after-ness.

2.4 Ignorance enables alienation in all forms, from seed to tree.

Hartranft has: "Not seeing things as they are is the field where the other causes of suffering germinate, whether dormant, activated, intercepted, or weakened." Patañjali alludes to a simple horticultural metaphor, but many translators don't draw it out. I believe that making it transparent ("from seed to tree") helps to demystify the complex forms of karma that Patañjali cites: prasupta (dormant), tanu (thin), vicchinna (interrupted), udārāṇām (activated).

2.5 Ignorance involves not learning about change in objects, ideas, sensations, or self.

Patañjali speaks of ignorance as the misinterpretation of objects. According to the sage, ignorance allows for the cognitive confusion between mutually dependent categories such as pure/impure, pleasure/pain, and soul/non-soul. He suggests that our problem is rooted in our tendency to confuse one for the other. My thread avoids the reification of these categories by simply naming ignorance as the stasis of non-learning. The original provokes an anxious black-and-white thinking: ignorance as the confusion of the self (the good) with the non-self (the bad). As Miller puts it: "Ignorance is misperceiving permanence in transience, purity in impurity, pleasure in suffering, an essential self where there is no self." In softening these loaded dichotomies, this thread implicitly suggests that an actual blending of the self and the non-self might provide a natural gateway to empathy. Failure to distinguish between two codependent categories becomes, simply, "not recognizing change".

2.6 Individualism sees things instead of relationships.

My critique of egoism is not, as is Patañjali-s, a critique of the fact or process of individuation *per se*, but rather a critique of how individualism tends to project its solitude outward onto a world of "things", when it would be both more accurate and relaxing to recognize interdependent relationships instead.

2.7 Addiction turns pleasure into a thing.

Patañjali and most translators implicitly condemn pleasure in this sūtra. I critique the mismanagement of pleasure through objectification and dependency. This view is actually more coherent with the Vedic view of the purusārtha-s, in which pleasure (kāma) is a necessary goal of living, though it can destabilize artha (necessary resources), dharma (personal path), and mokṣa (the capacity for freedom) when pursued to excess. I am depathologizing rāga (attachment to pleasurable experiences in the past), while pointing out the potential pathology of imbalance through addiction-driven or neurotically-driven repetition. Any repetitive form of rāga gives diminishing returns, and often leads away from relationship and into the traps of fetish and objectification.

2.8 Dissociation runs away from experience.

In a similar vein, I have no problem with aversion (dveṣa), which is as natural as desire. I am more concerned about dissociation from negative experiences, which leads to splitting and suppression, and so have positioned it as the kleśa in question. "Aversion stems from [experiences] of pain": Bryant's traditional translation describes an origin of discomfort, but not the problem of substance, in my view. Psychologically, aversion is rarely as damaging as splitting.

2.9 The "afterlife" devalues life.

Miller has: "The will to live is instinctive and overwhelming, even for a learned sage." My thread ignores the absurdity of labelling fear of death as a problem, and directly attacks its artificial solution: metaphysical speculation. Again: I posit the kleśa of ""afterlife"" as a knife to the heart of existential authenticity.

2.10 The causes of alienation are interwoven. Loosening one begins to unravel them all towards empathy.

2.11 Concentration stills alienating thoughts.

2.12 Fruitlessly seeking consolation, alienating patterns of thought tend to repeat.

Prabhavananda translates: "A man's latent tendencies have been created by his past thoughts and actions. These tendencies will bear fruits, both in this life and in lives to come." I avoid speculation on the theory of reincarnation by simply invoking "repetition". Patterning does not need past and future lives for meaning and context: it simply needs time. I also avoid another implicit impression, not unique to the good Swami: that "latent tendencies" are entirely self-created, rather than an inseparable weaving of interpersonal and personal conditions.

2.13 This repetition can impede self-perception, relationship to time, and the capacity for enjoyment.

The original states that afflictive karma causes rebirths of differing types and lengths. After subtracting the unprovable metaphysics of rebirth, this rendition substantially agrees: that the flaws of consciousness distort present capacities. The notion of rebirth in different forms (Taimni, Miller, and others) is thus reworked as an impediment to clear self-perception, for example.

2.14 Alienating patterns predispose you to continued alienation.

Alienation, like karma, is a feedback loop.

2.15 For one who takes responsibility for his or her existential condition, life will be felt fully as ever-changing, echoing with loss, limited, unknowable, and chaotic.

Miller renders: "All life is suffering for a man of discrimination, because of the sufferings inherent in change and its corrupting subliminal impression, and because of the way qualities of material nature turn against themselves."

In most previous translations, the original communicates a pessimistic theme that rallies towards a transcendental escape: if you are intelligent, you see suffering in everything. Further: the very dynamic qualia of existence (the guṇa-s of gravity, urge, and resolution), being in continual conflict, imprison us. Implicitly: we are in a flawed or mistaken place, compelled to search for another. Here I make an existential stand. The description of life's conflicts and sufferings is not an invitation to dissociate. It is actually our call to participation. To realize the condition of consciousness is to take responsibility for improving it. The guṇa-s move without end, and so do we, and there's nothing wrong with this at all, for those willing to let life be *felt fully as ever-changing.*

2.16 But the future is unwritten.

Here I modify the positive side of Patañjali-s false choice (stay in a flawed world, or escape into private bliss). The original suggests that pain can be "discarded" (Aranya) "escaped" (Miller) or "avoided" (almost everyone else). I see no evidence for the cessation of pain, because I cannot imagine any part of life that is not growing and learning, stimulated by dissatisfaction and impeded by struggle. With this remixed thread, I wish to simply open the future to a sense of creative and flexible agency into which rajas is inextricably woven and the dialectic of evolution is invigorated.

2.17 Pain is caused by the blurring of authenticity with fabrication.

Throughout, Patañjali seems to suggest that the blending of nature with our awareness is the insufferable flaw of human experience. This is a traumatized and suicidal view, implying that our basic ecodynamism, which has evolved precisely to blend nature and awareness, is an abomination. Instead, I focus on a particular challenge of modern consciousness: our cognition of objects is so efficient and seamless that it creates a potentially artificial and alienating web of simultaneous projection, interpretation, and abstraction. The problem is not that the seer has become "defiled" by the seen, but that the seer can't know that it is seeing/cognizing/

re-cognizing, and tends to unknowingly blend the seen (authenticity) with its own meanings (fabrications).

2.18 We feel gravity, urge, and resolution surge through the elements, and these feelings can lead to ecstasy.

Taimni's translation typifies the traditional narcissism of this sūtra: "The Seen (objective side of manifestation) consists of the elements and sense organs, is of the nature of cognition, activity, and stability (sattva, rajas, and tamas) and has for its purpose providing the Puruṣa with experience and liberation." In other words, Patañjali suggests that human consciousness should live parasitically upon the oscillating qualia of life while surfing towards isolated transcendence, at which point the guṇa-s are discarded like so much dross. By contrast, I suggest that the guṇa-s (which I translate as the qualia of gravity, urge, and resolution) are the very texture of experience, and feeling them fully can be blissful.

2.19 Gravity, urge, and resolution appear in all stages of form, from the object we name and hold to the nameless quanta coursing through it.

Gravity is the mood of sinking towards stasis. Urge is the dissatisfaction that compels movement, down to the level of autonomic self-regulation (heartbeat, breath, peristalsis). Resolution is the buoyant plateau of momentarily satisfied desires. These three qualia seem to cycle choicelessly through all internal and external media.

2.20 Consciousness seems distinct from the flesh, and yet pours through it.

Here I allude to the apparent separation between consciousness and the other media of experience. Patañjali holds that this separation is real and should be accentuated to the point of utter isolation. My assertion, derived from a phenomenological perspective and immersed in neuroscience, is that the feeling of separation is illusory, and can be softened.

I use the word *flesh*, which Merleau-Ponty introduces (*la chair*), to label our psycho-somatic experiential medium, which is utterly contiguous with "the world". In *The Visible and the Invisible* (1964/68), he writes: "There is a body of the mind, and a mind of the body.... The essential notion for such a philosophy is that of the flesh, which is not the objective body, nor the body thought by the soul as its own (Descartes), [but] which is the sensible in the two-fold sense of what one senses and what senses" (259). In the same text, he writes: "One can say that we perceive the things themselves, that we are the world that thinks itself—or that the world is at the heart of our flesh" (136).

2.21 Consciousness delights in giving meaning to the flesh, as though it were its source.

Sacchidananda renders: "The seen exists only for the sake of the Seer." As I reverse the direction of this thread, I also poke gentle fun at consciousness: it prides itself on giving meaning where meaning always-already resides. The original introduces a master/slave relationship between puruṣa and prakṛti, in which the former waits upon the latter for amusement and self-discovery. I turn the focus to the mysterious relationship between consciousness and perception, which is the more deeply problematic dualism. The introduction of the term "meaning" here will carry through to thread 2.26, denoting a primary function of consciousness: to give meaning.

2.22 As consciousness evolves, meanings change or are taken away, for different people at different times.

Bryant has: "Although the seen ceases to exist for one whose purpose is accomplished, it has not ceased to exist altogether, since it is common to other puruṣa-s." This is one of the most nihilistic/narcissistic aphorisms of the original. After setting up the master/slave dichotomy between puruṣa and prakṛti, which the practitioner is to first cognize and then exploit for the purpose of soul-enlightenment, Patañjali then claims that the very makeup of the world shifts according to this exploitation. In a wild paradox, he says that the world (prakṛti) ceases to exist materially for the enlightened, while remaining in place for the unenlightened. In this thread I place the focus instead on what I feel to be the actual challenge of describing how we change: that consciousness evolves at different rates for different people, creating a polymorphous plurality of experience.

2.23 Consciousness projects meaning onto things but then, forgetting its projection, assumes those given meanings belong to those things. But the conjunction of consciousness and things invites both to feel their interdependence.

Hartranft has: "It is by virtue of the apparent indivisibility of the phenomenal world and pure awareness that the former seems to possess the latter's powers." Vivekananda has: "Junction is the cause of the realization of the nature of both the powers, the experienced and its Lord." I combine these meanings in this thread.

If this remix identifies a core flaw in the structure of human experience, it is the fluidity with which consciousness abstracts itself from its material/perceptual source, and then makes outrageous claims about its precedence and even mastery over this source. This process seems to correlate to early ego-formation in developmental psychology, in which the infant creates an individuated, self-soothing identity (the "inner mother", cf. Louise Kaplan) in order to form the seeming autonomy we find so necessary to personhood. As the ego is to the psyche, so is consciousness to the fullness of the experiential spectrum. Both run into trouble when they try to run away from home. It seems to happen so quickly and seamlessly.

2.24 These assumed meanings are another kind of ignorance.

2.25 When ignorance fades, the original source of projected meaning is seen as consciousness and not the thing. A burden lifts.

Rather than advocating the "dissociation" (Taimni uses this very word!) of consciousness from its object, my focus is on the recognition of their necessary relationship, and a more honest account of how meaning is generated. Suffering in my view does not arise from the blending of consciousness and the world: such blending is simply an evolutionary fact. The difficulty comes when consciousness casts a narcissistic palimpsest over the world, as in the Borges story ("On Exactitude in Science") famously embellished by Baudrillard in *Simulacra and Simulation* (1994). A king wished for the most accurate rendering of his kingdom, and so commissioned his cartographer to create a map on a 1:1 scale. The map was impeccably accurate. But of course its size demanded that it cover over the land that it depicted, denying it sun and rain. The king could then see an exact representation of what he possessed, but as he gazed at the picture of his land, the land itself perished, along with his wealth. In our context, the king might be consciousness, the cartographer his cognitive faculty, and the land he covers over and kills with his representational fetish is, tragically, his livingworld. This thread offers another possibility: if we recognize the difference between the map (*projected meaning*) and the land (*the thing itself*), the map will be lifted away to more clearly reveal what it was meant to represent.

2.26 This becomes clear through contemplation on the difference.

2.27 As veils of assumption fade, the depth of perception expands, and begins to explore the unknown.

2.28 The practices of yoga diminish alienation, allowing for the radiance of clear sight.

2.29 The eight practices are relationship to other, relationship to self, poise, freedom of breath, freedom of senses, focus, contemplation, and integration.

Prabhavananda says: "The eight limbs of yoga are: the various forms of abstention from evil-doing (yama), the various observances (niyamas), posture (āsana), control of the prāṇa (prāṇāyama), withdrawal of the mind from sense objects (pratyāhāra), concentration (dhāraṇā), meditation (dhyāna) and absorption in the Ātman (samādhi)."

My names here for the eight limbs (aṣṭa-aṅga) privilege the intersubjective and avoid the language of constriction: using "relationship" twice, rejecting "control" and "withdrawal" (as prāṇāyama and pratyāhāra often convey), and using "poise" for the more conventional "posture" to signal that aligned carriage and gait not only give health and comfort, but can also produce social warmth and promote good communication.

2.30 Good relationship to others requires protection, honesty, fair trade, sexual responsibility, and self-possession.

By translating ahiṃsā as "protection", instead of the conventional "non-violence", I try to mitigate Patañjali-s drive to ascetic withdrawal by distinguishing between forms of violence that re-establish justice, and forms of violence that oppress the safety or rights of others. By translating asteya as "fair trade", I broaden the aspiration beyond the usual translation of "non-stealing" to gesture towards holistic economy. By translating brahmacarya as "sexual responsibility", I widen the yogic path to include people at all stages of sexual maturity, expression, and orientation. By translating aparigraha as "self-possession", I affirm the grasping nature of desire as an intrinsic catalyst to growth and learning, but gently limit its scope to the field of self-responsibility. The kind of grasping we should most discourage would be that which arises from compensatory need.

2.31 These five means of good relationship work for everyone, all the time.

2.32 Good relationship to oneself requires ecology, contentment, endurance, learning, and commitment.

Śauca (which I render as "ecology") is often translated as "cleanliness", which in our age is an insufficient and self-centred goal to the challenges of ecological destruction, insofar as our attempts to "clean" (from chemistry to antibiotics) often pollute our broader context. Svādhyāya is typically translated as "study of scriptures and chanting of mantras" (Aranya), or "study of spiritual books" (Sivananda). I democratize this into "learning." Īśvara praṇidhāna is translated as "devotion to god" (Aranya), "self-surrender" (Taimni), "worship of God" (Sivananda), and "orientation towards the ideal of pure awareness" (Hartranft). I demystify and secularize this into "commitment".

2.33 Negative thought patterns can be altered by embodying what balances them.

Bryant renders this sūtra as: "Upon being harassed by negative thoughts, one should cultivate counteracting thoughts." This might imply that Patañjali is anticipating cognitive behavioural therapy in this sūtra: the idea that psychological change can be initiated by changing the tone of one's self-talk. What might be a problem with this view is that "pratipakṣa bhāvanam" in the broader literature has the more generalized meaning of "cultivating the opposite", which is by no means limited to cognitive acts. It is a phrase used in Āyurveda, for instance, to define the terms of multifaceted therapies: the qualia of an etiology (dryness, coldness, hypermobility) is treated with the opposite qualia (moisture, warmth, stillness), applied through diet, herbs, movement, and daily rhythm. Āyurveda cautions that thinking is not necessarily the most effective way to treat thought. Thus I have chosen: "embodying what balances them."

2.34 When thoughts of oppression in any degree are held, acted upon, delegated to another, or colluded with, whether through greed, anger, or delusion, one must realize this pattern leads to shared suffering and ignorance, and work hard to reverse it.

My choices here do not deviate too far from other translations, except for the fact that I emphasize the socialization of ethics to encourage broad responsibility for the multiple human systems in which we are each enmeshed. When we see corporate, governmental or social abuses, we must respond: "Not in our name."

2.35 When one protects others from harm, this produces a feeling of connectedness and safety.

The original fosters magical thinking: "When a man becomes steadfast in his abstention from harming others, then all living creatures will cease to feel enmity in his presence." (Prabhavananda). Worse than being completely untrue, it supports the implicit argument that a violent encounter is the victim's fault. As in: "You must not have been steadfast in your abstention from harming others—no wonder you were beaten/assaulted/oppressed."

Molding ahiṃsā into "protection" (which may require physical violence in its enforcement) calls out at least three implications: pure non-violence does not exist (consider the immune system); violence is not the problem, but oppression is; and the ideal of pure non-violence is based upon a metaphysics of disembodiment which denies the power differentials that grind out change and time. Decriminalizing "violence" might also implicitly criticize rigid vegetarianism, which is not appropriate in all ecosystems, often depends upon agricultural imbalances, and anthropologically arises out of metaphysical cleanliness taboos and at least in part the wish that we can somehow avoid our predator/prey relationship with the other.

2.36 In the aura of honesty, causes and their results make sense.

Bryant has: "When one is established in truthfulness, one ensures the fruition of actions." The suggestion here is that truth becomes a spell when spoken aloud, causing things to happen effortlessly. As I will develop further in the third pāda, I reject the magical thinking of the yogi-superpower-wish. For me, true words are not magic words that change reality: they are simply true. Honesty allows for a clear sharing of how things work, which biases the communal over the private. I hear in this thread the potential for an implicit yogic endorsement of the standards of peer-review, in which truth is established by the honesty of a consensus method, the results of which can be shared. Truth is interdependent.

2.37 When you practice fair trade, your feeling of wealth is enhanced.

2.38 Sexual responsibility enables intimacy.

Prabhavananda double-negatives intercourse: "When a man becomes steadfast in his abstention from incontinence, he acquires spiritual energy." Here I reject the numerous problems of the original and most translations: bodily distrust, the privileging of asceticism over householding, and the archaic naturopathic belief that orgasm is necessarily devitalizing. Whether we are partnered or not, conventional or not, heteronormative or not: intimacy is a fundamental need. Intimacy allows us to pacify the often-traumatizing oscillation between union and individuation. To take interest in and responsibility for each other's sexual integrity makes intimacy safe.

2.39 Self-possession allows you to define yourself according to your own actions, while revealing your interdependence with all things.

Mature yoga seeks to avoid the compensatory behaviours of grasping to develop a centred sense of self-reliance that acknowledges our immersion within time, relationship, and livingworld. From this groundwork, I can resonate with Sacchidananda's more orthodox translation: "When non-greed is confirmed, a thorough illumination of the how and why of one's birth comes." Interdependence is both how, and why.

2.40 Ecology allows you to honour your flesh, and the flesh of others.

Here I emphatically reject the most egregious example of the body-hatred that characterizes most ascetic worldviews of Patañjali-s era. The original praises śauca ("purity", "purification", "cleanliness") for its ability to make the flesh appear revolting, i.e., something we should desperately seek to escape. The original message is unambiguous: "By purification arises disgust for one's own body and for contact with other bodies" (Sacchidananda). I feel that this view cannot help a disembodied culture reconcile itself to its material sources, nor will it increase trust and familiarity amongst practitioners. I offer the opposite view.

2.41 Ecology enables clarity, brightness, joy, insight, sensual harmony, and inquiry.

2.42 Contentment makes one at home in the world.

2.43 Endurance allows the flesh and senses to be more fully enjoyed.

In rendering tapas as "endurance", I turn away from the penitential indicators used by most translators: "austerity" and "mortification". My aim is to bring out the positive meanings of effort. Tapas is envisioned as the heated exhilaration of the bodymind in full participation.

2.44 Learning connects you with your archetypes.

I've already discussed the broadness of "learning" as a translation for svādhyāya. The original invokes the principle of iṣṭa devatā: the particular representation of metaphysical energy that resonates most deeply with a yogi's psychology. Sacchidananada translates: "By study of spiritual books comes communion with one's chosen deity." Indian cosmology is peopled with infinite deities to serve every possible purpose. It is assumed that each practitioner will find his or her own divine "handler"—or that they will attract such a being by virtue of their ardour. For most contemporary people, these legions of old deities are far less accessible than the archetypal figures that emerge in our art and dreams. I believe, however, that they serve the same function: as intermediaries between the unconscious and the conscious. My choice is to liberalize the concept with a nod to Carl Jung. But the thread is still limiting. Learning does so much more: it's at the very heart of yoga, I believe. I'll explore this more thoroughly in the Coda.

2.45 Commitment to relationship invites integration.

2.46 Poise is steady and well-spaced.

Hartranft is rhythmic and eloquent: "The postures of meditation should embody steadiness and ease." In my thread, I feel that "poise" allows for more movement than "posture" suggests. With movement implied, my rendering of āsana more readily includes what is now the majority of yoga practitioners: women who do vinyāsa, who are actively hybridizing the more static vocabulary of meditation/purification postures of the hatha tradition with elements of modern gymnastics and dance. "Well-spaced" is a more direct translation of sukha than "pleasant" (Vivekananda) or "comfortable" (Sacchidananda) or "agreeable" (Aranya). Su = "good"; kha = space.

2.47 This occurs when restlessness fades and feeling is boundless.

2.48 Then, even oscillations are peaceful.

The dynamic movement of the triguṇa-s (gravity, urge, resolution), and the binary impressions of the twenty qualia (hot/cold, wet/dry, smooth/rough, etc.) are often highlighted in Indian psychosomatology as irritants to transcendent peace. As we saw in 1.16, Patañjali describes the higher meditative attainments as characterized by the evaporation of the guṇa-s. Here, I suggest that these natural oscillations do not disappear in the full expression of āsana practice (for clearly, movement never stops), but that experiencing them becomes enjoyable.

2.49 Breath is free when its movement is first easy and then voluntary.

"Voluntary" breath for me expresses a positive and natural view of prāṇāyama , which has been more faithfully rendered as "cessation" (Aranya), "interruption" (Houston), "control" (Miller, Sacchidananda), and "stopping" (Prabhavananda). Having observed no instance in which vigorous and willful control of the breath leads to *less* anxiety in a practitioner, I suggest to students and clients a much more observant approach to the study and quieting of breathing. In deep states of parasympathetic relaxation, in which the "rest and digest" nervous functions are active, breath may indeed slow and pause for substantial moments. But forcing this phenomenon to occur would be contrary to the ideals of steadiness and spaciousness that govern āsana. Further, any willful cessation of breath seems to me a clearly separative gesture: an assertion that one's life force can be enhanced by removing it from relationship. When breath is stopped, a clear boundary between self and not-self is asserted. I'm not sure what the utility of this would be, except perhaps in homeopathic doses: that the experience of willful separation between internal and external forms of prāṇa might show the practitioner the extent of his or her alienation.

2.50 You can feel yourself making the breath smooth and subtle by observing the number, length, and placement of inhalations, exhalations, and pauses.

2.51 Breath observance can also suspend the division between what is inside and what is outside.

Here I explicitly make breath the physiological hinge of intersubjective realization. Breath is never possessed, but always shared.

2.52 This feels like an unveiling of light.

For the object of the sentence, prakāśa, Miller translates "the light of truth". Sacchidananda translates "the inner light". I resist overdetermination here by not abstracting "light" at all, whether as a metaphor or as though it were coming from a location, such as the soul or ātman.

2.53 And concentration blossoms.

2.54 As consciousness draws inward, it becomes the object of the senses.

Taimni says: "Pratyāhāra or abstraction is, as it were, the imitation by the senses of the mind by withdrawing themselves from their objects." This remix proposes a different direction: that even consciousness itself can become the object of phenomenological inquiry. It feels like something, it is sensible, it is an inner landscape to sensually explore. These days I wonder if the sensations of focusing upon consciousness alone—buoyancy, a sense of the luminous—are actually what arise when we attune ourselves closely to our autonomic movements.

2.55 When the senses are free, they will not disturb contemplation.

The Patañjali-an view of the senses is coherent with much of Indian philosophy: they are five wild horses that need vaśyatā: "obedience, subservience" (Hartranft), "supreme control" (Aranya), "complete mastery" (Prabhavananda). I continue to avoid all dominant/submissive language: my aim is towards the contemplative flexibility that can rise when sensory action is not driven by compulsion.

5.15 the song of practices

Yoga applies endurance, learning,
and commitment.
It reduces alienation and cultivates empathy.

Ignorance, individualism, addiction,
dissociation, and the "afterlife": these alienate.
Ignorance enables alienation in all forms,
from seed to tree.
Ignorance involves not learning about change
in objects, ideas, sensations, or self.

Individualism sees things instead of relationships.
Addiction turns pleasure into a thing.
Dissociation runs away from experience.
The "afterlife" devalues life.

The causes of alienation are interwoven.
Loosening one begins to unravel them
all towards empathy.
Concentration stills alienating thoughts.
Fruitlessly seeking consolation,
alienating patterns of thought tend to repeat.

This repetition can impede self-perception,
relationship to time, and the capacity for enjoyment.
Alienating patterns predispose you
to continued alienation.

For one who takes responsibility for his or her existential condition,
life will be felt fully as ever-changing, echoing with loss,
limited, unknowable and chaotic.
But the future is unwritten.

Pain is caused by the blurring
of authenticity
with fabrication.
We feel gravity, urge, and resolution
surge through the elements,
and these feelings can lead to ecstasy.
Gravity, urge, and resolution appear in all stages of form,
from the object we name and hold
to the nameless quanta coursing through it.

Consciousness seems distinct from the flesh,
and yet pours through it.
Consciousness delights in giving meaning
to the flesh, as though it were its source.

As consciousness evolves, meanings change
or are taken away,
for different people at different times.
Consciousness projects meaning onto things
but then,
forgetting its projection,
assumes those given meanings belong to those things.
But the conjunction of consciousness and things
invites both to feel their interdependence.
These assumed meanings are another kind of ignorance.

When ignorance fades, the original source
of projected meaning is seen as consciousness,
and not the thing.
A burden lifts.
This becomes clear through contemplation on the difference.
As veils of assumption fade, the depth of perception expands,
and begins to explore the unknown.

The practices of yoga diminish alienation,
allowing for the radiance of clear sight.
The eight practices are
relationship to other,
relationship to self,
poise,
freedom of breath,
freedom of senses,
focus,
contemplation, and
integration.

Good relationship to others requires
protection, honesty, fair trade, sexual responsibility, and self-possession.
These five means of good relationship work for everyone,
all the time.

Good relationship to oneself requires
ecology, contentment, endurance, learning, and commitment.
Negative thought patterns can be altered
by embodying what balances them.
When thoughts of oppression in any degree
are held, acted upon, delegated to another, or colluded with,
whether through greed, anger, or delusion,
one must realize this pattern leads to shared suffering and ignorance,
and work hard to reverse it.

When one protects others from harm,
this produces a feeling of connectedness and safety.
In the aura of honesty, causes and their results make sense.
When you practice fair trade, your feeling of wealth is enhanced.
Sexual responsibility enables intimacy.
Self-possession allows you to define yourself
according to your own actions, while revealing your interdependence
with all things.

Ecology allows you to honour your flesh, and the flesh of others.
Ecology enables clarity, brightness, joy, insight,
sensual harmony, and inquiry.
Contentment makes one at home in the world.
Endurance allows the flesh and senses
to be more fully enjoyed.
Learning connects you with your archetypes.
Commitment to relationship invites integration.

Poise is steady and well-spaced.
This occurs when restlessness fades and feeling is boundless.
Then, even oscillations are peaceful.

Breath is free when its movement is first easy
and then voluntary.
You can feel yourself making the breath smooth and subtle
by observing the number, length, and placement
of inhalations, exhalations, and pauses.
Breath observance can also suspend the division
between what is inside and what is outside.
This feels like an unveiling of light.
And concentration blossoms.

As consciousness draws inward,
it becomes the object of the senses.
When the senses are free, they will not disturb contemplation.

6. pāda three: wonders

6.1 the book of wonders

3.1 Focus can channel diffuse thoughts into one theme.
3.2 Contemplation is focus that attunes to its object.
3.3 Integration can dissolve the subject-object barrier through attunement, allowing both to share a single form.
3.4 These three work together.
3.5 They give flashes of brilliance and understanding.
3.6 They unfold in stages.
3.7 They are more internal than the first five limbs.
3.8 Yet they can feel external to even deeper states.
3.9 Deeper states build momentum and depth through feedback, changing hidden patterns.
3.10 Meditative feedback can create a continuous flow that overwrites alienation.
3.11 As this happens, wandering thoughts find their home, and the feeling of integration deepens.
3.12 As integration deepens, there is equanimity between things rising and dissipating.

3.13 Such practices give insight into what we sense, how we sense, and the passage of time.

3.14 All forms share the same basic particles through time.

3.15 The sharing and recycling of particles in various patterns causes different forms to continually emerge.

3.16 Understanding what we sense, how we sense, and the passage of time can yield narrative intuition.

3.17 Deconstructing the blend of sounds, meanings, and intentions within language gives insight into the grammar we share with all beings.

3.18 Uncovering your latent patterns gives insight into your past.

3.19 Understanding your mind gives insight into another's mind,

3.20 but not insight into the things that Other sees.

3.21 Meditating on flesh resolves the feeling of being objectified.

3.22 Understanding the narrative of events gives insight into how things end.

3.23 Contemplating the grace of others strengthens you.

3.24 Meditating on the non-human world gives shamanic energy.

3.25 There is an intuitive relationship between internal light, atoms, hidden things, and things that are far away.

3.26 Meditating on the sun gives insight into the earth.

3.27 Tracking the moon teaches you the stars.

3.28 Meditating on the North Star reveals how we move.

3.29 Meditating on the core shows the elegance of physiology.

3.30 Meditating on orality gives insight into appetite.

3.31 Focus on the thyroid can give bodily stillness.

3.32 Meditating on the halo connects you to the heritage of genius.

3.33 All such insights can be spontaneous.

3.34 The heart shows you thought.

3.35 Seeing the difference between consciousness and the self-sufficiency of things sharpens self-awareness.

3.36 From this can come heightened sensuality.

3.37 But such peak experiences are not always the point.

3.38 When the flesh is free and relaxed, you are open to intimacy.

3.39 Rising energy can make you buoyant amidst oppressors, thieves, and puritans.

3.40 A shining core can be seen.
3.41 The art of listening is the marriage of ear and space.
3.42 Movement feels like flight when the flesh is wedded to space.
3.43 Abstract consciousness seems to blaze with light.
3.44 By living intimately with nature and learning the large and the small, the still and the dynamic, and how things work together, one feels blessed by the world.
3.45 Experience can then shrink into a bead of pleasure, or countless other things.
3.46 The freed flesh pulses through the facets of beauty, grace, and glowing strength.
3.47 When you see how the sense organs work, weave you together, and commit you to the world, they become gateways of pleasure.
3.48 These gateways can also encourage the exploration of internal worlds at the speed of light.
3.49 Seeing the difference between consciousness and the self-sufficiency of things makes all of these experiences possible.
3.50 Equanimity towards even these wonders, while burning the seeds of alienation, grants even deeper liberation.
3.51 Otherwise, one can become seduced by spiritualism.
3.52 Meditating on both a single moment and the flow of time gives insight born of différance.
3.53 This insight deconstructs experience down to its raw data.
3.54 This raw data communicates to consciousness all possibility at once.
3.55 Then consciousness can be aware of even itself as raw data, co-creative with materiality.

6.2 meditation, magic, magical thinking and existential radiance

For Patañjali, the wonders of meditation present a fork in the road of the evolutionary path. In pāda three, he describes the "supernatural" powers of transformation and insight granted by the narrowing of consciousness into single-pointed focus. But he also warns (in 3.37) against becoming overly enthralled with these powers, as they might distract us from the ultimate goal he presents in pādas one and four: the reorientation of personal experience towards perfect and unchanging peace through the final separation of puruṣa from prakṛti. Patañjali offers meditation *magic* in pāda 3, and meditation *salvation* everywhere else.

I believe that what we as postmodern practitioners can reasonably expect and enjoy from meditative discipline lies somewhere in between these two anachronistic goals of superpower attainment and blissful withdrawal. If the meditative results described in *the book of wonders* have anything to offer us today, it is to inspire our capacity for entranced learning and the endless connections possible through the schooling of our intuition. It celebrates the possibilities of what we may become. If the results described in *the book of overflowing* speak to us, it is to draw out love for our existential condition: that we are patterned energy, brightly dissolving. It celebrates the inevitable uncertainty of our condition. The pāda-three form of meditation is ecstatic and effusive. Pādas one and four describe the radiant pause that attends understanding so deep and familiar it feels remembered.

Clearly we don't currently believe that meditation can allow us to fly (3.39), or take possession of other people's bodies (3.38), as the more faithful translations of these sūtra-s preserve. The strange thing is that Patañjali probably didn't either, but was himself referring to a mythological tradition of superheroes, which held such sway over the imagination of his culture that he had to rationalize their lauded feats in some way. He wasn't an eyewitness to levitation and bodysnatching, because nobody has ever been. He seems to stand in an awkward developmental stage of human inquiry, in which the new discipline of philosophy feels compelled to explain and reconcile older mystical paradigms. He uses an archaic metaphysics to reverse-engineer levitation, bilocation, shrinking the body to atomic size, and invisibility. It's not dissimilar from an early-Renaissance proto-science being used to rationalize Jesus' resurrection from the dead.

Philosophical speculation always precedes scientific testability. What we see so often in the yoga tradition is philosophical speculation that has not yet been vetted by scientific inquiry, and is nonetheless given an evidence-free reality-pass. It's relatively easy to tell a story about how quantum indeterminacy (pāda four) might imply that a yogi who had understood it could attain the physical strength of an elephant (pāda three). Proving it according to current consensus reality is something else entirely. And this is where we as postmodern yogis have to become really clear on the vast differences between our current epistemic reality (how we know what we know and how we verify it as true) and that of the archaic culture we have inherited. Failing this clarity, we will find ourselves deeply split between demanding rigorous testing of our seatbelt strength and road safety, and trusting blindly when some charismatic yoga teacher tells us that we are the angels of kaliyuga.

Even if in our most sober consideration we balk at the myths of levitation or the ability to shrink our bodies down to a bead of light, we have to admit that we still harbour many stubborn parcels of magical thinking. Contemporary yoga culture, as it indistinguishably intertwines with new age spirituality, is filled with wishes for internal heaven and peace on earth—or worse, attempts to impose these by fiat through the cognitive and emotional bullying of "It's all good". We put "love" stickers on bottled water to "change the molecular structure" of its contents. We sing the names of Hindu deities we know nothing about, asking for grace. We "tune our cakras" with crystal bowls. We receive downloads of reiki healing power in weekend workshops. We organize global meditations to psychically stop nuclear reactors from melting in Japan. We do sun salutations *en masse* in public parks and feel that a new age of equality, environmental protection, and late-capitalist politeness is somehow dawning. Our yoga clothes look like Star Trek uniforms: we're about to explore the universe.

These are rich and compelling fantasies, and completely understandable given how complex our world is and how comforting it can be to regress into a child-like paradigm. But we must be clear that they are personal and private consolations that at best enrich a hopeful attitude, and at worst may dissociate us from real solution-seeking. Whether he earnestly believed in what he was writing or not, Patañjali is wrong: we cannot learn to fly by meditating. As for us: we won't solve homelessness in Manhattan by doing tree pose in Times Square. We won't reverse global warming with śītalī-prāṇāyama or moon salutations. "Mindful shopping" will not reverse our terrible wealth inequities. We know absolutely, and uncomfortably, that for every serious issue we face as a culture and a species the time-consuming and unglamorous evidence-based and peer-reviewed protocols that we have developed over the last two hundred years are our best hope at systemic improvement.

It's very easy to attribute mystical, magical, and metaphysical attributes to meditative states. We mute our senses, still our breath, and plunge deeply into what seems to be infinite internal space. It's easy to convince ourselves that consciousness is endless, because the *content* of thought is logarithmically expansive—thinking begets thinking. We can easily naturalize this limitless feeling with magical or mystical sentiment, i.e. that which we can neither define nor understand. Internal journeying therefore seems to provide a road map for the "soul", not because the soul exists as a verifiable entity, but because "soul" is our best effort at naming the sensation of limitlessness. Equipped with an undying and luminous soul, what can we not do? Does it not feel it can fly? Can it not dream a body the size of a mustard seed? Once consciousness crowns itself as the source of the limitless soul, it begins to forget that the *form* or basis of thought is materially dependent. This is the fallacy of consciousness-presumptuousness, which I've described earlier: the feeling that interiority is so vast and seemingly different from immediate sensual experience that it fosters the unwarranted conviction that it is *a priori* to physical presence, perhaps in the same way that space is *a priori* to the formation of planets.

But if we really look around, private fantasies of internal limitlessness are no more dazzling than our everyday eyes-wide-open livingworld. At this very moment, I can see limitlessness everywhere, from the edges of every tree-leaf swaying outside my window to the countless threads of my shirt, from the inscrutable eyes of my cat to the thousand movements of my partner's flesh. Why do we bias our spiritual sentiment towards our internal evidence? Why did we create the *inner* soul, and then put it in a cage? Was it because self-consciousness comes late to us, both individually and as a species, and we're trying to catch up with its novelty? Or was it because we find it easier to turn away from interpersonal and sensual complexity, and hide ourselves "inside"?

What, then, is meditation for? Can it show us something "more real" than what we otherwise see? Does it lead us to the "soul", or towards a fantasy/fetish that separates us from the intersubjective? Does it facilitate delusions of internal grandeur? Can it harmonize and resolve internal and external stimuli? Can it inspire us without deluding or disconnecting us? (This would be a new goal for pāda three.) Can it draw out our existential wonderment? (A new goal for pāda four, perhaps.)

6.3 on the other hand: magic resists the banal

Hand in hand with alienation is the depression of the banal. If the old yogi came out of the forest and had a look at my iPhone, he would fall on the ground in full prostration at my mystical virtue that I had been granted this boon, or that perhaps I had even made it. But not only do I not associate the iPhone's power with myself, I don't have the slightest clue as to how it works, nor have I retained my post-purchase glow for more than a few hours—I also have no real idea as to where it even came from. In fact, it actually came from nowhere (having been made in 40 different countries), and it was made by "no one" (between our hidden slave-wage economy and robots guided by theta-waves of Steve Jobs). Because *it* came from nowhere, I'm not entirely sure where *I* am.

In the old days, an instrument with similar mystical powers would be thought to be accessible only through years, if not lifetimes, of intense spiritual practice. But today I basically got it for free because I bought a phone plan, because I had some money, because I either earned it from someone who borrowed it from someone else, or because I borrowed it myself directly from a computer in outer space. This means that this device, totally miraculous to my ancestors, and briefly miraculous to me, can hold no magic anymore. I'm holding a thing in my hands that came from nowhere and was made by no one, and thus has no history, and is infinitely replaceable. It is impossible for me to form an emotional relationship with this object beyond the order of the fetish. But at the same time, it soon ends up holding and representing and controlling a huge chunk of my life. The thing that runs my life is mass-produced and completely alien to me, except on the level of the brand interface. I am hovering in the world of the banal. Only fascination with animals, plants, and my breath could possibly restore the magic now. It might just be a pleasure to dream in Patañjali-s world.

6.4 what is meditation for?

Meditation is the willful exercise of our most recent faculty. To meditate is to consciously choose to enter an evolutionarily new internal space. Why? We have evolved to show ourselves a new ocean within. We want to dive in and observe its dream-like corals and currents. We have become aware of turbulence underneath us. It seems that by watching the movement, the movement becomes quiet. And the horizon of consciousness always recedes: there is always farther to swim. However, it would be good to be aware of when our exploration of consciousness becomes circular.

Consciousness, built upon the flesh, can spiral stubbornly towards disembodiment. We are easily confused.

I've written that consciousness is the youngest child of the flesh, developmentally and anthropologically. And that a kind of forgetfulness amounting to arrogance leads it to believe that it came first, that it is the creator-god. This is the basis of much metaphysical posturing. But we are gifted with a natural constraint upon this presumption. Because the fact is that as we become self-conscious, we develop a more and more refined capacity to observe our phenomenological origins. The poignancy of this is on display in the laboratory as the geneticist peers through a microscope at the strands of her own DNA. She does not forget that she is looking at her origins through the lens of what her origins have evolved. She has many skills and a vast intelligence, but she knows she is looking at the source-code that has produced her very eyes, and, by extension, her microscope. She is humbled by knowing she is just learning to read herself, and will never know the full story. Her continued learning expands the curriculum. As she learns, she expands the promise she can see glowing on the slide. She engages in a sublime feedback loop: each new datum of learning about her DNA expands the horizon of what she knows DNA to be capable of.

This might constitute one strand of meditative pursuit: to use consciousness to look at where you have come from and what you consist of, and how you became and remain conscious. It consists of contemplating this history and function of flesh: the very basis for your being able to contemplate at all. In practice terms, we might say that this strand is covered by the "mindfulness" category in contemporary meditation culture, in which consciousness does nothing active, but merely observes with quiet fascination where it comes from, what it rests upon, and the undercurrent waves of psycho-somatic sensation that ripple through it. This happens most easily through conscious focus on the breath, which is not only microcosmic to our entire livingworld, to how we relate, but also the immediate source of life. To watch the breath is to look at DNA as it rhythmically unfolds its code. And in the midst of watching breath, we feel things rise or pass through or wash over us. What are these things? Instincts, habits, sensations, memories of place and others, the autonomic roots of emotion. And we just watch.

At times, mindfulness meditation feels like gazing at a newborn, except that you are not the parent. You watch the beautiful simplicity of breath, the eyes finding focus, the twitches of digestion and spontaneous muscular expression and development. In time, baby finds your eyes. You look at him with love and tenderness, and he grows very still, and then the mutual reflection of gazing begins to fill and overflow you both. You are both watching what you came from. He is watching his father. You are watching the root of being alive.

But there is another strand of meditation, in which consciousness surreptitiously becomes its own object through a learned process of substituting ideas and symbols for phenomenological experience. For instance, legions of gurukula students in generations past have been asked to memorize the Sāṃkhya system of 25 tattvas: a conceptual map of being that proposes to describe everything we experience—from lowly earth element to unspeakable puruṣa. After memorization, a kind of analytical review of the presumed categories of matter and consciousness is encouraged, so that by repeated contemplation an internal experience begins to develop that seems to validate the model. In effect, consciousness is being told a story about itself, and training itself to believe it. The mood of the contemplation embodies the same quietude and non-reactivity with which we experience the objects of the mindfulness strand—breath and sensation—and this seems to bind "realization" of the concepts to autonomic contentment. The calmness of the flesh seems to endorse the self-organizing puzzle of cognition.

This conceptual or analytical meditation was the main technique to which I was exposed through my 20s and 30s. I began with Tibetan Buddhism, and learned a typical series of contemplations on orthodox topics: the parts of a spiritual path, the inevitability of death, the inherent dissatisfaction of life, various proofs of past lives, categories of karma, proofs of selflessness. I was instructed that each topic should be contemplated until "realized as true". It seemed to take about six months for each topic, one to two hours every morning, before dawn. I was taught good posture for meditation, and asked to watch my breath briefly to calm my mind. Quickly, I was then to embark upon a series of preparatory mental exercises that cued a psychic posture of devotion and receptivity. I was taught to visualize my teacher as a perfected person, to fantasize that I was making offerings to him, to confess my behavioural failings, and to ask him to help me understand the subject matter at hand in the coming meditation. I was meant to arouse a devotional feeling towards the subject matter by glorifying where it came from. (Mindfulness, by contrast, seems to arouse a devotional feeling towards where *I* come from.)

There was something about sitting very still with my breath that amplified my capacity for devotion. For me, simply sitting quietly aroused profound feelings of being loved and taken care of. But I believe that I began to misattribute this love and care as emanating from the teacher and the subject matter, when in fact my conscious self was being held and loved by my phenomenological reality. Quietude and breath gave me direct experience of the support of the world beneath me and around me and within me, but the abstract technique made me think that the subject matter was in fact my world, my source of support.

The teaching went so far as to explicitly degrade my lived reality. My teacher would say: "Watching your breath is a good way to begin to calm down your mind, but your transformation really begins when the object of meditation is more virtuous than you are. Your breath is not a virtuous object. It comes and goes. It is impermanent. It will end one day. But the truths of Buddhist teachings are proven to be stable and can resolve your suffering forever." I bought it at the time, because I was depressed and ungrounded. For about ten years, I believed that a set of ideas was more important than my lived experience of breath and sensation and relationship. I believed that "transformation" was a higher purpose than presence. And so I learned a lot about Buddhist metaphysics, but very little about myself. I learned about putative layers of "the mind", qualities of mental activity, alternate realms of being, and of course the terrible risks of not meditating as I was instructed. I translated most of the concepts of my Catholic upbringing into this format: little changed on the psychological level. The confusing thing was that I *thought* I was learning about myself. But I was simply reinforcing what I had always been taught. Somehow it was consoling for it to come from a new cultural source.

The abstracting meditations became more complex over time, and began to demand increasing levels of emotional commitment and psychic contortionism. By the time I was fully entrenched in the vajrayāna tradition, I was completely overwriting my own lived experience with intense visualizations of myself as a Tantric deity, and my surrounding world as my maṇḍala. The prescribed details of visualization and fantasized sensation were baroque and absorbing to the point of mental overload. Meditation felt like leaving my flesh and experience to inhabit another plane—which of course was the intention of the underlying transcendental philosophy. Eventually, spending time with my breath and simple sensation seemed to be boring, lazy, and irresponsible: it could not fuel my meditational fantasy life. I floated in this florid abstraction until I took my first āsana class, and realized that there was a universe of wordless and embodied sensation available to me, which I had been neglecting. Within an hour, I re-entered my flesh, and I have tried not to leave ever since.

I've said that in this second, abstract strand of meditation "consciousness surreptitiously becomes its own object." Why surreptitiously? Because it is easy to think we are thinking about "the world" when in fact we are thinking about a *model* of the world, or a language about the world, or symbols that stand in for the phenomenological experience of the world. Through this unexamined confusion, a kind of structural narcissism takes hold: the conscious mind begins to investigate its own creations as though they were as substantial as the facts of perceptual and autonomic groundwork. Contemplating a philosophical argument creates a kind of enclosed hyper-subjectivist loop of a self-sense that investigates, debates, and validates its self-thoughts. This can even happen within the practice of bhakti yoga, in which the devotional attitude is focused upon a deity or one's guru. The attraction to worship is sparked by an embodied connection: one feels a personal resonance with the story or the aesthetics of the god, or one feels an emotional connection to the presence of the teacher. But neither circumstance offers ongoing relationship in the same way that breath and sensation can—the god is stagnant in his iconography, and the guru is often unapproachable. Inevitably, bhakti meditation must fight against becoming abstract. It fights against ennui to stay in love, to keep that initial embodied fire. But it is hard to be in active loving relationship with a concept, or an icon, or the mere image of a person.

The mindfulness strand maintains a porous, constant, dialogical boundary between the faculty of observation and what it observes. I watch breath, I feel pressure from the floor and air on skin, I listen to heartbeat. Mindfulness is biased towards a self-and-other dialogue (in which sensation is "other", and "I" am learning my "self" by becoming intimate with it) that progresses towards intersubjectivity, whereas abstract meditations seem to bend towards self-isolation.

The circularity of subjective-only meditation is vulnerable to a potentially dissociative infinite regress that the simple mindfulness of presence won't indulge. Consider meditating on the principle of puruṣa. We learn the principle from a book or teacher. We learn how to language it: "Puruṣa is the seer, and prakṛti is the seen." We learn how to visualize it: behind everything that happens and appears, there is a witness, a watcher. We sit down and watch the breath: we make a phenomenological start. But soon, we elide the process of actually observing the breath with the principle of observation. It feels as if we are gaining insight into puruṣa. But behind this insight is an awareness of having an insight. Is this not a deeper manifestation of puruṣa, we wonder? The levels of meta-observation have no end: every postulated observer presumes yet a further layer of observation to make sense of it. *Who is watching the watcher?* is a question with infinite and invariable answers: there's always another watcher. Meanwhile, the breath, sensation, and the entire livingworld continue on underneath, increasingly unnoticed.

Infinite regressions of this type may be intoxicating. But we also have to look very carefully at whether this stream of multiple watching-selves provokes a feeling of paranoia within the meditator. If it does, it might serve mechanisms of social control within the spiritual cultures that promote it. I have personally experienced both sets of feelings: the bliss of falling into the mirrored hall of my seemingly endless identities, and the unease of feeling trapped by an aspect of myself standing behind me with legions of gurus and saints, watching my every movement in sanctimonious silence.

In my opinion, a key problem in contemporary meditation instruction is that we are as consistently unclear in distinguishing between these two strands of meditation as we are unclear about the interdependence of perception and consciousness. When we engage in abstracting meditations, we often fail to see that we are pulling ourselves away from our phenomenological foundation into the sky-castles of thought. You can contemplate presence and being directly, and then you can slide into the contemplation of ideas without realizing it. It doesn't matter if those ideas are *about* presence and being. Both can be covered over by the language, symbols, and concepts that represent them. All too easily, we can feel homeless with abstraction.

Occasionally it can feel as though we are meditating on both together—that the inhale elides with some idea of expansion, for instance. Perhaps this is where we can actually open meaningful dialogue between perceptual and conscious realms. I think we need to if we would like to reverse our habitual splitting. My maxim for meditation instruction would be: *Every idea gains meaning through the support of a phenomenological root.* Connect the ideas of "blessing" and "grace" to inhaling. Connect "surrender" and "release" to exhaling. Connect the passion of devotion to your earliest childhood bonds. Connect the blue sky above to the dissolution of identity at death. "Only connect" is the epigraph to E.M. Forster's *Howard's End*. His heroine finishes the sentiment: "Only connect the poetry and prose of life." Perception is like poetry: immediate, visceral, and irreducible. Consciousness is like prose: grammatical, narrative, seeking the resolution of knowledge. I propose that connecting them gives birth to awareness, and heals an evolutionary trauma.

The threshold between mindfulness and abstract forms of meditation mirror the threshold between perceptual and conscious faculties. Transparency with regard to this threshold is the key: feeling when one is in the connective phenomenological mode, and feeling when one begins to detach and move into the enclosure of abstraction. To cross this threshold with awareness is like travelling to another country but knowing that you will return home. To know when one is in which realm, and to be able to bring insight from one into the other. To hear the constant perceptual-conscious dialogue within.

I felt this dialogue most strongly through one particular form of meditation I practiced. For several years while studying Āyurveda and Jyotiṣa, I practiced mantra for about an hour per day, before dawn. Chanting the names of moon, for example, were said to activate an innate capacity for lunar intelligence. *Oṃ somāya namaḥ. Oṃ candrāya namaḥ.* I sat in siddhāsana, as I always had for meditation, watched my breath until it was still and even, and then began to chant aloud, keeping track of my rounds with a yak-bone mala between the thumb and third finger of my left hand. The sublingual tremor of my typical cognition was overwritten by the syllables, and I felt the different consonants and vowels reverberate in different areas of my flesh. My voice was like an internal ultrasound for the flesh: I felt every vibration, and where things flowed, and where they landed, or stopped.

Above the rolling drone that energized my flesh, my cognitive faculty would drift to the meaning of the sounds. I found that I had several layers of meaning accessible, from meanings I was taught to meanings that seemed to spontaneously emerge from the texture of sound. The emotion of ō was distinct from ā. Round sounds, round mālā beads, round moon, the round vault of sky, and water is symbolized with a circle. The circle rolls as ō's roll into ā's, and water shifts with tide, and the moon waxes and wanes. Repetition of the mantra reflects itself like a lunar surface, luminous and relaxed. Flesh and consciousness sang through each other here, but even so I found it was possible for consciousness to float away from the palpable root of sound. Sometimes I would find myself in a reverie completely distinct from the meaning of the mantra, and yet still reciting. But all I had to do once I recognized the split was to chant a little louder, feel the beads in my hand with a slightly tighter grip, and I was soon back in relationship with my fuller presence, mediated by sound, where flesh and the thing that rides on flesh are inseparable and indistinguishable.

It feels as if I continue to spend most of my mornings on this same mantric threshold as I write this book. There are conscious projects and goals, cognitive decisions, the details of language. And underneath, the rhythm of my typing fingers, waves of bodily sensation that fuel intuitions that blossom into arguments; periodic blankness as words disappear, alternating with flooding as they pour out. Thinking rolls on the tides of livingworld. I wouldn't know any other way of writing about yoga.

6.5 epoché

Epoché: from the Greek. The moment in which experience reduces to seamless phenomena through the suspension of cognition. Said to happen when all ideas are "bracketed" and set aside for the sensory truths of relationship to emerge. A key motif in the phenomenology of Husserl. A contemporary and western concept for samādhi (integration).

[pause]

You begin to lengthen a muscle. At the first pulse of pleasure it takes the reins and lengthens itself. Your breath seeps into a forgotten place. A limb straightens. A network of unseen contractions disengages. Flesh and thought soften to neutral. Thought pauses its forward rush, and flesh reverses its retreat. A page goes blank in the script of identity. Pain diffuses with a flush of hot circulation. The pregnancy of future concern delivers the presently known and felt. Yoga happens to you.

Living forces honesty. Answers are seasonal, losing their sense precisely as they become scripture. You will die: this is the first meaning. The world around you seems to bear helpless witness to your wandering. Other people suffer in the same way, and yet this seems to increase loneliness. But you can welcome despair like gravity, for at some point the sheer pressure, tectonic in the soma, compels a violent break in pattern: running through the woods, making love with an utter loss of self. The reality of your condition offers a stark gift you accept through sudden discharges of rage and rage's joyful shadow: this is the only life you know, and it fills you to overflowing. You live your life, yoga happens to you.

You thought you were alone. You tried to be independent. Then, standing in the market with your hand on an orange, children underfoot, traffic humming, conversations blending with the radio by the cash register, shoes you did not make on your feet and clothes you did not sew on your back, sun slanting through rips in the tin awning, you're almost late for meeting someone, always almost too late. You know this orange will give you life, and that you did not grow it. Someone else gave it to you, it will become your flesh. Its colour adds immeasurably to your language and dreams while its name rhymes with nothing, and you did not conceive of it. The old grocer's hands have become gnarled through a lifetime of handling boxes of oranges for you to eat. Someone else gives you your flesh. They could not give what they do not have. Someone else holds their flesh forth until it becomes your flesh.

A child triggers an internal laugh. A dog slaps her thick tail against your shin. Every single object that gives you life surrounds you. If you really were alone you would not exist. You did not make the air you breathe. You can't say where the inside of your flesh begins. You are naturally reaching out as something reaches into you. No one and everyone taught you this. You surrender to the always-already-there, and yoga happens around you, through you.

6.6 karma as feedback

Patañjali lays out his notions of the effects of meditation upon karma (the causal flow of experience) in three passages. His focus is upon the modulation of saṃskāra-s—"latent impressions" (Hartranft's phrase, where I use "traces"), thought to be carved into consciousness like grooves through which future actions must flow. In pāda one (1.45 to 1.51), he says:

> In deep meditation you can witness
> how experience is woven together.
> Such witnessing leaves traces.
> Your hidden aspects become integrated.
> A feeling of authenticity arises.
> It is deeper than what you can hear or study.
> It begins to unravel future patterning.
> Bearing no future patterns, you become unbound.

To bear witness to one's phenomenological base (*how experience is woven together*) begins to re-write experience itself (*witnessing leaves traces*), so that a fuller view of life begins to saturate memory (*hidden aspects become integrated*). Simple mindfulness of subjective experience brings what is conventionally forgotten—our ecological and relational immersion—into present awareness (*a feeling of authenticity*). This contemplative moment slips below our cognitive cloak (*it is deeper than what you can hear or study*), and begins to deconstruct neurotic habits (saṃskāra-s) to the extent that we are no longer reliant upon them (*bearing no future patterns, you become unbound*).

In pāda three, (3.9 to 3.12), he says:

> Deeper states build momentum and depth
> through feedback, changing hidden patterns.
> Meditative feedback can create a continuous flow
> that overwrites alienation.
> As this happens, wandering thoughts find their home,
> and the feeling of integration deepens.
> As integration deepens, there is equanimity
> between things rising and dissipating.

We have considered "alienation" in its twofold form: the abstracting separation between perceptual and conscious modes (leading to *wandering thoughts*, unrooted) and the subsequent fiction of the individual distinct from relationship. Mindfulness (and other *deeper states*) triggers a self-reflexive loop—*feedback*—in which becoming aware of autonomic and perceptual processes calms and soothes these processes, which then become continued objects of awareness. Feedback initiates a self-perpetuating development between one stage (some degree of *alienation*) and the next (some degree of *integration*), in which information about the change is used to accelerate and stabilized the change. Conscious resting into the phenomenal root bears a bright flower that begins to unfold kaleidoscopically. *As integration deepens*, the stresses of consciousness—maintaining a self-sufficient story along with an identity to tell it—resolve into *equanimity*, so that the changes of life, *things rising and dissipating*, are not only tolerated, but expected, and perhaps even quietly enjoyed. Like watching waves on the sea.

Finally, in pāda 4 (4.8 to 4.11), he says:

> Past action binds a memory; present circumstance unlocks it.
> Memory can outshine the details of identity.
> Memories, like desire, are without beginning.
> An undigested memory resolves when
> its cause, effect, context, and neurosis are
> integrated into present awareness.

Patterns roll with internal logic and rhythm. Karma leaves latent impressions—*past action binds a memory*—that are triggered by *present circumstance*, and can then cover over the clarity of presence, outshining the current *details of identity*. In other words, patterns embedded in memory can obstruct us from living now, if current circumstance provokes them. We can find ourselves suddenly living in two time periods, applying the habits and strategies of past trauma-responses to entirely inappropriate contexts. Into this theme we may interpolate our current understanding of psychotherapeutic treatment, in which either the conscious re-telling of a traumatic memory, or an unconscious transference of a traumatic world of relationship onto the client/therapist dyad, may trigger the present experience of the memory. In early schools of psychoanalysis, it was thought that this re-emergence of memory through conscious or unconscious stimulation was key to the resolution of trauma. My understanding of contemporary neuroscience suggests that we now know that to introduce new tools of self-regulation during the controlled invocation of habitual stress patterns can deactivate hard-wired reactive responses, and forge new non-reactive pathways (Doidge, 2007). *An undigested memory resolves.*

We would do well to pay close attention to the power of our metaphors. In many Indian philosophies of mind, agricultural images are used to describe the causation of thoughts and behavioural patterns. Saṃskāra-s are often likened to "seeds". Karma is not only the experience of sprouting and ripening seeds, but continued action is said to harvest and sow new seeds in an unending cycle of production and reproduction. The most lauded forms of virtuous action are said to arrest the cycle by "roasting seeds" (pācaka karma) in the fire of ardour (tapas), leaving nothing to grow and take root. Patañjali-s ultimate goal is nirbīja samādhi (integration without seeds). The "karmic purification" of such practices are symbolized in yoga's cultural memory by the actual seeds—mustard, lotus, rudrākṣa—that are the primary offerings to the sacrificial fire of the Vedic pūjā.

As any farmer knows, seeds, especially those of invasive species, are notoriously difficult to eradicate, and the potency of a seed can lie dormant for generations before the right germination conditions stimulate its growth. Inherent as well to the metaphor is the feeling of an endless and impossible task—a common sentiment to every crusty farmer. Given an infinite number of past lives, the quantity of seeds in the individual karmāśaya ("storehouse") is limitless. A farmer's work is never done. But the yogi hopes to finish the work through fire, in the external ritual of puja, and the internal effort of tapas. The lotus and rudrākṣa seeds that form his mālā are sterile: the germ has been killed by boring a whole for the thread.

Neuroscience does not offer a metaphor of accumulating things, but ways of measuring habituated experiences. Distinct neural pathways are located as memory-seats, and the intensity and regularity of their stimulation can be directly observed, along with specific changes brought about by various therapies and interventions. As we transition from an agricultural metaphor to the direct observation of neuroplasticity in our consideration of memory and trauma recovery, I believe that we'll carry a more nuanced view of how memory resolves and heals into our yoga practice. No longer will it be as simple as endlessly dividing the bad from the good for incineration. We'll be looking for feedback patterns that entrap us, and through cognitive and sensory inputs we'll alter the feedback. We'll understand that we are altering old patterns, and creating new ones. There is no storehouse but "flesh"—just as endless, but more palpable, than what we once separated out as "the mind".

6.7 piercing the ādhyātmikā bubble

Karmic theory within Indian philosophy is rich and complex, but it has been grossly simplified in contemporary culture, thanks in part to misunderstanding that the hyper-personalist presentation of Patañjali is but one view. His concentration on the inner causes of actions and experience (saṃskāra) makes sense for the yogi who has presumably narrowed his range of relational contingencies through social and even physical withdrawal. And it makes sense that the alienated postmodernite would want to take up this view. Given the complexity of our world, it seems for a time far more consoling to believe that we are individually responsible for our realities, and that our positive acts of internal will are "manifesting abundance". "As I think, so I shall be", and a thousand quotes from *The Secret* splash themselves across the Facebook status-updates of yoga culture. I think that these are actually the sentiments of those caught between trauma and guilt. On one hand, asserting absolute self-responsibility seems to provide a measure of control in an unintelligible world. It narrows the variables to one. On the other hand, we must actively suppress the guilty knowledge that the only reason we can even begin to think that we alone control our destinies is because we benefit without reason or merit from massive political-economic advantages. The platitude cannot withstand the honest appraisal: "As I think, so I shall be, as long as no one holds a gun to my head, pollutes my river, and steals my land."

We must recognize that Patañjali is reflecting quite economically on only a single aspect of cause and effect. In the broader sweep of Indian traditions, this aspect is called ādhyātmikā : those actions attributable to your discrete person. Ādhyātmikā karma is counterposed with ādhibautika karma (the actions of others that impact you) and ādhidaivika karma (literally, "acts of God", but we can make do with "environmental factors"). "What happens" within the larger Indian framework is an inextricable weave of the desires and impulses of self-action, other-action, and world-action. Focusing on the ādhyātmikā alone creates a bubble of neurotic self-regard.

The question is: what do we have control over? What can we change? A surfing metaphor may help to unfold subtleties we may contemplate for the rest of our lives.

You want to go surfing: this is self-action (unless you were inspired/provoked by a surfing buddy). You strap your board to your car. Other-action invades: who made the car? Who made the board? You drive to the beach. Choosing your route is self-action interacting with the other-action of traffic, which is impacted by the world-action of windstorms, which may have made certain roads impassable. You arrive and assess the surf, which is pure world-action. You paddle out and look for your wave. Self-action paddles on the other-derived board over the waves of world-action. You choose a wave and make your stand—this seems to be self-derived, but to the extent that you learned to surf from someone, even your technique is other-dependent. As is your flesh. And so on.

The threads cannot be separated. We are riding waves of interdependence, making small and influenced choices within a range of possibility framed by others and the world. We are definitely acting, but not with anything that approaches the fiction of "free will". If we have freedom, it is not the freedom to do things, but the freedom to work with others and the world.

6.8 my choices: the book of wonders

3.1 Focus can channel diffuse thoughts into one theme.

This pāda focuses upon dhāraṇā (focus), dhyāna (contemplation), and samādhi (integration): the last three of the eight limbs of Patañjali-s system.

The placement of mental focus (dhāraṇā) is usually given a spatial indicator. Hartranft has "area", and Bryant has "place", both accurate presentations of deśa. I'm using "theme" to de-atomize, de-localize and therefore de-isolate consciousness, a measure I'm taking against transcendental imagery. Focused consciousness does not "go" to a single "place", but rather experiences a coherence of content.

3.2 Contemplation is focus that attunes to its object.

Patañjali and his translators describe the difference between dhāraṇā and dhyāna as a matter of intensity of focus. Some oral lineages I have learned from offer terms of time-measurement to discern the two. Dhāraṇā is said to consist of unshaken focus upon a single area of concentration for over a minute, while dhyāna engages a smaller object of focus more than five minutes. (Subsequently, samādhi is said to last for around twenty.) From my own experience in contemplation, but also in therapy and as a therapist, it seems to me that there's another quality at play besides time. Time spent absorbed in an object seems to generate an energetic dialogue that cannot be measured by a clock. Dhyāna (what I'm translating as "contemplation") is an enrichment of "focus" (dhāraṇā), such that empathy (or "attunement") begins to vibrate between subject and object. This also colours the consideration of meditative context with the feeling of the interpersonal sphere: attunement is felt when gazes meet.

3.3 Integration can dissolve the subject-object barrier through attunement, allowing both to share a single form.

Patañjali presents focus (dhāraṇā) as the meditative "lock" of consciousness into a single area, contemplation (dhyāna) as single-pointed concentration on one object, and integration (samādhi) as the merging of consciousness and its object, such that consciousness disappears, as per the self-annihilatory goal of isolation (kaivalya). Because intersubjectivity is the evolutionary focus of *threads*, I present integration as an increase of empathetic attunement of subject and subject to the point of experiential coherence between them.

The highest form of integration, in my view, would be saturated with feelings of love. This is most easily felt on an interpersonal level, and then with practice might be generalized to relationship with the world at large. I remember sitting with my partner on a restaurant patio in the twilight, halfway through our first pregnancy. Our tumultuous year together came to a radiant pause. Soft light and street noise swirled around us as our gazes met and locked and our emotions mirrored their rising to overflow. So many feelings: a shared story, both apart and together, a sense of knowing who baby might be, a sense of completely not-knowing who baby might be, knowing we were making something, someone, life itself, feeling the countless actions and decisions and blindnesses that had drawn and thrown us together, feeling the weight of time and the buoyancy of the timeless, feeling the life of our parents and friends and history flow through us to an unknown end, knowing we will love and enjoy and lose and long-for, feeling those who have died pouring through us as well. Tears streamed through expressions of delight and mystery as we emptied ourselves of the forms that distinguish us (svarūpa śūnyam). As we mirrored each other, sharing flesh, our realizations expanded in intensity.

I imagine my experience of integration will advance to the intensity that Patañjali points towards when I am able to feel such interactive communion with a tree or river. I have in small pieces so far, which encourages me to wait with patience and openness. I'm sure that my path back to coherence with the livingworld begins with other people.

3.4 These three work together.

3.5 They give flashes of brilliance and understanding.

"Prajñā" is usually translated with overdetermination: "light of knowledge" (Aranya), "brilliance of insight" (Houston), "light of wisdom" (Miller). With "flashes of brilliance and understanding", I seek to avoid irreducible signifiers, and broaden the description to include an experience that is palpable to most people at some point in their lives.

3.6 They unfold in stages.

3.7 They are more internal than the first five limbs.

The first five limbs (*angas*) consist of relationship to other, relationship to self, poise, freedom of breath, and freedom of senses.

3.8 Yet they can feel external to even deeper states.

The original distinguishes saṃyama—the combination of focus, contemplation, and integration—from actions that invoke even subtler states. Hartranft has: "Even these three are external to integration that bears no seeds." While saṃyama is said to create karmic feedback, it is claimed that subtler states do not. I avoid the speculative metaphysics of this distinction by simply referring to the layered feelings of meditative integration: the deeper one goes, the more stillness envelops, making the possibility of continued reactivity (karma) seem more and more remote.

3.9 Deeper states build momentum and depth through feedback, changing hidden patterns.

"Feedback" will be my material metaphor for karma as Patañjali begins his discussion of the saṃskāra-s ("hidden patterns" here, though I will also use "traces" for poetic value, while many other translations use "latent impressions") that are built and changed by focus, contemplation, and integration. In this sūtra, the original suggests that meditation begets and amplifies meditation. In this sequence, Patañjali brilliantly predicts much of our current understanding of the action of memory-release in the context of psychotherapeutic trance, in which an extra-cognitive or hypnotic state can allow for the safe re-experiencing and re-visioning of past relationship impressions, ranging from deep love and acceptance to trauma. The re-experiencing of the nurturing impressions is felt to slowly rewire present feelings of alienation, while the safe re-experiencing of a trauma allows for its reintegration into conscious experience, and a reduction in emotional reactivity compelled by unconscious drives.

3.10 Meditative feedback can create a continuous flow that overwrites alienation.

Miller renders: "From subliminal impression of these moments, the flow of tranquility is constant." With "overwrites", I'm alluding to current notions in neuroplasticity that suggest that repeated willful mental actions begin to literally rewire the neurological pathways responsible for habitual responses (Doidge, 2007). This invocation works against the more static view of mind/brain that Patañjali holds, in which thought can receive training, but only up to the point at which it realizes that it is eternally separate from puruṣa.

3.11 As this happens, wandering thoughts find their home, and the feeling of integration deepens.

Patañjali-s approach to what should happen to non-integrated thought and feeling is mostly subtractive. Miller has: "The transformation of thought towards pure contemplation occurs when concern for all external objects declines and psychic focus arises." In choosing to render samādhi as integration, my bias is conjunctive, reflecting a central tenet of psychotherapy: neurotic thoughts are not to be avoided or discarded, but reconciled. "Wandering thoughts find their home."

3.12 As integration deepens, there is equanimity between things rising and dissipating.

3.13 Such practices give insight into what we sense, how we sense, and the passage of time.

Miller renders: "By extension, these transformations of thought explain the transformation of nature's properties, characteristics, and conditions, which occur in material elements and sense organs." Here I elide internal inquiry into memories and thoughts with a sharpened insight into our "external" relations with livingworld.

3.14 All forms share the same basic particles through time.

Here begins the introduction to vibhūti (special powers), which builds its fantastical claims upon the notion of sentient atomism. Hartranft renders: "The substrate is unchanged, whether before, during, or after it takes a given form." I have adventurously remixed Patañjali-s magic to reflect the new magic of the intersubjective, as part of a general thrust to re-locate the mystical in the material. Considering this thread we might say that Patañjali-s general notion of "substrate" (dharmī) remains thrillingly current, especially if we emphasize the notion of forms "sharing" particles through fields and field-activities—which contemporary physics points to through the recent Higgs boson discovery. The Higgs boson points to the existence of a hypothetical unified field at the heart of our matter-energy complex—a kind of syrupy substrate by which elementary particles acquire mass—that would answer the previously metaphysical question: "Why is there something rather than nothing?". With things mutually sharing their parts, and consciousness moving towards intersubjective empathy, what might be possible?

3.15 The sharing and recycling of particles in various patterns causes different forms to continually emerge.

3.16 Understanding what we sense, how we sense, and the passage of time can yield narrative intuition.

The original claim here is that the yogi attains omniscience (atītānāgata-jñānam) with regard to causality. "Narrative intuition" softens this fantasy into the kind of thing we see fine novelists do as they shape storyline according to the rhythm of the learning heart.

3.17 Deconstructing the blend of sounds, meanings, and intentions within language gives insight into the grammar we share with all beings.

The original suggests that saṃyama (focus, contemplation, and integration) on the parts and agencies of language allows us to understand the speech of every animal. I feel no need to overreach here. I find the discoveries of Noam Chomsky, who proposed a "generative grammar" innate to language acquisition, and Steven Pinker, who enriched this model with the narrative of evolutionary psychology, are mystical enough. We sing in chorus with the earth.

3.18 Uncovering your latent patterns gives insight into your past.

To again avoid speculation into reincarnation, I offer "insight into your past" in place of "knowledge of past life" (Vivekananda and others).

3.19 Understanding your mind gives insight into another's mind,

"Gives insight" softens the common renditions of para citta jñānam, which tend to imply that meditation can give you mind-reading skill. Miller has: "Through direct perception of cognitive process, one has knowledge of the thoughts of others."

3.20 but not insight into the things that other sees.

Bryant has: "That knowledge is not accompanied by its object since this object is not the object [of the *yogi*'s mind]." Negating the prospect of magical mind-reading in 3.19 opens a path for me to emphasize the otherness of the other in this thread. At the heart of the intersubjective attitude is the recognition that perfect empathy does not involve perfect knowledge but rather a surrender to the unknowability of another's internality. Ideally, this feeling does not alienate, but invites ever deeper levels of dialogue and intimacy.

3.21 Meditating on flesh resolves the feeling of being objectified.

This is a radical revisioning of a sūtra that traditionally promises bodily invisibility through meditation. Miller renders it: "From perfect discipline of the body's own form, one can become invisible by paralyzing the power to perceive one's body and blocking the contact of light from one's eyes." My deepest experience of meditation is not that it makes me invisible (although I might not be trying hard enough), but that it changes the way in which I see and am seen by reducing the edge of separateness that visual form seems to etch around my presence. When I get very still, I feel a softening of my silhouette.

3.22 Understanding the narrative of events gives insight into how things end.

This is a generalization of the magical power (siddhi) that purportedly allows the yogi to predict the time of his death.

3.23 Contemplating the grace of others strengthens you.

3.24 Meditating on the non-human world gives shamanic energy.

This generalizes a verse that traditionally promises the yogi the physical strength of an elephant if he meditates fully on the physical strength of an elephant. I choose rather to invoke the figure of the shaman, who in earlier cultures negotiated communication between human and non-human realms—usually by learning the language or dances of animals or plants or weather patterns. The shaman is a threshold figure. Today she might be found standing between cultures, histories, languages, technological paradigms, or the space between the city and the countryside. She cultivates her mirror-neurology responses to everything around her, and uses these responses to inspire her fellows towards deeper relationship.

3.25 There is an intuitive relationship between internal light, atoms, hidden things, and things that are far away.

This thread introduces a sequence of reflections resonant with the Vedic principle of "yat piṇḍe tat brahmāṇḍe"—as above, so below. The oscillation between microcosmic and macrocosmic views provides one of the deepest forms of meditative pleasure: to see an oak tree in the nervous system or in the bronchioles and alveoli of the lungs. To see a galaxy in a fingerprint. "To see a World in a Grain of Sand" as Blake writes, "And a Heaven in a Wild Flower, / Hold Infinity in the palm of your hand / And Eternity in an hour."

3.26 Meditating on the sun gives insight into the earth.

The original promises the yogi full knowledge of the cosmos. I generalize this to a coherent insight into one's present location.

3.27 Tracking the moon teaches you the stars.

3.28 Meditating on the North Star reveals how we move.

Tradition provides that sūtra 3.27 refers more specifically to the constellations and asterisms (rāśi and nakṣatra) of Vedic astrology, while 3.28 focuses on stars collectively. Side by side, they seem uncharacteristically redundant for the aphoristic form. I am taking the liberty here to add something new: that the relative stillness of the North Star can act as a touchstone for our own endless motion. If we meditate upon it.

3.29 Meditating on the core shows the elegance of physiology.

Patañjali refers to nābhi cakra here: the navel plexus. This siddhi is not so fantastical. It is well-known in Āyurveda that the entire health of a person may be discerned from studying the functions of his or her agni: the digestive fire that "sits" within the lower abdomen.

3.30 Meditating on orality gives insight into appetite.

Here I take a Freudian turn, in order to side-step Patañjali-s original claim that the pit of the throat can erase the need to eat and drink—an unfortunate temptation to a culture prone to disordered eating. Freud suggests that our desire-drives begin with a concentration on oral sources of stimulation and satisfaction through breastfeeding, along with sensual exploration of the world in general with the mouth and tongue. "Appetite" suggests the entire spectrum of drives. In Āyurveda, emphasis is placed upon lingual experience of the six tastes (sweet, sour, salty, pungent, bitter, astringent) as one of the roots of digestive therapy. It is said that meditation on the root of the tongue allows one to intuit the best medicine. This thread appends a psychological meaning here as well.

3.31 Focus on the thyroid can give bodily stillness.

Translators have struggled with the bodily location of kūrma nāḍī. The best evidence suggests that Patañjali is referring to the thyroid area. Kūrma means "tortoise". Reptiles can suspend their metabolism: literally checking out for long periods of time extends their longevity. As the thyroid regulates metabolism and therefore motivation, quiet meditation upon it might well produce palpable sensations of deep stillness.

3.32 Meditating on the halo connects you to the heritage of genius.

The original describes the attainment of being able to see "siddha-s" (Aranya), "celestial beings" (Prabhavananda), "perfected beings" (Taimni), "masters and adepts" (Sacchidananda), after attaining integrated meditation on light in and around the head. A phenomenological perspective does not look for other realms, but rather enjoys the bright sensation of intergenerational mentorship. We learn from the dead in every moment.

3.33 All such insights can be spontaneous.

3.34 The heart shows you thought.

This is a poetic simplification of the more typical: "From perfect discipline of the heart, one has full consciousness of one's thought" (Miller).

3.35 Seeing the difference between consciousness and the self-sufficiency of things sharpens self-awareness.

Miller translates: "Worldly experience is caused by a failure to differentiate between the lucid quality of nature and the spirit. From perfect discipline on the distinction between spirit as the subject of itself and the lucid quality of nature as a dependent object, one gains knowledge of the spirit." I feel my rendering is more aphoristic, ignores the speculation of the first sentence, and avoids the hard dualism of the second.

3.36 From this can come heightened sensuality.

The original describes supernormal and intuitional sense powers. "From this knowledge arises superphysical hearing, touching, seeing, tasting, and smelling through spontaneous intuition" (Sacchidananda). I intend for my abbreviation to have a more direct and embodied feeling.

3.37 But such peak experiences are not always the point.

The warning of this sūtra is traditionally taken to mean that the enjoyments of meditation can distract the yogi from the ineffable stillness of enlightenment. But I somewhat ambiguously steer this thread in another direction. It's not that I feel that wonderful sensations are obstructive to higher experiences, but that they may well seduce us away from the sacred normalcy of life.

3.38 When the flesh is free and relaxed, you are open to intimacy.

Miller translates: "From loosening the fetters of bondage to the body and from awareness of the body's fluidity, one's thought can enter into the body of another." Bodysnatching was commonly believed to be a core yogic behaviour (White, 2009). Today, intersubjectivity is our response to body-possession. In empathetic recognition of each other, we mingle experientially with each other, combining our oneness with our twoness. We long to create community through the honouring of flesh. The era of zombies is over.

3.39 Rising energy can make you buoyant amidst oppressors, thieves, and puritans.

"From mastery of the vital breath rising in the body, one does not sink into water, mud, or thorns, but rather rises above them", writes Miller. This is Patañjali-s levitation sūtra. He speaks of how udana vāyu (the "upward moving wind" responsible for exhalation, vomiting, and transcendence) can raise the yogi's flesh over swamps and thorns. Some translators (Aranya, Sacchidananda, Prabhavananda) interpolate here to suggest that mastery over this same vāyu allows the yogi to choose the time of his death by willfully projecting what is envisioned as a seed-pod of a soul out through the cranium at an auspicious time. I sidestep both of these facets of magical thinking with some textual levitation of my own. Since no one literally levitates ("yogic flying" aside), I see no reason to preserve what Patañjali says one may levitate above. I rather choose to describe a confidence that allows one to rise above various social pathologies, rather than literally floating in the air. The ecological obstacles of "water, swamps and thorns" are revisioned as of "oppressors, thieves, and puritans."

3.40 A shining core can be seen.

This refers to the development of samāna vāyu: the centripetal and equalizing breath, which pulls prāṇa to the centre of the flesh to enhance digestive fire, to project a radiant aura outwards.

3.41 The art of listening is the marriage of ear and space.

Instead of the promise of supernatural hearing, here I offer a therapeutic aphorism that refers to both the elemental link said by the Saṃkhya system to exist between space and the faculty of hearing, and non-violent communication. The primary principle of Non-Violent Communication, as taught by the innovator Marshall Rosenberg (2003), is that the first need that any speaker has is the need to be heard. This is fulfilled, he says, through communicational rhythms that allow for various types of interpersonal and internal space. Interpersonal space is injected between a statement and its response, for example, so that the feeling of the original statement can be empathetically resonant for both communicants. Internal space is also utilized to broaden the gap between "your story" and "my story". This space is most commonly disrupted by communication habits that fail to nurture the gap of otherness. For instance, if one friend begins to tell another friend of her marriage problems, the second friend can begin to "hold space" for the first by simply reflecting the feelings she hears. This allows the first objective of communication—being heard—to be fulfilled. But if the second friend begins to "false-empathize" with the first by immediately saying, "Oh I know what you mean: let me tell you what my partner did", she has blocked the space of otherness through a pattern that Miles Sherts (2009) calls "automatic self-referral". The first friend will not feel heard, and her feelings will become more isolated and compressed, a combination that invites suppression.

3.42 Movement feels like flight when the flesh is wedded to space.

In this thread, Patañjali tells the yogi how to literally fly: by meditating on the relationship between flesh and space. I am more reality-based, choosing only to describe how the movement one is already doing can be enhanced by reverie upon spaciousness.

3.43 Abstract consciousness seems to blaze with light.

Miller translates: "The turning of thought without reference to the external world is called 'the great disembodied thought'; from which this veil that obscures the light is destroyed." My abbreviation here removes the implicit praise of disembodiment: "the great discarnate" (Aranya), "bodilessness" (Sacchidananda), "great disincarnation" (Prabhavananda).

3.44 By living intimately with nature and learning the large and the small, the still and the dynamic, and how things work together, one feels blessed by the world.

The original offers "mastery over the elements" (most translations). I avoid this fantastical grandiosity in favour of describing what I have personally experienced: that wonderment at phenomena makes everything responsive. In other words: meditate on the details of the world, and the world will seem to begin to communicate with you as the larger you that it is.

3.45 Experience can then shrink into a bead of pleasure, or countless other things.

This is my rendering of the promise of being able to physically shrink to atomic size through meditation.

3.46 The freed flesh pulses through the facets of beauty, grace, and glowing strength.

3.47 When you see how the sense organs work, weave you together, and commit you to the world, they become gateways of pleasure.

Another strong alteration, courtesy of my phenomenological bias. Patañjali posits a controller-function that would master the senses. Miller writes: "From perfect discipline of the receptive, intrinsic, egotistic, relational, and purposive functions of the sense organs, one attains mastery over them." We must remember that the language of domination used here is driving towards an ultimate separation of puruṣa from prakṛti, and that sensory contact with the world is considered a serious impediment to the transcendent freedom of the soul "entrapped" by sensual reality. Moving downwards and horizontally, I advocate celebration of the senses as conduits of ecology: if there is a soul, it is not found through extraction but through awareness of interdependence.

3.48 These gateways can also encourage the exploration of internal worlds at the speed of light.

Sacchidananda has here: "From that, the body gains the power to move as fast as the mind, the ability to function without the aid of the sense organs, and complete mastery over the primary cause (prakṛti)." Because I haven't allowed for "mastery" over the senses in 3.47, I continue to explore what role the senses may play in the exploration of internal space.

3.49 Seeing the difference between consciousness and the givenness of things makes all of these experiences possible.

In the original, we find one of the most grandiose statements of the entire text. Miller writes: "For one who is attentive to the distinction between the lucid perception of nature and spirit, omniscience and power over all states of existence result." Rather than claiming that the attainment of separative discernment between puruṣa and prakṛti grants omniscience, I opt for a somewhat inverse view. If we become clear that consciousness argues with perception, and that awareness of livingworld resolves enough tension between them to allow for a blossoming of intuition, then we may well come to the splendid gifts this pāda describes.

3.50 Equanimity towards even these wonders, while burning the seeds of alienation, grants even deeper liberation.

Bryant has: "By detachment even from this attainment [i.e., omniscience and omnipotence], and upon the destruction of the seeds of all faults, kaivalya, the supreme liberation ensues." To the extent that "supreme liberation" implies an end to evolution or learning, I reject it. We have no evidence anywhere for any static state of anything.

3.51 Otherwise, one can become seduced by spiritualism.

The original warns the yogi not to be enticed by the celestial beings to join in their hedonism. I haven't noticed this problem amongst the practitioners I know. What I have seen, however, is many practitioners who are more attached to the narrative and pageantry of spiritual life than to the uncertain, dirty, and very material work of personal evolution.

3.52 Meditating on both a single moment and the flow of time gives insight born of différance.

Miller has: "From perfect discipline of moments and their sequence in time, one has the knowledge born of discrimination." I return to an invocation of "yat piṇḍe tat brahmāṇḍe": as in a single instant, the whole is revealed. I then replace "discrimination" (viveka), which echoes all of Patañjali-s separative languaging and techniques, with the dynamic neologism of Jacques Derrida—*différance*—a term that implies a dialectical rhythm to the evolution of thought, and which resists the fantasy of completion. *Différance* does not settle for describing the yogi's capacity to distinguish the good from the bad or the true from the false, but rather the more refined skill of recognizing that thought grows and changes through a mechanism of comparison (differing) that unfolds endlessly, so that ultimate meaning is constantly deferred.

3.53 This insight deconstructs experience down to its raw data.

Hartranft has: "This insight allows one to tell things apart which, through similarities of origin, feature, or position, had seemed continuous." *Différance* is a fulcrum of deconstruction. Deconstruction places the presumption of our labeling under sharp scrutiny, breaking apart things, situations, and thoughts we have held together out of habit. This might include personal narratives, tissue injuries, emotional traumas, and fears.

3.54 This raw data communicates to consciousness all possibility at once.

3.55 Then consciousness can be aware of even itself as raw data, co-creative with materiality.

Patañjali reiterates his central (d)evolutionary claim in this thread: "Absolute freedom occurs when the lucidity of material nature and spirit are in pure equilibrium"(Miller). Given the preceding exploration of the interaction between consciousness and materiality, I am drawn here to summarize the dynamism of their relationship, as opposed to describing the improbable event of their stasis. To me, the high point of phenomenological *gnosis* would be consciousness realizing its complete dependence upon and immersion within its tangible constituents. Further: that consciousness continually dances with its root—leading and being led in equal and inseparable measure.

6.9 the song of wonders

Focus can channel diffuse thoughts into
one theme.

Contemplation is focus that attunes to its object.

Integration can dissolve the subject-object barrier
through attunement, allowing both to share a single form.

These three work together.
They give flashes of brilliance and understanding.
They unfold in stages.
They are more internal than the first five limbs.
Yet they can feel external to even deeper states.
Deeper states build momentum and depth
through feedback, changing hidden patterns.

Meditative feedback can create a continuous flow
that overwrites alienation.
As this happens, wandering thoughts find their home,
and the feeling of integration deepens.
As integration deepens, there is equanimity
between things rising and dissipating.

Such practices give insight
into what we sense,
how we sense,
and the passage of time.

All forms share the same basic particles through time.
The sharing and recycling of particles in various patterns
causes different forms to continually emerge.

Understanding what we sense,
how we sense,
and the passage of time
can yield narrative intuition.

Deconstructing the blend
of sounds, meanings, and intentions within language
gives insight into the grammar we share with all beings.
Uncovering your latent patterns gives insight into your past.
Understanding your mind gives insight into another's mind,
but not insight into the things that other sees.
Meditating on flesh resolves the feeling of being objectified.
Understanding the narrative of events gives insight
into how things end.
Contemplating the grace of others strengthens you.
Meditating on the non-human world gives shamanic energy.
There is an intuitive relationship between
internal light, atoms, hidden things,

and things that are far away.
Meditating on the sun gives insight into the earth.
Tracking the moon teaches you the stars.
Meditating on the North Star reveals how we move.
Meditating on the core shows the elegance of physiology.
Meditating on orality gives insight into appetite.
Focus on the thyroid can give bodily stillness.
Meditating on the halo connects you to the heritage of genius.
All such insights can be spontaneous.
The heart shows you thought.

Seeing the difference between consciousness
and the self-sufficiency of things
sharpens self-awareness.
From this can come heightened sensuality.
But such peak experiences are not always the point.

When the flesh is free and relaxed,
you are open to intimacy.

Rising energy can make you buoyant
amidst oppressors, thieves, and puritans.
A shining core can be seen.

The art of listening is the marriage of ear and space.
Movement feels like flight when the flesh is wedded to space.
Abstract consciousness seems to blaze with light.

By living intimately with nature and learning
the large and the small,
the still and the dynamic,
and how things work together,
one feels blessed by the world.
Experience can then shrink into a bead of pleasure,
or countless other things.

The freed flesh pulses
through the facets of beauty, grace, and glowing strength.

When you see how the sense organs work,
weave you together,
and commit you to the world,
they become gateways of pleasure.

These gateways can also encourage
the exploration of internal worlds
at the speed of light.
Seeing the difference between consciousness
and the givenness of things makes all of these experiences possible.
Equanimity towards even these wonders,
while burning the seeds of alienation, grants even deeper liberation.
Otherwise, one can become seduced by spiritualism.
Meditating on both a single moment
and the flow of time
gives insight born of différance.
This insight deconstructs experience down to its raw data.
This raw data communicates to consciousness
all possibility at once.
Then consciousness can be aware of even itself as raw data,
co-creative with materiality.

7. pāda four: overflowing

7.1 the book of overflowing

4.1 The wonders of integration can also come through the conditions of one's development, intimacy with plants, conscious communication, ardour, or meditation.

4.2 Evolution is an overflow of identity.

4.3 The overflow is natural, and only needs gardening.

4.4 Individuation creates selves.

4.5 These selves share collective consciousness.

4.6 Of the means towards wonder, meditation is the most stable.

4.7 For those experienced in integration, the judgment of moral actions becomes subtle.

4.8 Past action binds a memory; present circumstance unlocks it.

4.9 Memory can outshine the details of identity.

4.10 Memories, like desire, are without beginning.

4.11 An undigested memory resolves when its cause, effect, context, and neurosis are integrated into present awareness.

4.12 A thing reveals its past and future as its particles dance.

4.13 The particles dance to the music of gravity, urge, and resolution.

4.14 The dance is so entrancing, a dancer appears.
4.15 Each person will see a different dancer.
4.16 But no single gaze can understand or define or possess her.
4.17 Things colour consciousness.
4.18 Matter produces and is known by consciousness; consciousness produces and is known by awareness.
4.19 Consciousness can be seen by awareness.
4.20 But it is difficult for consciousness to be aware of itself seeing.
4.21 The attempt can lead to a hall of mirrors and an alienation from time.
4.22 When consciousness is still, it can become aware of itself.
4.23 Consciousness is fulfilled when it warmly intermingles with matter and awareness.
4.24 It delights in being seen.
4.25 Being aware of this process imbues individuation with connection.
4.26 This awareness re-integrates the part and the whole, and feels inexorable.
4.27 At this point, alienating thoughts are fleeting memories.
4.28 And you already have experience in releasing them.
4.29 The exalted is common, and the common exalted, and living feels like a summer downpour.
4.30 Standing in it washes away alienating thoughts and isolated footprints.
4.31 Under a clearing sky, the desire for knowledge wanes.
4.32 Within you, gravity, urge, and resolution integrate.
4.33 You can see the flow of time behind you, and you know how it happened.
4.34 Immersed in integrated relationship, consciousness sees itself evolving.

7.2 overflow and the intersubjective

In his fourth chapter, originally entitled kaivalya pāda, Patañjali diminuendos towards the final "isolation" (kaivalya) of puruṣa from prakṛti. But along the arc of pādas three and four, *threads* surges towards the pleasurable excesses (the overflow) of the intersubjective. I've framed the "wonders" of pāda three as the pleasure of learning about the other: *Meditating on the non-human world gives shamanic energy.* In pāda four, I allude not to the separation of consciousness from awareness but rather a necessary love affair between the two: *When consciousness is still, it can become aware of itself. Consciousness is fulfilled when it warmly intermingles with matter and awareness. It delights in being seen.*

I've named pāda four "overflowing" after the feeling of love's mutual gaze. Between parent and child, or two lovers joining, or two lovers parting, the gaze meeting the gaze creates a feedback loop of recognition, identification-with, longing, and empathy. Tidal, tears rise up and spill over.

7.3 against isolation and the extraction urge

Not only is Patañjali-s thrust towards isolation incompatible with our most pressing aspirations, it is also a fantasy that conspires with an unconscious drive that is pushing our global culture to the brink of ecological disaster: the extractive drive. I believe that our desire for sweeter sweets, hotter fuels, higher speeds, more potent foods and medicines is inextricably intertwined with our quest for some irreducible internal essence, be it either the positive or negative signifiers of the soul: ātman or anātman. The extractive drive is also at the heart of the creation of "garbage", or that which we reject and leave behind or refuse to digest. Extracting the sugar from the sugar beet and throwing away its grounding fibre reflects the fantasy of extracting the soul from the husk of the flesh.

But the extractive drive cannot be amputated. Extraction is essential in our crush of white noise. We spend the majority of our sensual time filtering for what we think we want. A brief evolutionary tour might explore the origins and possibilities of this extractive drive.

As our primate neurology developed a more refined sensual sensitivity, we also evolved in aesthetic sensitivity. This begins with our sense of taste and a refinement in the logistics of eating. Our earliest hominid forebears had massive jaws and molars, and were quite content to munch for hours on bland grasses, astringent twigs, and revoltingly bitter leaves to procure their nutrition. But at some point, someone wanted something else—something a little sweeter, a little more rich. (In the paradigm of Āyurveda, the craving for sweet taste is analogous to a craving for intimacy.)

We had to grow our brains to satisfy this desire for sweetness, because finding sweetness requires even more discrimination and memory, as well as complex and staged choices in migratory feeding. But the skull can only expand so much before it becomes unstable on the cervical spine. So we traded the weight of crushing jaws and grinding molars for expanding craniums. Over countless generations, we transformed from beings who physically chew all day to beings who mentally chew all day, as we ruminate on how to experience more sweetness.

As previously noted, an essential instruction in āsana is to release the jaw during the execution of any posture, and when sitting for meditation. If you manage to relax the hinge of the jaw, the digestive tract releases, peristalsis softens, and you can begin to explore the next layer of relaxation: the soft palate. If you can allow the soft palate to relax upwards, in the same way the respiratory diaphragm rests upwards on the exhalation, you might be able to feel the perineum disengage from some low-level tension. Once this happens, the groin also tends to soften, and the hip joint can open more fully into both external and internal rotation. Such instructions, refined in our present generation by yoga practitioners who study structural alignment and visceral contiguities, are actually echoes of our early hominid evolution. Somehow we remember that mandibular tension keeps the nervous system on high alert, and obstructs receptivity to internal and external experience. This tension can arise from either needing to eat all day, or to think all day.

Shrunken (and relaxed) jaws and expanded brains gave not only the capacity to become more discriminating about what we put into our mouths, but also the mandate to find richer sources of nutrition. We now needed our meals to come in more easily digestible forms, and to be higher in calories, to compensate for our weaker mastication. And we now had the smarts to make this happen. We sought out more succulent vegetation and berries over our former massive amounts of stringy and taste-poor fibres. We designed sharp tools to harpoon the sweetest fish. We began to mentally catalogue where the fruit hangs lowest, and when it is most ripe. Thus: territory and calendars.

We found and controlled fire to aid in our task of procuring higher nutrition from ever more potent sources. We learned to reverse-engineer the process of photosynthesis, using the sun in the form of cooking fire to extract what the sun in the form of its rays had bestowed upon vegetation, and through vegetation, upon animals. We learned that heat releases things. We learned that it opened us up: the tissues softened with our sweat, and our tongues loosened around the campfire. We gazed at the fire for hours, seeing in its dance something strange, familiar, utterly necessary.

We felt the first stirrings of four essential drives in human experience: an increase of conscious actions in relation to instinctual actions, an orientation towards goal-driven behaviour, a renewed fixation upon comparison and difference, and the compulsion to plan. As we began to more rigorously seek out the sweet and the shiny to the exclusion of the bitter and dull, we laid the groundwork for language and the most basic economy: how to find, store, protect, and tabulate what we consciously desire.

As we chose berries over bog grass, we began our endless search for essence. In choosing the food that is harder to find, we began to look through the shadows, for the hidden thing, for the jewel in the lotus, for the sacred heart, for the Self enshrouded in matter, etc. We began our training in the essential human behaviour of extraction (a behaviour that surely informs the later philosophical technique of not-this, not-this).

The principle of extraction creates agriculture, refined sugar and wheat, theologies of the soul, the accumulation strategies of capitalism, all technologies of distillation, fossil fuels, herbology, and transcendental forms of yoga. We seem evolutionarily hard-wired to seek the essence of things, a mandate which bestows great rewards and exacts steep debts. It also creates something that never existed before: *garbage*—the residue of our search for essence. The peel, the packaging, the flesh shucked away from the soul. It would not be until the golden age of tantrism that the difference between essence and garbage would be questioned, and then rejected, leading to a fuller embrace of all aspects of life.

The thought that drives extractive intelligence with tantalizing and painful regularity is: *There is something better than what I have and am already.* This thought reaches a dizzying apex of complexity in the levels *of samādhi* proposed by Patañjali. The first time we reached into a tree and pulled out our hand covered in honey, the seeds of the idea of transcendence were born. The honey may have been ecstatically sweet, but we now had an intractable internal training to believe *there must be something sweeter still,* for which honey would become a symbol.

A key result of the extractive drive is that it turns the inhabitant of the world into a consumer of the world. It creates, stimulates, and perpetuates conscious desires, which motivate actions towards fulfillment. But fulfillment is unstable, and only feels like fulfillment if it incrementally intensifies. And so the search for sweet must itself intensify.

It is well worth noting that this *precise* description of the problem of desire is at the root of every Eastern mode of spiritual therapy / psychological readjustment. The feedback loop of accelerating needs fulfilled by extraction must be deconstructed, and its energy redirected to the cultivation of the soul or self. But as yogis realize that extraction of sugar leads to a greater desire for sugar, and wish to no longer participate, a strange paradox ensues. They begin to use the same extractive principle to remove themselves from the cycles of desire. They nurture the fantasy of a difference between the "common" extractions of pleasure, and the "final" extractions of moksa, nirvāna, etc.

The practice of yoga can mimic the continually dissatisfying extractive habit it is meant to curb. Our question for Patañjali and all other ascetics might be: when are we pure enough, sweet enough, high enough, and enough apart?

We didn't simply seek our sweetness in food and other comforts. We also sought it from each other by employing other sensual faculties. As our eyes sharpened in focusing capacity to distinguish the sweet berries from the poisonous, we also used them to probe the eyes of potential mates. We developed a language of winks and seductive glances so powerful that we became the only mammals to turn around and copulate face to face. We could now gaze into each other's eyes as we tasted pleasure, interacted with essences, and created new life. The erotic gaze gives an auxiliary meaning and purpose to sexual activity, parental activity, and, by extension, all human interaction. The autonomic extractive drive is now mediated by an emotional extractive drive. We discover (or create freshly) needs and nuances of communicative pleasure of which we were previously unaware. By gazing into each other and trying to understand what we love and how we create together—this might be a good translation for namaste—we are provoked to a core yogic action: gazing into ourselves.

What do we want, other than to draw out the wholeness of each other? We used to use metaphysics as our extractor. But now I think metaphysics is itself what we must extract presence from. The sky castles crumble into dust. The words fall off our flesh like so many raindrops, into the earth.

7.4 lubricating the threshold between polarities: a samādhi on saṃdhi

It is obvious that we need to deconstruct the artificial dichotomies of "mind" and "body", "matter" and "spirit": they have driven us away from our wholeness. They have denigrated our perceptual connectivity, unfairly privileged the conscious over the autonomic, and created an upside-down hierarchy of authority. The root of hard-dualist philosophy is likely a dissociative trauma, and its compost is the developmental failure of ambivalence. There is a paradox: splitting is both our wound, and how we often cope with wounds.

But as I've spent year after year with the hard dualisms of Christianity and Patañjali, connecting these to both the signs of hard dualism in our present culture and my own vulnerability to black-and-white thinking, I've come to sense that the radical deconstruction of dualism is not a whole answer. In fact, pursuing it with rigour creates yet another false dichotomy—between the "dual" and the "integrated", where "dual" is categorically useless or false. But daily experience does not bear this out. Life seems to oscillate in a rolling dualism between twoness and oneness, between the separate and the whole. Perhaps our greatest task is to pay close attention to the transitions between the two.

My training as a practitioner of Āyurveda, for example, has shown me a benign usage of the dualism impulse. The twenty qualia of prakṛti are my primary therapeutic tools. Conditions are perceived as hot or cold, wet or dry, heavy or light, clear or cloudy, still or mobile, rough or smooth, dense or flowing, soft or hard, sharp or dull, gross or subtle. Every perception is contingent: nothing is "hot" except in relation to the temperature of other things. Binary language is used to bounce between unfindable poles to find a resonant description of the given perception. In other words, we use "black" and "white" not to foster black-and-white thinking, but to navigate our infinite areas of grey.

The dualistic impulse also carries a sense of play. Nursery rhymes and songs overflow with *this* and *that*, *up* and *down*, *here* and *there*. I remember the theory of signs from my early studies in semiotics: Swiss linguist Ferdinand de Saussure showing the dialectic of meaning-creation through opposition. The "moon" is not the moon without the "sun". Our experience is comparative, and becomes meaningful upon a scale of polarities, and both our language and language acquisition reflect this through an endless play of differences that we don't in our hearts feel to be concrete, because the learning process never ends.

This is at least the elementary level of what Jacques Derrida implies with his neologism *différance* (first "translated" into English in 1978, and included in *Margins of Philosophy*, 1984): that not only is meaning generated in dynamic comparison (differing), but that, being constantly confounded by the gap between the name and the thing, and the gap between the I and that I saying "I", and perhaps also the gap between neuroception and the after-life of cognition, we are compelled to keep searching and speaking to narrow the seemingly insurmountable gaps between us, both interpersonally and internally. The sharing of absolute meaning is never quite within our grasp: it is deferred by the endless play of difference. We play until we're exhausted. Perhaps you remember playing in the late summer evening. It seemed that pleasure was both endless but also endlessly pursuable. As you became more and more tired, you wanted ever more to stay awake, to run around the yard for *just ten more minutes, Mummy!* to capture the last juice of the day, being but one day in a lifetime of days you could never fully grasp. You were happy being on the very edge of happiness, and then you dropped down into deep sleep, as the crickets sang.

The play of differences has deep and tender roots. I remember painting a fence with my ex-wife. She told me that from childhood, activities like these, which involved working with repetition or a series of similar objects, seemed to immediately suggest a game to her: some of the fence-slats were "good guys" and some were "bad guys". The good guys might deserve nice smooth and flowing strokes of the paintbrush, but the bad guys might really call for some rough daubing, and even a few wet slaps, if they really got out of line. We laughed and laughed at the game. There stood the fence-slats, all equal and dead as doornails, but we amused ourselves with fantasies about their manners. Contrast made the job fun. It made me remember similar silent games of my own childhood: separating out cans of food in my mother's kitchen, making different piles to dole out to imaginary recipients. I would give more cans to some invisible person I imagined I liked better than someone else.

Such games are simultaneously learning tools for the faculty of discrimination and projections of the good-self/bad-self dynamism of childhood development. As the toddler attains agency, she encounters approval for some actions, and disapproval for others. We soon begin to internalize approval and disapproval as if they referred to different people within us: a good-self, and a bad-self. The good-self is happy enough. But moving towards integrity involves accepting the bad-self as part of the whole-self. Repression arises when the disapproval (first external and then internal) is so onerous that we reject the bad-self as though it were an intruder. We accuse, imprison, and finally ignore a part of ourselves to relieve the incompatibility.

Play is a natural and inborn tool to counter dualistic repression. Derrida writes: "The concept of play keeps itself beyond this opposition, announcing, on the eve of philosophy and beyond it, the unity of chance and necessity in calculations without end" (1981). As a boy, I was a very fast runner. I would practice on my own, timing myself over a set distance. With no one else around, I played out one of two fantasies as I ran towards the finish line. I was either the victor or the defeated, by a hair's breadth either way. I would decide which one I would be almost randomly, depending upon whatever emotions arose as I ran. The victorious self received praise and admiration from the invisible crowd while an orchestra played, and a gold medal from a girl with red ringlets. The defeated self felt waves of empathy from the stands, and a brunette girl with big brown eyes patted my shoulder in consolation. It actually felt better to fantasize about *losing*: it invited more identification from those I fantasized were watching. After all, the winner is alone. Most of us understand much more clearly the feeling of losing, of not being the best. However I repressed my bad-self in other areas of my inner life, I seemed to have had this inner self-regulatory faculty that was able to elevate the part of me that failed, and to even regard the difference between success and failure as a game to be held lightly. Good-self and bad-self were reconciled with the birth of my sense of irony. Winning and losing were, in part, a performance.

But the dance of binaries is not just the pleasure of a language game, or a dialectic of psychic structures. We are inundated by binary experiences. Interior meets exterior. Self meets other. We individuate and we merge. Parents and children define each other. We move inexorably from sleep to waking and back again, from night to day, and from rainy to dry. We join together in intercourse, and we fall away into relative isolation. Through pregnancy and birth, a woman's flesh is one thing, and then two things, and then becomes one thing again, though a changed oneness. And, as I've tried to show throughout this text, we move back and forth between raw perception and consciousness, with consciousness grasping at our attention with great stubbornness and presumption. But is the *tension* necessary? Is it possible to resolve into enjoying the play between perception and consciousness? In this desire we might take inspiration from the (ideally) seamless interaction of our hemispheres through the corpus callosum.

The dynamic pulse between polarities is not the problem. The problem is the stress of the transitions. Instead of feeling like a play of twoness, the transition from one to two can feel like a rupture. I now wonder if failing to resolve the stress of transition by failing to feel its play encourages the natural and playful dynamism of polarity to calcify into philosophical dualisms. We go from children playing with *here* and *there* to adults paralyzed between "earth" and "heaven". The question is: how do we cross the many thresholds of our lives, from one state or experience to another? Patañjali suggests (with a little help from the 2.0 crowdsource) that poise is key: *Poise is steady and well-spaced. This occurs when restlessness fades and feeling is boundless. Then, even oscillations are peaceful* (2.46–8). Without poise, our transitions are traumatic, our thresholds are terrifying.

In Āyurveda, we pay a lot of attention to the thresholds, which are said to be governed by vāta dosha ("the force of wind" is as good a translation as any), the psychosomatic principle of change embodied in the elements of air and space. Vāta governs empty spaces in the flesh such as the ear canal, hollow organs such as the bladder, autonomic impulses, nervous response, and, it is said, thought itself. Its constant movement endows us with a pervasive pulse, from kinesis to cellular respiration. It governs the places where types of tissues conjoin and bones hinge at the joints. In fact, the "joint" is simultaneously an expression of and the perfect metaphor for vāta's function: air and space elements pervade and conjoin all others. The smooth flow of vāta's connective purpose is most easily disturbed at the numerous thresholds of our days and lives. The thresholds between sleeping and waking, biorhythmic periods of the day, ovulatory and menstrual periods, and even the broader transitions of life: these can all disturb vāta dosha. Serious disturbances trigger the stress responses of circulatory contraction, reduced circulation, compromised metabolism, neurological confusion, coldness, dryness, anxiety, and perhaps even dissociative imagination. Chaotic energy at the "joint", both in the flesh and its livingworld, is catabolic to the wider system, and portends a centrifuge away from groundedness. Yeats: "Turning and turning in the widening gyre / The falcon cannot hear the falconer; / Things fall apart; the centre cannot hold...".

The majority of Ayurvedic therapies centre upon the goal of "pacifying" vāta dosha: slowing, smoothing, and regularizing its movement, generally by applying the qualities of the non-vāta category elements: stillness and weight of earth, moisture and expansiveness of water, and the warmth and dilation of fire. These three come together in the therapeutic application of warm oil, massaged into the skin, or cooked into a soup. Warm oil is the perfect reduction of every quality that would pacify vāta dosha. It weighs down, moistens, and holds the diffusive spin of air and space elements close to the radiant heart. It lubricates the thresholds of change. Oiling the passage between one state and another helps us to achieve the continuity that is the healthful bulwark against change. Hard dualism is anti-continuous. Good and bad, night and day, human and divine, mind and body: these are mutually exclusive to the extent that we were not able to see or accept the smooth elision between them. Western intellectual history might be different if Descartes had received a warm oil massage every day. We might not have had to wait another three hundred years for phenomenology to emerge.

The power of the threshold and the importance of its resolution in yoga are hinted at by the etymological bond between two critical Sanskrit terms. Saṃdhi means "joint" or elision. It is used to denote the literal joints of the skeleton, but also the phonetic elision of smaller words into compounds. It also denotes the transformational gap between periods or fields: sunset is a brief window of saṃdhi, and when a planet passes from one astrological house to another, it is said to be in saṃdhi. Saṃdhi is where the magic and vulnerability of change occurs. Its roots are sam, which means "together", and dhī, which means "holding". Saṃdhi is almost samādhi, but minus an ā. The ā of samādhi means "towards": the word, which I and others have translated as "integration", literally means "moving towards holding together". Saṃdhi is that which holds together, and samādhi is that which moves towards holding. Saṃdhi is samādhi without the interference of the preposition. Invoking samādhi on the fact of saṃdhi would suggest that the coherence we seek through yoga is most in reach at those places and in those times in which things are most likely to fall apart. This is why in Vedic culture, the most powerful times for the fire ritual are dawn or twilight. As our livingworld offers up its polarities, we can slide into the gap to find the continuity of our own growth.

7.5 reverie on "cleave"

In section 4.8, I wrote: "Yoga has so far not escaped this pattern of cleaving, but now it might." I was writing of my main theme: that hard-dualist positions inevitably separate—*cleave*—consciousness from perception, and ourselves from our world, and that this is not yoga.

But the journey of this book has weathered my argument, and the word "cleave" calls me up short. I've slowly come to recognize that the twoness of things is also a function of play, language, and *différance*. Twoness is a tango between the benign unconscious and the scattered and scattering conscious, between the malignant unconscious and the empowered conscious, between what we feel and what we think, between what we think we feel, and what we feel we think. Hard dualism as a philosophical trap is perhaps the fossilization of a naturally productive polarity: like pinning two butterfly wings to a mounting board, where their colours can only dream of intoxicated flight.

Does yoga invite us to join, or not to join? Does this very question calcify a polarity? Is yoga's real gift given by allowing us to recognize that we both join and not-join as persons, that every communion and solitude are interdependent, that the guṇa-s are interwoven, that differentiation and empathy mutually mirror?

Yoga implies joining, which presupposes the not-joined. The word contains its opposite, as does its practice.

Our word "cleave" goes even farther. In a recent conversation with a friend, I learned that "cleave" holds two opposite meanings within its single spelling. Firstly, it comes from the Old English *cleofan*—"to split, separate", itself from the Proto-Indo-European root *gleubh*—"to cut, slice". Secondly, it means "to adhere", from the Old English *clifian*, the Old High German *kliban* and *kleben* "to stick, cling", themselves from the proto-Indo-European *gloi*—"to stick", which descends into English as "clay".

"Cleave" means to separate *and* to connect. A river cuts a cleft in the stone; the water courses over its clay bed to connect the banks. The chest is cloven where the ribs meet, and beneath this we find the heart. We reach towards the cleft of everything, to enter the dark crevice where we meet and part. We live in the cleaving between this and that, and this-becoming-that, separating and joining in an endless weave.

"From clay am I formed as well as thou, and we are formed from the same" (Job 33:6, Septuagint).

7.6 left to right: the psychogenic triptych of perception, consciousness, and awareness

Again: in pāda four Patañjali returns to his project of prying puruṣa clear of prakṛti, as though our most recent evolute of consciousness—the capacity for buoyant and broad awareness—could be isolated from its phenomenological/perceptual base. Again: my position is that this is neither possible nor helpful, and that the very drive to do so is likely motivated by trauma and other developmental handicaps from which humanity is slowly recovering. In contemporary Western yoga, we are telling a story that no longer applies.

Still, the fact remains: we have perception, consciousness, and awareness, all working, all influential, and all mutually co-reflective. Awareness of perception soothes and grounds conscious action. A conscious choice to be aware of perception roots us to the present. A conscious choice to be aware of consciousness itself catapults us into abstraction, some of which is creative, and some of which is masturbatory.

Perhaps we can consider these three aspects as a triptych: a painting suggesting a beginning, middle, and end. The first panel of perception (on the left) depicts simple origins: a timeless garden, a flowing stream, primary colours and meandering design. The centre panel of consciousness shows action and industry, role-playing and production, coupling, family life, attainment, and loss. The right panel of awareness is a kind of mural of sentient connective patterns, perhaps an Escher-like spray of beauty looking at beauty looking back at itself, as fish turn into swans and the sea becomes sky.

The triptych is read from left to right. As with a written sentence, meaning begins in an intuitional cloud, progresses towards structure, and resolves in self-reflective cadence. (The word at the end of this sentence is a kind of *resolution*.) As the left eye is privileged to read the left panel, the right brain vibrates with perceptual timelessness and subconscious phenomenal connection. The centre panel mingles both hemispheric functions as the gaze shifts to both eyes, and finally moves to right-eye predominance to satisfy the left hemisphere with yet more abstract cognitive function. Our waking, working, public lives are enmeshed in the central panel. The peripheral left panel engages the right brain. The peripheral right panel engages the left. Subconscious and meta-conscious data flow into the centre, into the heart of our action. We have left-hand sources and right-hand sources.

I saw my first triptych when I was five, but it wasn't a painting. It was a three-panelled mirror in my family's bathroom, with each of the side panels hinged so that they could turn in towards the centre. I spent hours swinging the panels towards the centre. As the angles approached ninety degrees, I could look into the sharpening corners and see an endless sequence of my heads receding into a grey-blue horizon. I turned back to the centre panel and saw myself quite plainly. I turned to the left mirror-corner and had the sense of "This is where I come from." Then I turned to the right mirror-corner and felt "This is where I'm going."

Until I left my parent's home, I was transfixed by this *trompe l'oeil* every single morning. Usually before dawn, as I was preparing for the long subway ride to my downtown Catholic school. I found out later that this particular time of day is called "brahmā muhurta" in the Vedic system: "the hour of expansion". It was my first meditation, with mirrors, before heading off to school, where I imperceptibly unlearned my wonderment, while learning to be guilty for the sins of men I never knew.

7.7 my choices: the book of overflowing

4.1 The wonders of integration can also come through the conditions of one's development, intimacy with plants, conscious communication, ardour, or meditation.

Sivananda has: "Siddhis are born of practices performed in previous births, or by herbs, mantra repetition, asceticism, or by samādhi." In this thread I again eschew reincarnation as an *explanation* for present circumstances to focus on the *nature* of present circumstances. To relate access to yogic benefit to "conditions of one's development"—with all of the economic, social, and political factors this entails—might open a much-needed discussion about the role of community, resources, public policy, and parenting in yoga culture. I've extended "herbs" (auṣadi) beyond its hallucinogenic meaning to "intimacy with plants", which I hope might include gardening. (For the urban alienated, there's nothing more integrating than gardening.) I've remixed "mantra" as "conscious communication", to be able to include intersubjective dialogue, and to allude to the work of Marshall Rosenberg (*Non-Violent Communication*, 2003), and Miles Sherts (*Conscious Communication*, 2009).

4.2 Evolution is an overflow of identity.

Hartranft has: "Being delivered into a new form comes about when natural forces overflow." This is a generalization of the original *sūtra*, which much more explicitly refers to the transmigration of souls, specifically across species, and hopefully in an ascent up the food chain. I like how Hartranft's rendition seems to suggest that this thread presents an opportunity to displace the meme of reincarnation with that of evolution, and to leave it frayed enough that it can refer to biology or psychology equally.

While Patañjali guides an evolutionary arc towards advanced consciousness through successive lives, he frames it within the devolutionary narrative of Saṃkhya philosophy, in which the tangible has been created out of the delusion of the intangible. In other words, Patañjali teaches evolution in the penitential context of clawing our way back up from a preternatural fall. This may be why his original text resonates so deeply with our vestigial Christianity of original sin, as Vivekananda understood and exploited so well.

The theory of reincarnation often serves as a consoling fantasy of long-term improvement that transcends the harsh limitation of our years. If you don't get or achieve what you want this time around, you can at least set up the causes for future happiness in lives to follow. That there is not a shred of evidence for future lives seems to make the psychological need for reincarnation all the more tenacious. The American dream is the inverse fantasy: this very life is an invitation to greatness, and there's nothing standing between you and your happiness except you—never mind your socio-political matrix. Both fantasies are grappling with the need and hope for positive change, and doing so by ignoring fundamental existential facts. Somewhere in between these two wishes lies authenticity: knowing that we are limited but interconnected. We are mortal yet eternal in ways that overflow our identities.

Also: somewhere between the patience of reincarnation and the anxiety of "must-change-now" lies the most efficient attitude towards evolution. We can make small choices every day towards greater interconnection, to open up our alienation bit by bit. Our time is limited. But as we forge connections, we may begin to relax in the shadow of death.

4.3 The overflow is natural, and only needs gardening.

The original stimulates an extensive discussion in the commentaries (cf. Bryant, p. 410) about whether virtuous or non-virtuous actions are the crucial causes of the arc of personal evolution. Does our evolution require our direct intervention, or simply a nurturing hand (gardening)? What seems to be at stake is the question of whether conscious behaviours can influence the ultimate attainment of a post-conscious state. This is the intractable problem of the transcendent view: it wants to claim that its goal—puruṣa —is a state both *a priori* and *a posteriori* to conscious experience—the vṛtti-s of prakṛti. But how can the intrigues of prakṛti lead to puruṣa, when they are of different orders of reality? Plainly: how can a body reach the soul? For this sūtra, Hartranft has: "The transformation into this form or that is not driven by the causes proximate to it, just oriented by them, the way a farmer diverts a stream for irrigation." The transcendent position must create a nebulous ground of active non-action as it conceives of how what is flawed might realize or produce what is perfect. In other words: we can't cause the perfect, but we can get out of its way. My thread simplifies the discussion radically, because it is not burdened with metaphysics.

4.4 Individuation creates selves.

4.5 These selves share collective consciousness.

The conventional translations and commentaries say that sūtras 4.4 and 4.5 describe how the accomplished yogi can multiply his body innumerable times through acts of mental projection—said to happen through the individuation principle of asmitā. The commentaries then go on to address the concern of whether each body has its own mind. Bryant has: "There is one mind, among the many [created by the yogi], which is the director in the different activities [of the different bodies]." The fantasy of becoming many different bodies and then discussing how many minds they might have amongst them, or how one might manipulate them all through remote-control, is really not worth humouring. My salvage job here intends to be intersubjectively useful.

4.6 Of the means towards wonder, meditation is the most stable.

This thread refers back to the five means towards integration mentioned in 4.1. The original privileges meditation as causing an integration that is anāśayam—"without the storehouse of karma" (Bryant). I am more conservative, preferring to suggest that amongst "conditions of one's development, intimacy with plants, conscious communication, ardour", meditation is the most dependable and self-sufficient route to wonderment.

4.7 For those experienced in integration, the judgment of moral actions becomes subtle.

Hartranft translates this sūtra as: "The actions of a realized yogi transcend good and evil, whereas the actions of others may be good or evil or both." My rendition dodges the question of "Who is a realized yogi?", and also rejects the concept of a person who has transcended ethics, as such a person would be dissociated from relationship. Everyone makes an ethical footprint.

4.8 Past action binds a memory; present circumstance unlocks it.

A rendition of non-metaphysical karma. It heralds a psychotherapeutic view: karma is memory, and relationship and/or circumstance can trigger its re-emergence, so that therapeutic alternatives may be offered, or so that new patterns of response can emerge of their own accord.

4.9 Memory can outshine the details of identity.

Prabhavananda renders this sūtra as: "Because of our memory of past tendencies, the chain of cause and effect is not broken by change of species, space or time." Continuing the demystification of karma into "memory", here I simplify even further, and again strip away the metaphysics of reincarnation. This more sparse thread simply asserts that who we have been can outshine (overshadow) who we might become.

4.10 Memories, like desire, are without beginning.

Bryant: "The saṃskāra-s are eternal, because the desire [for life] is eternal."

4.11 An undigested memory resolves when its cause, effect, context, and neurosis are integrated into present awareness.

The original advocates the "absence" (Vivekananda), "removal" (Prabhavananda), and "disappearance" (Aranya, Taimni, Hartranft, and others) of cause, effect, etc. Sacchidananda has: "The impressions being held together by cause, effect, basis and support, they disappear with the disappearance of these four." This remix expresses a standard truism of contemporary psychotherapy. Memory isn't the problem: undigested memories are. Memories cannot be removed any more than injuries can. But both can be digested or healed through integration. With this change I continue to move the text out of an age in which psychic splitting and suppression is preferred or even possible. My interpolation of "neurosis" is inspired by Sacchidananda's use of the word "support" for ālaṃbana. The neurosis that develops as a coping strategy for any undigested memory can become over time a source of support for that memory.

4.12 A thing reveals its past and future as its particles dance.

4.13 The particles dance to the music of gravity, urge, and resolution.

4.14 The dance is so entrancing, a dancer appears.

4.15 Each person will see a different dancer.

4.16 But no single gaze can understand or define or possess her.

With threads 4.12 through 4.16, I have interpolated the metaphor of dance and dancer to elucidate Patañjali-s discussion of the guṇa-s, and his primordial reach towards quantum theory. The dance of particles (dharmāṇām) reveals predictive and retrodictive patterning. Like everything else, this patterning is enthralled by gravity, urge, and resolution. While in constant movement, this patterning interacts with the personal memory of the viewer, who from it seems to create a definable thing (a dancer). But this thing-ness is established by viewers who each experience a different view. Finally, the text suggests that beyond different views, the thingness yet contains something unnameable that survives being unobserved. The dancer is self-sufficiently other: she does not need an audience to exist. For 4.16, Hartranft writes: "But the object is not dependent on [any] of those perceptions; if it were, what would happen to it when nobody was looking?" Śiva Naṭarāja provides a cultural-religious mnemonic for a number of these ideas: his dance, frozen into the tāṇḍava mudrā, allows us to intuit the steps that come before and after. At various cadences he pauses (tamas), accelerates (rajas), and resolves (sattva). The meaning and teaching of his dance are said to be different to each devotee, depending upon what they are inclined towards or need to see.

4.17 Things colour consciousness.

Although this book strongly criticizes the transcendent idealism of Patañjali, we must credit him with being less radical in his idealism than other thinkers of his day. The original version of this sūtra is his critique of the idea that physical objects are creations of thought. With this sūtra, he concretizes the notion of a real consciousness encountering real objects that go on existing beyond the instance of that encounter. Vivekananda says: "Things are known or unknown to the mind, being dependent on the colouring which they give to the mind." Patañjali-s pragmatism is as relevant today as it was then, given the pervasion of radical idealism that characterizes new age thought.

4.18 Matter produces and is known by consciousness; consciousness produces and is known by awareness.

The original is a reiteration of the changing vs. unchanging prakṛti/puruṣa paradigm. Taimni expresses the hard-dualist view: "The modifications of the mind are always known to its Lord on account of the changelessness of the Puruṣa." My thread here may contain the boldest remixing of this whole project. It is a materialist flag in the ground, stating the evolutionary-biological view that will be prominent in the next few threads. My progressive staging holds that "awareness" is an evolute of consciousness. Consciousness is thinking that pours through a self-structure, while awareness is the recognition of thinking through a self-structure. Consciousness itself arises from biological roots in successive forms, from bacterium to mammal.

4.19 Consciousness can be seen by awareness.

4.20 But it is difficult for consciousness to be aware of itself seeing.

4.21 The attempt can lead to a hall of mirrors and an alienation from time.

The original warns that the feedback loop of consciousness regarding itself will "confuse memory", presumably because the act of self-recognition itself creates memory. I'm suggesting that this feedback loop can become an obstacle to presence. I agree with the original that a distinct faculty is required to hold the space of witnessing. We can feel it—awareness—as we practice mindfulness meditation: the ability to witness our thinking while adding a minimal amount of content to it.

4.22 When consciousness is still, it can become aware of itself.

4.23 Consciousness is fulfilled when it warmly intermingles with matter and awareness.

In the three-part psychogeny I've presented so far, "consciousness" stands between the "flesh" as its phenomenological basis and ancestor, and "awareness", its more advanced faculty. Consciousness remains our predominant mode of experience, and is happiest when it feels interdependent with where it came from and where it can go. Perception grants groundedness, and awareness gives hope.

4.24 It delights in being seen.

The original reiterates the idea of the puppet-master puruṣa ("awareness" in our terms), along with the earlier chauvinistic claim (2.21) that the world exists for the sake of awareness. I continue to reject this position: obviously things exist with or without being seen by human eyes. I add a further, almost erotic suggestion: that consciousness and awareness are mutually enthralled.

4.25 Being aware of this process imbues individuation with connection.

Here the original begins its march towards the conclusion of kaivalya ("isolation"). "To one who sees the distinction between the mind and the Ātman, thoughts of mind as the Ātman cease forever", as Sacchidananda translates. To me, the oscillation between consciousness (which seems to move towards individuation) and awareness (which seems to move towards connection) would not necessarily end "the ongoing construction of the self" (Hartranft). Rather, the oscillation would serve to blur the hardened distinctions between the individual and the livingworld. To nurture the smoothness of this oscillation might strengthen the root of empathy.

From here on, I am inverting the original thrust of kaivalya/isolation towards connection/interpenetration. I have arrived again at my main thesis: yoga philosophy that distinguishes awareness from matter merely names the problem. The many means of integration actually work on the problem.

4.26 This awareness re-integrates the part and the whole, and feels inexorable.

Hartranft's version reads: "Consciousness, now oriented to this distinction, can gravitate toward freedom—the fully integrated knowledge that pure awareness is independent from nature." Whereas the original continues in the extractive stream, my thread continues to posit freedom as the re-integration of parts: consciousness, awareness, and ecology.

4.27 At this point, alienating thoughts are fleeting memories.

Bryant has: "During the intervals [in this state of discriminate awareness] other ideas [arise] because of previous saṃskāra-s." Patañjali has moved into describing the vestigial disturbances to a yogi who has almost achieved complete rest—in his view, by withdrawing himself completely from prakṛti. Whereas the sage impugns the remaining thoughts that suggest puruṣa and prakṛti are yet conjoined, I impugn the opposite: lingering thoughts that continue to separate them from each other.

4.28 And you already have experience in releasing them.

That is, if you worked through "the book of practices".

4.29 The exalted is common, and the common exalted, and living feels like a summer downpour.

"Summer downpour" is my rendition of dharma-meghaḥ ("the virtue-pouring cloud"—Aranya; "a cloud of irreducible experiential substances"—Hartranft). As I was finishing this book, the late summer rain woke me very early one morning. I got up to write. My partner got up a half-hour later and sat on the couch in the dark with her hands on her pregnant belly. I went to sit with her for a moment. Half-asleep and radiant, she said "I love the rain. It makes me feel like many ages at the same time."

4.30 Standing in it washes away alienating thoughts and isolated footprints.

Bryant has: "From this comes the cessation of the kleśa-s [impediments to yoga] and karma."

4.31 Under a clearing sky, the desire for knowledge wanes.

4.32 Within you, gravity, urge, and resolution integrate.

The original suggests that the guṇa-s end their endless movement in the experience of the accomplished yogi. As I've expressed in many places, I believe that true integration is not about the ending of life-processes as we know them, but about lubricating the transitions between seemingly contradictory energies.

4.33 You can see the flow of time behind you, and you know how it happened.

4.34 Immersed in integrated relationship, consciousness sees itself evolving.

We are not content to end with a static state. Research will continue.

7.8 the song of overflowing

The wonders of integration can also come
through the conditions of one's development,
intimacy with plants,
conscious communication,
ardour, or meditation.

Evolution is an overflow of identity.
The overflow is natural, and only needs gardening.
Individuation creates selves.
These selves share collective consciousness.
Of the means towards wonder,
meditation is the most stable.
For those experienced in integration,
the judgment of moral actions becomes subtle.
Past action binds a memory;
present circumstance unlocks it.
Memory can outshine the details of identity.
Memories, like desire, are without beginning.
An undigested memory resolves when
its cause, effect, context, and neurosis are
integrated into present awareness.
A thing reveals its past and future as its particles dance.
The particles dance to the music of gravity, urge, and resolution.
The dance is so entrancing, a dancer appears.
Each person will see a different dancer.
But no single gaze can understand
or define
or possess her.
Things colour consciousness.
Matter produces and is known by consciousness;
consciousness produces and is known by awareness.

Consciousness can be seen by awareness.
But it is difficult for consciousness
to be aware of itself seeing.
The attempt can lead to a hall of mirrors
and an alienation from time.
When consciousness is still,
it can become aware of itself.
Consciousness is fulfilled when
it warmly intermingles with matter and awareness.
It delights in being seen.
Being aware of this process imbues individuation
with connection.
This awareness re-integrates the part
and the whole, and feels inexorable.
At this point, alienating thoughts are fleeting memories.
And you already have experience in releasing them.
The exalted is common, and the common exalted,
and living feels like a summer downpour.
Standing in it washes away alienating thoughts and isolated footprints.
Under a clearing sky, the desire for knowledge wanes.
Within you, gravity, urge, and resolution integrate.
You can see the flow of time behind you,
and you know how it happened.
Immersed in integrated relationship, consciousness
sees
itself
evolving.

8. coda

8.1 how do we learn and continue to learn?

See how a child chooses shells on the beach. The precious ones are precious for no reason we can fully know. She reaches for them with a mind empty, but for a little rhythmic song. Her small shivering flesh forgets about cold and snack time. This shell has a fleck of turquoise, this one has thicker pearlescence, this one is a hundred times smaller than the rest. She makes a small pile in the sand, contiguous with the shells beneath it. She'll have to sort them again when it's time to go, but with little concern: an hour has shown her the beach is infinite.

Hers is research driven by fascination alone. She doesn't need perfect shells, but simply the right shells for her. Each shell she picks speaks to a unique interest: her friend may pick up other shells, and they may quarrel about which are better, but neither will truly believe their arguments. An hour has shown them both that the beach is infinite. Bickering is boring: every ringing claim will be one-upped by another, until both children tire of proving things, and shrug and go back to combing the sand with empty minds and half-sung songs.

The child is feeling her neurology blossom. The infinity of shells intimates infinite systems. Attraction that flows over a sequence of particulars is the beginning of pattern recognition. Things repeat, things vary, things disappear, things return. It is blissful and commonplace, because she feels the beach and experience mirror each other. This is why she forgets time, loses self-consciousness, and doesn't really care how many shells she brings home. Her mum gave her a bucket to put them in, and after her infinite hour the bucket is full and heavy. But dad doesn't want the shells in the car, so she has to choose "just three". She chooses in an instant and happily dumps the rest at the tidal line. Within a day, the shells will be lost in her room amongst books and clothes. Her room is an internal beach, a ground of memory. Years later, a good therapist might comb through its artifacts with the same wordless wonder.

Her fascination with shells wasn't about collecting. It was about the infinite hour, the pleasure of resonance between mind and beach, and the exercise of pattern recognition. Detail and number melt into the immersive flow. It wasn't about preserving, but about noticing with the whole being: sand between toes, surf in her ears, sun on her back and cold spray on her shoulders, eyes scanning for what dazzles and fingers digging through what's hidden. Quiet ecstasy, quiet entasy, and humming, humming. It all takes place in the safety between two mothers: the mother her flesh came from standing behind her on the dune, her call-outs like a gossamer umbilicus. And the mother of the sea, the one her primal life came from, with open arms of blue and green.

When do we experience this as adults? The best artists are doing it all the time: a mood of engagement overtakes them, and provokes an intuitive harvest of images, sounds, and turns of phrase. An entranced poet is like a five-year-old child on the beach of words. The documentary filmmaker shoots an entire shoreline of footage, and then picks up her shells in the editing room. If she had a specific story she wanted to tell when she started, the shells and how she chooses them will rewrite it. Painters tease patterns out of the ocean of paint. The research of creativity is a simple and primal wonderment with connection, through any mode: shape, through-line, colour, resonance. "Let my playing be my learning, and my learning be my playing," writes Josef Huizinga (1949).

There's something about time as well. Limiting the shell-gathering to that infinite hour prevents fatigue and banality: doing something because one should, or because no other options are apparent. For us, what could be more oceanic than the web? And who can surf intuitively from interesting shell (or link) to shell for more than an hour or so, before the infinite roll of the digital beach provokes anxiety? The shift from pleasure to dis-ease is marked by the emergence of a controlling self: the person who, dissatisfied with textures, must comb through and distill meaning from the entire web, and who suffers because he cannot. This is the self of metaphysics: stuck in despairing confrontation with a complete mystery, which will kill him because he can't solve it. At this juncture, the wonderment of "what is this?" turns into the oppression of "what am I supposed to *do* with this?" But the child didn't collect shells for the sake of collection or interpretation. The infinite beach did not expose her insignificance, but rather provoked and magnified her very circulation, her very breath.

Post-traditional yogis are admonished: *Don't pick and choose from the tradition according to your attractions.* But isn't this precisely our first yoga? Weren't we drawn, inexplicably, to that shell, to that book, that friend, that lover, to that method of breathing, to that twist, that teacher's language, to another teacher's radiant movements? Have we not so far trusted the attractions of our infinite hour? Was it even a question of trust? Did the abandonment of that hour release our self-healing skill? Did the flesh not reach for what pleased it, and the empty mind for the shape that would kindly sculpt how it filled back up? And did that hour not hold more than any memento we brought back from it, to lose on our shelves?

The beach is data. Shells of biology and history. The skeleton is driftwood on the dune. Technology glints in the sand beside ethics and cognitive science. There are also spiritual shells: a sūtra, a proverb, a visualization. How could we pull these shells apart into subjects and disciplines? Why would we? What would we exclude from our infinite hour? Aliveness is the complete path you wouldn't even think of completing. You walk it by living, sand between the toes, finding what glints.

The creative posture in yoga practice is a squat on the beach. Its wandering focus prevents a system from hardening. Baffled by infinity and patterns, femurs fully grounded, the senses absorbed in continuity, mostly naked, unashamed. The reverie can last for about an hour. Hum along with every connection. You know you can't bring everything home. You don't have to count every shell on the beach. It's perfect to just love the ones in your hands. It's getting late. There will be another day. Find one last really nice shell. Run to mum when she calls.

8.2 the love of not-knowing

Before speaking, before time, before individuation—we begin with the ground of embodied sensation. Lips wrapped around the nipple, flesh moulded to the mother's side. One continuous flesh with the origin, with the world. The eyes do not sharpen upon objects, and sound is everywhere. We begin with sensations, oceanic, and carry these as implicit memory. We may become distracted from embodiment, but as sure as we read this, it has remained. The light and the marks and the hum of space pre-exist whatever sentences this text will structure.

We can recapture this coherence through the yogas of sensation and presence: āsana and breath.

As self-consciousness blossoms between eighteen and twenty-four months, sounds become words, silhouettes become objects, and feelings become a body: you are capable of explicit memory—the eye that captures the whole of you against the whole of everything else, taking the picture of the first thing you remember, a crystallization of self. Words become sentences, sentences become propositions. Descriptions, reasons, and instructions are added to the ground of perception. A maternal fleshed connection fades, and a paternal tether of words replaces it. On top of sensation, thought gathers like pixels to be organized into internal pictures that mirror or dispute what now seems outside.

We begin with sensations, and continue with what we are told. The world is carved out by the words of others. The software of language and culture is given and installed. Words become sentences. Sentences become strategies. Strategies become beliefs. The majority of early cognitions are taught. This teaching establishes knowledge as other, from another place, something received.

More than this: teaching is something that protects and explains and makes for survival. From the breast to the word, the given nurturance of mother and father is the root of maintenance, the assumption of safety, the ground of faith.

Quite naturally we believe in gods and heroes, or any ordering principle that is given to us whole, before we have the tools to take it apart, examine it, reverse-engineer it, or redesign it for another purpose. Mother knows by holding. Father holds by knowing. (And the reverse.)

Early consciousness, informed by teaching, feels theological. After āsana, so are our first steps in the study of yoga. It comes through a given language, fully formed. We go for yoga "teachings", and some of us recapture early memories of being held by simple words that told us we were safe, and that our parents had power and strength to transfer into us.

The *Upanishads* are exactly this: fathers giving sons perfect theological teachings. *Everything is Brahman. You are that very Self.* The son melts into the father's knowing gaze, and feels eternally held. We remember this. Or for those of us who were abandoned, we wish we could remember this. And there are others who feel eternally bound and compressed by this same power.

The given teachings of yoga are theological. Sometimes they are literally "words (*logoein*) about god (*theos*)". But even when they are not about god, as when Patañjali says that nature exists for the sake of awareness (2.21), the teaching conveys a theological *structure*, performing the same functions of simplification and security as anything that is given whole.

Theology confers safety as time dries the mother's milk. But time also kills both parents. Time shows the teacher to be a person, struggling, just like yourself. Time and experience smash all words, even words about god.

When you are broken, when you have lost safety, when you are dying to yourself, there is yet an "incredible need to believe" (Kristeva, 2009) that throws you hurtling towards the creation of new meanings. But new meanings require new language. A language that recreates what is given. The words that you once used, the given words, the words about god or reality or how things are, have been taken away. In the emptiness they leave, another seed of yoga swells with life. It is philosophy: "love (*philos*) of wisdom (*sophia*)".

Words about god can throw us, as they break, into a love for wisdom.

The love of wisdom is not given. It is not testimony. It is not a teaching. It does not say: "In the beginning, god created the heavens and the earth." It rather says: "The first thing I remember was a feeling." The love of wisdom carries *Thus I have heard* into *What can I learn*? The love of wisdom is an activity you surrender to when you realize you have no choice but to become your own mother, your own father.

Where do we start in yoga, as in life? We start with sensory perception, which is never lost, though easily covered over. We continue with philosophy, which can ground a given safety, but can also distract us from original perception. The need for this safety is never lost. This need pushes up a flower from the compost of rotting words: *love*. Love for what happens, love for confusion, love in pain: the love of not-knowing. Love feels like a return to perceptual immersion. The mouth stops speaking, filled with the breast of wisdom. The flesh stops aching, moulded to another flesh, a remembered flesh of coherence. The world enwombs, as it always did.

8.3 homo accipiens

Latin. Contemporary. "The human who learns, receives, and considers oneself indebted." A neologism for a person that eschews the fantasy of an ultimate state or final rest.

Life is experience. All experience is learning. Learning is the food of life, its central pleasure. The yoga 2.0 mind mud-bathes in uncertainty.

Enlightenment is a 1.0 construct, like a singular god or soul. The erotic of evolutionary learning knows that something always remains, concealed, that the twoness of dialogue is always on the verge of bursting out, fuelled by the unconscious.

We learn what we do not know. Therefore, what we do not know is the food of our life. Therefore, we depend on what we do not know to continue living. What we do not know gives us life.

We move towards what we do not know, breathing air we have never breathed. We receive what we do not know in every moment. We are indebted to the unknown for this gift of life. We chase the unknown through desire for experience, rendering implicit and baffled praise to we know not what.

The familiar is but a subtler texture of the unknown.

We think we are ambivalent towards the unknown, or we think we might fear it. Such fear is but excitement, misunderstood. In our former self-definitions, we emphasized what is past and static by taking the name of *homo sapiens*. This moniker presumes knowledge, rather than the process of continual learning. *Homo accipiens* envisions the sense of self as neither solid (accomplished/ātman) nor transient (illusory/anātman), but rather porous. Water darkens the unfired clay pitcher. I'm leaking meaning and it feels like love.

Recognizing our secret love for what we do not know, we assert our learning-life, our devotion to the infinitely receding horizon, through which we gambol and pause in wonder at every blade, clod, feather, twitch, colour, guṇa, odour, texture, tremor, swirl, breeze, drop, other drop, and drop that announces the next drop, each a mirrored pearl of a world slipping from unknown into the known and back again, always promising more. The unknown outruns us. We are breathless, exhilarated.

Remaining this indebted and gratified depends on recognizing when each learning episode has come to its natural conclusion, and then turning away from the empty stare of the text or idol and seeking the next flow of juice. For instance, the "truth" of Gaṇeśa breaking his tusk to pen the poetry of humanity is a pleasure to imbibe, evoking the wonderment of a childhood story. But when the juice of that imagery is fully squeezed (and we know this not through scientific measure but through our appetite for the story, and its taste), we are left with a rind that becomes iconic, which suggests the meanings of another time, or a series of venerable rituals, philosophical speculations, awkward and embarrassing prayers with the hand over the heart, or the object of any static dogma—none of which retains the contact of childhood learning. As the pleasure of a particular learning encounter evaporates, so too does its truth. If the children and teenagers are sniggering during church, they are compensating, trying to supplement the thrill of learning that the ritual has emptied out for them, even as it tries to rekindle wonderment.

The end of each learning arc heralds the twilight of the idol. You know you are no longer learning when the rind is dry. Jesus stops bleeding on the cross—there's no more blood to pour out. The tears of Mary looking up at him stop flowing—the sun is setting, the dusk is cold, and she sobers to the task of burial.

It is congesting to the dance of consciousness to freeze this tableau in place, to varnish his streams of blood, to cast his broken flesh in plaster or bronze, to fossilize Mary in her hopelessness and strip away her maternal pragmatism, and to generally demand that your heart and mind continue to venerate what it is no longer learning. Worse—if your emotions no longer open to the icon, you blame yourself, tragically believing you have failed this thing that ironically has been bled dry. It's like blaming yourself for not finding a plate of plastic food to be appetizing. Meanwhile, your hunger increases.

No wonder the medievals hallucinated the bleeding of statues and communion wafers. The heart's guilt at not finding connection with what it is told is holy is too grave to bear. Thoughts, through pure force of will, must make that image seem to live, so that learning can be renewed. *Homo accipiens* will go to any length to continue to receive.

To what extent can the sensation of my breath alone evoke the same wonderment and fascinating absorption that I felt when my father told me my first story? To what extent can the absolutely familiar regain its status as the unknown?

Because we do not know the world, the world is creator.

Because we do not know ourselves, we are creator.

Because we do not know each other, we are co-dependent and co-creative.

Food for each other. Earth for each other. Yoked to each other through ethics, breath, poise, our innate theory of minds and empathy, and contemplation. In endless and edgeless learning.

8.4 a brief review, and notes for future study on the neuroscience of yoga and meditation

I've approached Patañjali-s yoga sūtra-s with tools long familiar to me—literary theory, continental philosophy, and many perspectives from the psychological literature. With these tools, I've tried to reorient the function of language and textuality in yoga discourse, deconstruct the hard dualisms of both the old text and its echoes within contemporary culture, and analyze the traumas, sorrows, and wishes hiding within yoga's history and our hearts. My intentions have been to energize both discourse and practice, to elide "tradition" with present need, and to bring more awareness to the intersubjective possibilities of what has long been an anti-social culture.

Neuroscience is a newer tool for me: one that I'm sure will take many years for me to begin to learn how to use and perhaps incorporate into a future edition. It's also a newer tool for contemporary yoga culture: so far, I am aware of no comprehensive inquiry into the neuroscience of yoga practice. Contemporary Buddhism seems to be leading the way in this field so far, especially through the work of Daniel Siegel (2007), and Rick Hanson with Richard Mendius (2009). But I have a few introductory notes from a yogic perspective that I hope may bear fruit.

So far, I've put a lot of effort into deconstructing the transcendental arc of Patañjali-s vision: that the human has fallen into flesh and must climb back out through the discipline of subtractive/extractive ascent. I've argued that this story contradicts every facet of accepted evolutionary theory, that it encourages a hierarchy of internal states that elevates the dissociative, the anti-ecological, and the anti-social as it unconsciously compensates for developmental traumas on both personal and anthropological scales, and that this "hierarchy of purity" is often mirrored in the vertical structures of yoga transmission and pedagogy. I've argued throughout for the demystification of internal states, and the democratization of individual integrative experience. I've tried to lay our old anxious vertical yearnings down to rest on the inconceivably older horizontal earth.

But as I start to learn the language of neuroscience just a little, I'm realizing that Patañjali-s upward wish mirrors a key contemporary insight, albeit in reverse. Whether it's the polyvagal theory of Stephen Porges (2011), or the triune brain model, or discussions of explicit vs. implicit memory, hemispheric laterality, mirror neurology, or the process of amygdaloid-hippocampal regulation (reviewed in Cozolino, 2010, and Siegel, 2007), a different hierarchical vision of how we experience life and self-awareness is emerging, which I think will cast new light on the stages of meditative insight that the yoga sūtra-s describe. As Patañjali yearns to consciously reach upward into "higher" realms of awareness, contemporary neuroscience seeks out the mechanisms that lie buried beneath conscious life. The old yogis looked upwards to a primal and pure originary condition—puruṣa—to resolve the whirls of consciousness. The psychoneurologists are looking downwards, layer by layer, to understand the primal brain, how it has evolved, and how it can learn to better self-regulate. Looking upwards or downwards, the goal is the same: the search is for the root of experience and how it may come to fuller coherence and resolution. Perhaps the highest levels of meditation in Patañjali-s system can be seen as access-points to the most primal layers of brain function. His upward reach may be seen as digging into the fertile mud of our evolutionary and developmental psychoneurology.

I haven't spent much time in this book on Patañjali-s baroque hierarchy of meditative states, mainly because I have believed for a long while that he is speculating on the ineffable, and that theoretical complexity confounds the basic mindfulness goals of meditation, especially for beginners. I've maintained a light touch on the final three limbs of focus (dhāraṇā), contemplation (dhyāna), and integration (samādhi): relating them to stages of intersubjective harmony by which the self enters into deepening relationship with other, to eventually discover other-as-self. But the vast and granular tradition of commentary on the yoga sūtra-s proposes no fewer than ten levels of samādhi alone, *prior* to full enlightenment (kaivalya). Feuerstein pulls them together from the commentaries of Mishra and Bhikshu, from lowest to highest: "ecstatic-coinciding with cogitation", "ecstatic-coinciding beyond cogitation", "ecstatic-coinciding with reflection", "ecstatic-coinciding beyond reflection", "ecstatic-coinciding with bliss", "ecstatic-coinciding beyond bliss", "ecstatic-coinciding with 'I-am-ness'", "ecstatic-coinciding beyond 'I-am-ness'", "supraconscious ecstasy", "cloud of dharma ecstasy", and "aloneness-liberation" (1998, 253).

What can we make of this dizzying ascent? So far I've shown first that the contemplative ideal is for conscious functions to either lose or broaden focus towards an ultimate abstraction: from cogitation to reflection to bliss to "I-am-ness", to "supra-conscious" states. Secondly, the karmic theory presented in pāda-s three and four suggest that each transition to a "higher" state reduces or even eliminates some of the unconscious motivators of the "lower" states—saṃskāra-s and vāsanā-s. But does the teleology really need to be seen as moving upwards? Patañjali may be presenting a transcendent path, but perhaps we can read him against his grain. When looking at his map against the maps of psychoneurology, it seems as though he is actually working his way *downwards* into the ground of precognitive and prelinguistic states. Perhaps Feuerstein's translation of "nirvitarka samāpatti" could change from "ecstatic-coinciding beyond cogitation", to "ecstatic-coinciding *before* cogitation".

A key promise of neurology-influenced psychotherapy is to be able to examine and rebuild the foundations of our responsiveness to the livingworld and each other through accessing realms of hidden memory and embedded trauma-responses that precede language and conscious tought (Cozolino, 2010). Perhaps meditation is doing exactly this, regardless of the anachronistic language of "rising". If anything, we are sinking down to a root. Perhaps this is why the encouragement towards "groundedness" is the *sine qua non* of most contemporary meditation instruction.

What is meditation reaching down into? Neuroscience offers several ways of mapping the route towards the "root brain". The simplest and perhaps most famous is Paul MacLean's vision of "the triune brain". Roughly put, MacLean describes the brain as though it were a series of nested dolls—an image that will make sense to those familiar with the Indian system of the kośa-s (or "sheathes"). The outermost layer—the cerebral cortex with its familiar walnut-like folds—is the last to develop amongst the higher primates, and in the human individual it blossoms in complexity and connectivity throughout life. In MacLean's terms, it is the "neo-mammalian" brain, responsible for everything that's allowing you to read and understand and contemplate and perhaps internally argue with the marks on this page. Underneath this largest of the sheathes sits the "paleo-mammalian" brain (or "limbic system"), holding memory and emotion, which rises in small wordless currents as you read. The limbic wraps around the core: the "reptilian brain, relatively unchanged through evolutionary history, responsible for activation, arousal, homeostasis, and reproductive drives" (Cozolino, 2010, 5). It's this first, innermost brain that holds the deep unconscious will to breathe, circulate blood and nutrition, find supportive contact with the livingworld, and seek out the other for communion.

What do we do in meditation if it's not to sit down in relative leisure and safety with neo-mammalian conscious will and expectation and instruction (from Patañjali or any other source) to feel and perhaps resist the rich roll of emotion and memory that we float upon, in order to access our mechanisms of arousal and refine them away from the unnecessarily reactive? Consider Cozolino's list of reptilian-brain functions: "activation, arousal, homeostasis, and reproductive drives". This last category stopped me short when I came across it. In my days of Tantric meditation in the Tibetan mode I was given a sādhanā in which I was to visualize myself in distinct detail as a female deity, sixteen years of age, nude, engorged and dripping with arousal, preparing herself to be penetrated by her divine lover. I was then to use the primal feelings of this process to contemplate the erotic nature of the philosophies of interdependence and no-self-existence. There were two competing rationales for the technique. The more orthodox and somewhat prudish explanation for the practice was that we were "using desire to eliminate desire". The more provocative explanation was that we were plunging into the mud of desire to recognize the polymorphous fertility of a philosophical truth. And now I have a third take: that *I was using my neo-mammalian brain to prod my reptilian brain into an integrating conversation across my developmental and evolutionary history that could rewire the ruptures between consciousness and flesh.* Indeed, my emotional and sexual life improved. And writing began to flow more easily.

Of course, Patañjali-s system does not explicitly direct practitioners towards erotic visualizations, though he is liberal with his advice towards objects of meditation, going so far as to suggest in 1.39 that any object of attraction or desire can serve as a basis for focus, contemplation, and integration. Meditation in the yoga sūtra-s seems to be most associated with the first three functions of the reptilian brain, as per Cozolino's list. Samyama (the three "final" limbs) is definitely targeted at the mechanism of "activation", insofar as abhiniveśa (traditionally translated as "the will to live") is seen as a primary obstruction to internal peace. In this sense, the neo-mammalian brain might be soothing whatever reptilian survival-anxiety which is no longer circumstantially appropriate. Samyama also targets "arousal", generally through its goal of quelling the vṛtti-s, and specifically through its promotion of vairāgya (traditionally translated as "dispassion"). Finally, samyama surely heads towards enhanced homeostasis through the avoidance of rāga and dveṣa (traditionally translated as "desire" and "aversion"). More clearly, the process emerges: in meditation we are not transcendentally fleeing the reptilian brain. This would be impossible. In meditation we are doing what we need to do with *everything* in our lives: entering a dialogue, forming relationships against all odds, coming to know, slowly, the other. And in this case, the many others within us. As Cozolino points out: "This conservation of our evolutionary history alongside our modern neural networks confronts the therapist with the challenge of simultaneously treating a human, a horse, and a crocodile" (Cozolino 2010, 6). Perhaps this is why, in part, we name our āsana-s after a broad variety of animals. We contain, as Walt Whitman says, "multitudes".

The tensions of the triune brain are collapsed into dyadic structure in several neuroscience discourses, all of which contrast the often duelling evolutionary perogatives of survival and introspection. One involves the distinction between explicit memory (what I am using to remember a quote from Walt Whitman) and implicit memory (the flesh-patterns that allow me to type out that quote without thinking of where each letter key sits in space). In his focus upon how saṃskāra-s and vāsanā-s continue to beget the turbulence of vṛtti-s, Patañjali is clearly interested in the role of implicit memory, and "subtler and subtler" forms of meditative attention (as we climb Feuerstein's ten-rung ladder) are thought to uproot these smaller and smaller seeds of future imbalance.

A second neuroscience dyad consists of the distinction between two branches of the vagus nerve at the centre of the autonomic nervous system—the dorsal vagal complex (DVC), and the ventral vagal complex (VVC)—as described by Stephen Porges (2011). Porges observes and describes a phylogenetic layering of these two nerve bundles within the contemporary human brain. The newer branch (VVC) is called the "smart vagus", and allows us to self-regulate in instances of social stress with self-soothing behaviours that attempt to create the most positive and productive frame of mind. The "tone" of this nerve complex—its strength, resilience, and the health of its mylenization—is, according to Porges, a critical factor in our ability to metabolize stress. If its function is overwhelmed, we revert to a kind of backup system—DVC—which we share with all vertebrates. In situations of grave stress the dorsal vagal complex "freezes" autonomic function with shock, sending us into a vegetative/dissociative state in which we shut down all conscious processing to focus on root survival. Using Porges' model, yoga can be seen as the nurturer of ventral vagal tone, and not just through meditation: we would have to consider the calculated stresses of engaged ethics and āsana as well. These would prove to be helpful within the mild to moderate "range (Cozolino, 2010, 20), in which the VVC is given a below-threshold task to test and improve its functionality without being overwhelmed. The fact that prāṇāyama has been shown to calm the heartrate would also be a key strategy for toning the ventral vagal complex, which is wired to act as a brake upon the cardiac rhythms associated with fighting and fleeing.

Both of these dyads present an "upper" system that must develop good resilience and tone in order to craft or mould or reconfigure or inhibit a "lower" system that functions beneath consciousness. The five dyads of saṃprajñāta samādhi that Feuerstein lists suggest the same dyadic structure. There is a state with (above) and without (below) cogitation, with (above) and without (below) reflection, etc. Perhaps the feelings of various meditative states (and that is all we have within the yoga tradition: self-reported feelings within practice) have this dyadic structure because they are mirroring the fundamental dyad of what is seen and what is hidden. I make sense of this in my own meditation experience, in which each new feeling of coalescence or harmony seems to have two distinct stages: one in which I cognize where or how I am existing newly, and a further stage in which the quiet language of cognition falls silent in the face of its own radiance. I never have had the feeling of ascending from the first to the second. It is always a feeling of stepping down onto a lower plane of earth, or settling in a softer seat, or slipping into a warm pool of water, where language dissolves into wetness.

Perhaps the most fruitful neurophysiological dyad for yoga practice to explore is one that implies no vertical hierarchy: hemispheric laterality. The language and subtle physiology of yoga is already obsessed with right and left distinctions. There are "right-handed" (orthodox) and "left-handed" (heterodox) practices. There are solar techniques for the right-flesh and lunar techiques for the left-flesh. While reciting mantra-s, practitioners are advised to hold the mālā in the right hand to sharpen the intellect (the neo-cortex?), and in the left hand to soften the heart (the limbic system?). Mudrā-s are carefully chosen for complementarity between the hands. There's nothing more balancing than nādī shodhana prāṇāyama (alternate nostril breathing). And, as every āsana practitioner knows, physiological health assumes structural symmetry between right and left sides of the flesh. All of these practices speak to the psychoneurological goal of the integration of brain hemispheres, which is said to be enhanced by a good balance between cognitive and perceptual tasks.

Although distinct brain functions are generally spread throughout many structures of the cortex and subcortex through redundancies that allow us to at least partially (and sometimes miraculously) recover from localized brain trauma, the left and right hemispheres do "contain" certain categories of action. The right hemisphere (which governs the left of our physical structure) figures prominently in our neonatal experience, attuning us to spatiality, proprioception, sensorimotor and emotional life. It processes holistically and in concert with the rich emotional valence of the limbic system. The left hemisphere (governing our right sides) kicks into high development mode with language acquisition in the second year of life, attuning us to symbology and the grammar of linear and sequential reasoning, erecting structures of consciously narrative time into perceptual space. Its functions are more centred in the cortex, and work to inhibit the perceptual overflow of right hemispheric exuberance. Slowly, the two hemispheres enrich their dialogue through the development of the corpus callosum, a connective tube of nerve tissue that joins one side to the other, deep within the cortex (Cozolino, 2010). We might say that a truly integral yoga would stimulate rich neurogenesis (the building of nerve tissue) in the corpus callosum, by highlighting and reinforcing techniques of lateral communion.

These threads of research may unfortunately be taken up and woven together under the accusation of "material reductionism". There is a very powerful sentiment within yoga culture that wants to shield yogic techniques from scientific inquiry out of the fear that something sacred will be lost. "The mind is not reducible to brain function," they will say, or: "The spirit cannot be explained by biology." With these arguments, traditionalists will attempt to defend two anachronisms. One is easy to see: the original "mind-body" hard dualism. The other anachronism is more obscure. By claiming that quantities such as "mind", "spirit", "soul", or "Absolute" are beyond analysis or experimentation, traditionalists defend the hierarchy of pedagogical power that presumes to tell us what these words mean, and how they must be understood. In my view, this defensiveness actually makes religious language reductionistic, because it inhibits the flow of thought and creativity. Beginning to understand the mechanisms of meditation and the feelings of selfhood through the insights of psychoneurology doesn't "lose" any of the mystery of the experience described. Just the opposite: it imbues mystery with ever-deeper mystery, within a shared language and method by which we can come to know ourselves and each other openly, without the anxiety of assuming there is some final answer to it all.

8.5 how I got here

In the section "what is meditation for", I described how I'd spent about ten years with meditation instructions that dissociated me from my ecology. But I've just remembered that that's not how it all started, exactly. I first began to meditate, and then do āsana, because I was in love.

I was twenty-three and living a long way from home with my ex-wife. I felt I'd lost all direction. Dublin was lonelier to me and far colder than Canada. I drank and smoked and worked on my very painful first novel while the rain battered the slate roof day after day. One day my ex heard that a meditation teacher was coming through town, and suggested that we go to hear what he had to say. Depression makes one intensely reluctant, but I trusted her, and I wanted to please her. I wanted to be a better person for her. If I could learn meditation, perhaps I could calm the whirlwind of confusion that seemed to swirl within me, between us, and resolve it into the love I knew lay underneath.

The organizers rented a cold stony room in the Kilmainham Gaol. I was introduced to meditation in an old jail that had been turned into a museum.

The teacher was Tibetan. I didn't know anything about Tibet, and didn't really care. His English was poor. I can't remember what he talked about. But after a while he said, "Okay: now we meditate. Close your eyes and breathe deeply. Through your nose is best." I did what I was told, feeling anxiety rise. After a few minutes, he said, "Okay: when you inhale, ask—*Who am I?* And when you exhale, give the honest answer—*Don't know.*"

I followed the instructions and almost immediately felt tears and snot streaming down my face. I didn't know what had happened to me. Somehow, in a single question and answer on a single inhale and exhale, I had begun to undo the knots of consciousness that had since early childhood kept me abstracted from my flesh and isolated into a rigid and self-protective identity. I walked home with my ex in the rain. For me, meditation began through relationship. And through becoming honest about not-knowing. I didn't stop weeping for days.

There was no one to follow up with. But what was there to follow up? The instruction was so simple and profound and left me reeling and unsure how to practice it. A few years later I met the teacher who taught me abstract meditation techniques. Somehow I thought that his more measured and intellectual approach would put that first experience in Dublin into perspective and open its mystery to me. It didn't. Rather, it triggered all of my latent convictions of low self-worth. My mind could never focus clearly enough. There was always another bit of dharma to learn and obey. I should always recite more prayers.

Abstract practice amplified my self-abstraction. I followed the instructions for a long time, but I remained disconnected from the flesh and heart. I lost weight and libido, and my joints began to crack. I got smarter in the head and stiffer in the spine. I studied and meditated voraciously, trying always to rise up out of my inadequacy, to wash away my original sin. I tried to believe I was happier, or becoming more integrated.

Years later we were in Manhattan. I was at another very low point. My body was in pain. My emotions were tangled, suppressed, and volatile. It was raining. She looked at me and said, "Let's go to a yoga class." She grabbed my hand and we went.

I remember rising up out of savāsana and looking at my hand, by which I had been led to this room, and crying in gratitude for simply having a hand, a wrist, hairs on my forearm. I was flesh, and here, and breathing held a secret joy I had forgotten, and there was a rush of warm blood from my heart to my fingertips.

We walked home through the rain. For me, yoga began through relationship, and rain:

> The exalted is common, and the common exalted, and living feels like a summer downpour. Standing in it washes away alienating thoughts and isolated footprints.

8.6 saving breath for what is to come

Every book must end. For me, the ending of a book is an invitation to lay all books down for a while, and live beneath and beyond the cascade of words.

The cortical symphony can resolve to the gentle hum of a soothed amygdala. Explicit memory can sink into implicit memory, and bring present peace to past chaos. The conscious can become porous to the perceptual, inviting the livingworld to flood the tiny room of the "I".

Patañjali and the other grammarians of his time were obsessed with economy in writing. One of them said that if the writer of a sūtra could eliminate a single syllable from his text, this was equal to gaining a child. For them it meant striving for perfection in philosophical precision. For me, and I imagine most of us today, it means willfully becoming silent in the knowledge that the work of thought and empathy will never be finished, and letting this silence somehow make room for all that is about to be born within us and around us.

My last syllable for now comes here. Jacob is crying. Jacob needs these hands, this voice.

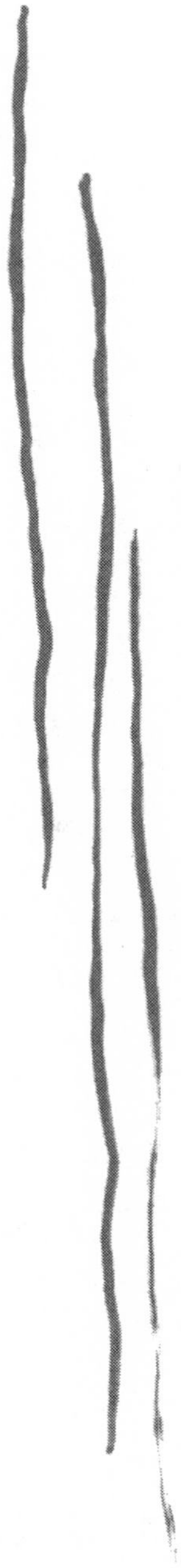

bibliography

Abram, David. *The spell of the sensuous: perception and language in a more-than-human world*. New York: Pantheon Books, 1996. Print.

Ballentine, Rudolph, Swami Ajaya, and Swami Rama. *Yoga and psychotherapy: the evolution of consciousness*. Glenview, Ill.: Himalayan Institute, 1976. Print.

Baudrillard, Jean. *Simulations*. New York: Semiotext(e), Inc., 1983. Print.

Coleridge, Samuel Taylor. *Bibliographia Literaria*. London.: Dent & Sons, 1817/1975. Print.

Cozolino, Louis J. *The neuroscience of psychotherapy: healing the social brain*. 2nd ed. New York: W.W. Norton & Co., 2010. Print.

Decety, Jean, and William John Ickes. *The social neuroscience of empathy*. Cambridge, MA: MIT Press, 2009. Print.

DeMause, Lloyd. *Foundations of psychohistory*. New York: Creative Roots, 1982. Print.

Derrida, Jacques. *Margins of philosophy*. Chicago: University of Chicago Press, 1982. Print.

Doidge, Norman. *The brain that changes itself: stories of personal triumph from the frontiers of brain science*. New York: Viking, 2007. Print.

Feuerstein, Georg. *The yoga tradition: its history, literature, philosophy, and practice*. Prescott, AR: Hohm Press, 1998. Print.

Hanson, Rick, and Richard Mendius. *Buddha's brain: the practical neuroscience of happiness, love & wisdom*. Oakland, CA: New Harbinger Publications, 2009. Print.

Harrington, Anne. *The cure within: a history of mind-body medicine*. New York: W.W. Norton, 2008. Print.

Hejinian, Lyn. *My life*. Los Angeles: Sun & Moon Press, 1987. Print.
Huizinga, Johan. *Homo ludens ; a study of the play-element in culture.* London: Routledge & K. Paul, 1949. Print.
Jaynes, Julian. *The origin of consciousness in the breakdown of the bicameral mind*. Boston: Houghton Mifflin, 1976. Print.
Jensen, Derrick. *Endgame*. Seven Stories Press 1st ed. New York: Seven Stories Press, 2006. Print.
Kaplan, Louise J. *Oneness and separateness: from infant to individual*. New York: Simon and Schuster, 1978. Print.
Klein, Melanie. *The selected Melanie Klein*. Juliet Mitchell, ed. New York: Free Press, 1986. Print.
Kramer, Joel, and Diana Alstad. *The guru papers: masks of authoritarian power*. Berkeley, CA: North Atlantic Books/Frog, 1993. Print.
Kramer, Joel, and Diana Alstad. *The passionate mind revisited: expanding personal and social awareness*. Berkeley, CA: North Atlantic Books, 2009. Print.
Kristeva, Julia. *This incredible need to believe*. New York: Columbia University Press, 2009. Print.
Merleau-Ponty, Maurice. *The visible and the invisible; followed by working notes*. Claude Lefort, ed. Evanston IL: Northwestern University Press, 1968. Print.
Pannikar, Raymond, and N. Shanta. *The Vedic experience: mantramanjari : an anthology of the Vedas for modern man and contemporary celebration*. Berkeley, CA: University of California Press, 1977. Print.
Petrie, Scott, and Matthew Remski. *yoga 2.0: shamanic echoes*. Toronto, graha yuddha press, 2010. Print.
Porges, Stephen W. *The polyvagal theory: neurophysiological foundations of emotions, attachment, communication, and self-regulation*. New York: W.W. Norton, 2011. Print.
Ramachandran, V. S. *The tell-tale brain: a neuroscientist's quest for what makes us human*. New York: W.W. Norton, 2011. Print.
Rosenberg, Marshall B. *Nonviolent communication: a language of life*. 2nd ed. Encinitas, CA: PuddleDancer Press, 2003. Print.
Sherts, Miles. *Conscious communication: how to establish healthy relationships and resolve conflict peacefully while maintaining independence, a language of connection*. Minneapolis, MN: Langdon Street Press, 2009. Print.
Siegel, Daniel J. *The mindful brain: reflection and attunement in the cultivation of well-being*. New York: W.W. Norton, 2007. Print.
Singleton, Mark. *Yoga body: the origins of modern posture practice*. Oxford: Oxford University Press, 2010. Print.
White, David Gordon. *Sinister yogis*. Chicago: University of Chicago

Press, 2009. Print.
White, David Gordon. *Yoga in practice*. Princeton, NJ: Princeton University Press, 2012. Print.
Winnicott, D. W. *The child, the family, and the outside world*. Harmondsworth, England: Penguin Books, 1964. Print.

source texts for Patañjali

Aranya, Hariharananda. *Yoga philosophy of Pantanjali: containing his yoga aphorisms*. Calcutta: University of Calcutta, 1963. Print.
Bryant, Edwin F. *The Yoga sūtras of Patañjali: a new edition, translation, and commentary with insights from the traditional commentators*. New York: North Point Press, 2009. Print.
Feuerstein, Georg. *The yoga-sūtra of Patañjali: a new translation and commentary*. Folkestone, England: Dawson, 1979. Print.
Hartranft, Chip. *The Yoga-Sūtra of Patañjali: a new translation with commentary*. Boston: Shambhala Publications, 2003. Print.
Houston, Vyaas. *The Yoga Sūtra workbook: the certainty of freedom : a translation of the Yoga Sūtras of Patañjali with word for word translation and grammatical index*. Warwick, NY: American Sanskirt Institute, 1995. Print.
Isherwood, Christopher, and Swami Prabhavananda. *How to know God: the Yoga aphorisms of Patañjali*. New York: New American Library, 1969. Print.
Miller, Barbara Stoler. *Yoga: discipline of freedom : the Yoga Sūtra attributed to Patañjali ; a translation of the text, with commentary, introduction, and glossary of keywords*. Berkeley, CA: University of California Press, 1996. Print.
Ranganathan, Shyam. *Patañjali's yoga sūtra*. London: Penguin, 2009. Print.
Satchidananda, Swami. *The yoga sūtras of Patañjali*. Yogaville, VA: Integral Yoga Publications, 1990. Print.
Taimni, I. K. *The science of Yoga; the Yoga-Sūtras of Patañjali in Sanskrit with transliteration in Roman, translation in English and commentary*. Adyar: Theosophical Pub. House, 1971. Print.
Vivekananda, Swami. *Selections from The complete works of Swami Vivekananda*. Calcutta: Advaita Ashrama, 1991. Print.

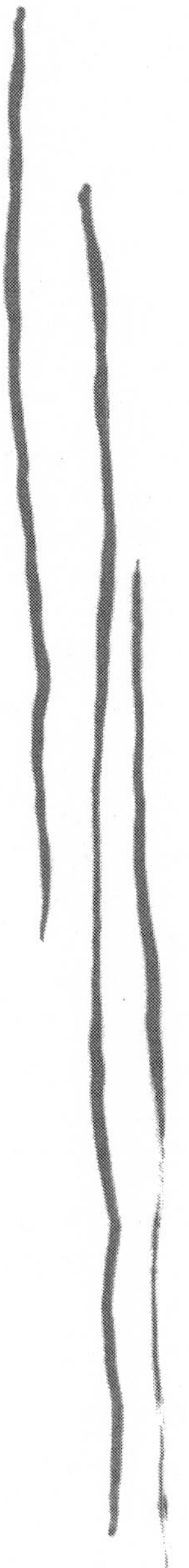

36620360R00144

Made in the USA
Middletown, DE
12 November 2016